CIPS Study Matters

Level 4

Foundation Diploma in Purchasing and Supply

Managing Purchasing and Supply Relationships

Second Edition

Mike Fogg
PMMS Consulting Group Limited

THE
CHARTERED INSTITUTE OF
PURCHASING & SUPPLY®

Published by

The Chartered Institute of Purchasing and Supply
Easton House, Easton on the Hill, Stamford, Lincolnshire PE9 3NZ
Tel: +44 (0) 1780 756 777
Fax: +44 (0) 1780 751 610
Email: info@cips.org
Website: http://www.cips.org

First published June 2006
Second edition published June 2009

While every effort has been made to ensure that references to websites are correct at time of going to press, the world wide web is a constantly changing environment and CIPS cannot accept any responsibility for any changes to addresses.

CIPS acknowledges product, service and company names referred to in this publication, many of which are trade names, service marks, trademarks or registered trademarks.

CIPS, The Chartered Institute of Purchasing & Supply and its logo are all trademarks of the Chartered Institute of Purchasing & Supply.

The right of Mike Fogg to be identified as author of this work has been asserted by him in accordance with the Copyright, Designs and Patents Act, 1988 in force or as amended from time to time.

Technical reviewer: David Chidley, Rubicon Training

Instructional design and publishing project management by Wordhouse Ltd, Reading, UK

Content management system, instructional editing and pre-press by Echelon Learning Ltd, London, UK

Index prepared by Indexing Specialists (UK) Ltd, Hove, UK

ISBN 978-1-86124-178-8

Contents

Introduction

This course book has been designed to assist you in studying for the CIPS Managing Purchasing and Supply Relationships unit in the Level 4 Foundation Diploma in Purchasing and Supply. The book covers all topics in the official CIPS unit content document, as illustrated in the table beginning on page xi.

Purchasing is about relationships! You as a person cannot be effective in a role within a purchasing team if you are not a relationship manager, you cannot represent your organisation to the supply market if you can't see both sides of a supply relationship and you can't work with the stakeholders of the purchasing process if you can't understand what drives them. One purchasing director known to the author believes that the sign on the door of the purchasing department of the future will be 'Relationship Management'.

A number of forces will act upon the relationships you will have to manage throughout your career and this syllabus includes them. Today, for example, technology is fundamental to all organisations and yet the electronic 'e-tools' that buyers use or misuse impact relationships in a way that some do not give enough attention to. Many buyers also underestimate the benefit to their organisation from understanding how they are seen by selling organisations and yet others fail to consider the people they meet on the other side of the table as *people*.

All of this is not to advocate a move towards 'partnership' for there is a spectrum of relationships and there is no one *right* relationship approach. The most appropriate approach at any one time will be contingent upon the existing circumstances which can change and change again. Frequently a buyer will have a number of conflicting objectives to manage within a relationship and to that extent they may feel like a juggler with several balls to keep in the air, while someone else tugs the carpet from under where they are standing. Managing purchasing and supply relationships is fundamental to all purchasing professionals.

How to use this book

The course book will take you step by step through the unit content in a series of carefully planned 'study sessions' and provides you with learning activities, self-assessment questions and revision questions to help you master the subject matter. The guide should help you organise and carry out your studies in a methodical, logical and effective way, but if you have your own study preferences you will find it a flexible resource too.

Before you begin using this course book, make sure you are familiar with any advice provided by CIPS on such things as study skills, revision techniques or support and how to handle formal assessments.

If you are on a taught course, it will be up to your tutor to explain how to use the book – when to read the study sessions, when to tackle the activities and questions, and so on.

If you are on a self-study course, or studying independently, you can use the course book in the following way:

- Scan the whole book to get a feel for the nature and content of the subject matter.
- Plan your overall study schedule so that you allow enough time to complete all 20 study sessions well before your examinations – in other words, leaving plenty of time for revision.
- For each session, set aside enough time for reading the text, tackling all the learning activities and self-assessment questions, and the revision question at the end of the session, and for the suggested further reading. Guidance on roughly how long you should set aside for studying each session is given at the beginning of the session.

Now let's take a look at the structure and content of the individual study sessions.

Overview of the study sessions

The course book breaks the content down into 20 sessions, which vary from three to six or seven hours' duration each. However, we are not advising you to study for this sort of time without a break! The sessions are simply a convenient way of breaking the syllabus into manageable chunks. Most people would try to study one or two sessions a week, taking one or two breaks within each session. You will quickly find out what suits you best.

Each session begins with a brief **introduction** which sets out the areas of the syllabus being covered and explains, if necessary, how the session fits in with the topics that come before and after.

After the introduction there is a statement of the **session learning objectives**. The objectives are designed to help you understand exactly what you should be able to do after you've studied the session. You might find it helpful to tick them off as you progress through the session. You will also find them useful during revision. There is one session learning objective for each numbered subsection of the session.

After this, there is a brief section reproducing the learning objectives and indicative content from the official **unit content document**. This will help you to understand exactly which part of the syllabus you are studying in the current session.

Following this, there are **prior knowledge** and **resources** sections if necessary. These will let you know if there are any topics you need to be familiar with before tackling each particular session, or any special resources you might need, such as a calculator or graph paper.

Then the main part of the study session begins, with the first of the numbered main subsections. At regular intervals in each study session, we have provided you with **learning activities**, which are designed to get you actively involved in the learning process. You should always try to complete the activities – usually on a separate sheet of your own paper – before reading on. You will learn much more effectively if you are actively involved in doing something as you study, rather than just passively reading the text in front of you. The feedback or answers to the activities are provided at the end of the session. Do not be tempted to skip the activity.

We also provide a number of **self-assessment questions** in each study session. These are to help you to decide for yourself whether or not you have achieved the learning objectives set out at the beginning of the session. As with the activities, you should always tackle them – usually on a separate sheet of paper. Don't be tempted to skip them. The feedback or answers are again at the end of the session. If you still do not understand a topic having attempted the self-assessment question, always try to re-read the relevant passages in the textbook readings or session, or follow the advice on further reading at the end of the session. If this still doesn't work, you should contact the CIPS Membership and Qualification Advice team.

For most of the learning activities and self-assessment questions you will need to use separate sheets of paper for your answers or responses. Some of the activities or questions require you to complete a table or form, in which case you could write your response in the course book itself, or photocopy the page.

At the end of the session are three final sections.

The first is the **summary**. Use it to remind yourself or check off what you have just studied, or later on during revision.

Then follows the **suggested further reading** section. This section, if it appears, contains recommendations for further reading which you can follow up if you would like to read alternative treatments of the topics. If for any reason you are having difficulty understanding the course book on a particular topic, try one of the alternative treatments recommended. If you are keen to read around and beyond the syllabus, to help you pick up extra points in the examination for example, you may like to try some of the additional readings recommended. If this section does not appear at the end of a session, it usually means that further reading for the session topics is not necessary.

At the end of the session we direct you to a **revision question**, which you will find in a separate section at the end of the course book. Feedback on the questions is also given.

Reading lists

CIPS produces an official reading list, which recommends essential and desirable texts for augmenting your studies. This reading list is available on the CIPS website or from the CIPS Bookshop. This course book is one of the essential texts for this unit. In this section we describe the main characteristics of the other essential text for this unit, which you are strongly urged to buy and use throughout your course.

The other essential text is *The Relationship-Driven Supply Chain: Creating a Culture of Collaboration throughout the Chain* by Barry Crocker and Stuart Emmett, published in its 1st edition by Ashgate Publishing, 2006.

Crocker and Emmett was published just as the present CIPS course book was going to press, so detailed references to it have not been possible. You should find that it provides very useful further detail or perspectives on many of the topics covered by this CIPS course book.

There are very few specific weblinks quoted under the further reading sections in each study session because these can change and frustrate students who cannot find them. All remaining links have been checked as at March 2009. However, students are advised to review the material on the CIPS website under the tab 'professional resources'. There are a large number of documents which can be down loaded by members in this area of the website. Again, specific named documents are not quoted as the continuous review process at CIPS may add, remove and change names over time.

Second edition amendments

As a result of amendments made to the learning outcomes and statements of practice, developments have been made to this course book. Additionally some of the CIPS topic reference files highlighted in the first edition have been replaced and time has required an update of other references to maintain currency.

Working with groups of students using the course book also made it obvious that it would enhance the student's learning experience if vital topics like supply positioning, supplier preferencing and the market management matrix were completely covered in a single study session rather than being separated to highlight their impact upon tactical and strategic relationships. Hence there have been amendments to study sessions 1, 3 and 4.

Unit content coverage

In this section we reproduce the whole of the official CIPS unit content document for this unit. The overall unit characteristics and statements of practice for the unit are given first. Then, in the table that follows, the learning objectives and indicative content are given in the left hand column. In the right hand column are the study sessions in which you will find coverage of the various topics.

Unit characteristics

This unit is designed to enable students to focus on developing and managing effective relationships, old and new, within the supply chain.

Students will be able to review and develop existing relationships and identify opportunities for establishing new relationships that will enhance the performance of the supply chain, while exploring the benefits and risks of establishing such relationships.

By the end of this unit, students will be able to apply a range of tools and techniques to manage relationships and explain how to exploit opportunities in order to maximise the effectiveness of the supply chain.

Statements of practice

On completion of this unit, students will be able to:

- Review the effectiveness of existing relationships and identify potential areas for growth and diversification in the supply chain
- Examine supply chains and appraise key relationships and growth opportunities
- Apply a range of techniques for supplier selection and assessment, for the provision of goods and services
- Appraise procedures to support the outsourcing of services
- Explain the use of a range of interpersonal and communication techniques required to develop personal effectiveness in relationships
- Identify supply chain problems and propose resolutions
- Explain how to monitor and review supply chain relationship effectiveness

Learning objectives and indicative content

1.0 **The context of relationships in supply chain management (Weighting 30%)**

1.1 Classify and describe the range of relationships that may exist within supply chains.   Study session 1
    - Definition of relationships in the context of supply
    - Overview of internal and external relationships

1.2 Evaluate the contribution of appropriate and well-managed relationships in achieving cooperation and collaboration between buyers and suppliers.
Study session 3
- The relationship spectrum
- Adversarial
- Arm's length
- Transactional
- Closer tactical
- Single sourced
- Strategic alliance
- Partnership
- Co-destiny

1.3 Evaluate or analyse the challenges in managing effectively the relationships between purchasers and suppliers.
Study session 3
Study session 4
- Supply positioning model
- Supplier preferencing model
- The reasons for changing the way in which a relationship operates
- Managing risk in commercial relationships
- Buyer and supplier behaviour in relationships
- Market management matrix

1.4 Define the natural life cycle of supply relationships and analyse the position of specific relationships in their life cycle.
Study session 6
- The concept of the relationship life cycle
- The stages of the relationship life cycle
- Linking the relationship life cycle to the relationship spectrum
- Understanding your position in the relationship life cycle

1.5 Differentiate between lean and agile supply philosophies on supplier relationships.
Study session 8
- Traditional supply philosophy
- Lean supply philosophy
- Agile supply philosophy

1.6 Analyse and explain corporate social responsibility (CSR) and ethical, technological, legal and environmental constraints on relationship development.
Study session 7
- Component parts of CSR
- The case for CSR
- The case against CSR
- CSR and supplier development

1.7 Evaluate the relationship between internal and external stakeholders in the supply chain and propose ways of maintaining objectivity within the relationships.
Study session 2
- Ways of maintaining objectivity in relationships
- Services versus manufacturing supply chain relationships
- Technical specialists versus purchasing specialists

1.8 Evaluate the role of culture and relationship values within supply networks.
Study session 16
- Organisational culture
- Relationship values and behaviours
- Managing buyer and supplier perspectives on values and behaviours

2.0 Assessing and selecting suppliers (Weighting 25%)

2.1 Formulate objectives for relationships with suppliers.   Study session 9
   - The impact of internal and external stakeholders on supplier selection
   - The impact of internal suppliers on supplier selection
   - The external supplier's view of the selection process
   - Manufacturing and service supply chains
   - Upstream and downstream supply chain activities

2.2 Evaluate and apply techniques for supplier appraisal and selection.   Study session 9
   - Supplier appraisal techniques
   - Vendor rating
   - Supplier auditing

2.3 Evaluate the effectiveness of the assessment process.   Study session 10
   - Supplier appraisal deliverables
   - Measuring the supplier appraisal process
   - Effect of supplier appraisal upon relationship development
   - Supplier appraisal in the context of the relationship cycle

2.4 Evaluate the constraints on supplier selection within the public sector.   Study session 11
   - Legislation affecting supplier selection
   - Supplier selection routes available to the public sector
   - The buyer's perspective on selection legislation
   - The supplier's perspective on selection legislation

2.5 Analyse the role of reciprocal trading in purchasing relationships.   Study session 12
   - Definition of reciprocal trading
   - Examples of organisations' policies on reciprocal trading
   - Managing reciprocal trading in the selection process
   - The impact of reciprocal trading on relationships during and after the selection process

2.6 Analyse and explain how to mitigate against the potential risks of a change of supply source.   Study session 13
   - Risks of change
   - Cost of change
   - Mitigation of risk and cost
   - Communication and stakeholder management

3.0 Managing outsourced relationships (Weighting 15%)

3.1 Develop and apply procedures for undertaking an outsourcing exercise and maintaining effective outsourced relationships.   Study session 14
   - The definition of and difference between service contracts, sub-contracting, outsourcing and insourcing
   - The outsourcing decision-making process
   - The outsourcing process
   - Legal implications of outsourcing

3.2 Explain how performance should be managed in outsourcing exercises.   Study session 15
   - Managing the outsourcing contract
   - Establishing and implementing performance measures

- Performance measures and their impact on the different parties within the supply chain, that is manufacturers, retailers, service providers
- The importance of measuring relationship development across the supply chain
- Difficulties involved in measuring performance across the supply chain
- The buyer and supplier perspectives on performance measurement

4.8 Evaluate a range of measurement tools to assess the performance of suppliers and the strength of relationships between purchasers and suppliers.   Study session 20
- Executive sponsorship
- Account management
- Continuous improvement programmes
- Service level agreements
- Key performance indicators
- Relationship assessment tools
- Feedback mechanisms

4.9 Review the circumstances in which supply relationships end, and select appropriate methods for their termination and, where appropriate, determine ways of retrieving and retaining the relationship.   Study session 6
- Resolving disputes
- Using the contract to terminate a relationship
- Maintaining a supply relationship post-conflict
- Ways of retrieving and retaining the relationships

4.10 Analyse the relationship challenges of multi-national suppliers in the context of a global supply chain.   Study session 17
- Barriers to successful ongoing relationship management
- Multi-national organisations as customers in local and national supply chains
- Multi-national organisations as suppliers in local and national supply chains
- The positive impact of multi-national organisations in developing economies

Study session 1

Definition and classification of purchasing and supply relationships

Introduction

Defining a subject is always the first thing to do before getting into the detail. The definitions have been placed at this point in the guide to form a point of reference at a place in the text which is easy to remember. Avoid the temptation to skip them – they are vitally important to your understanding!

Session learning objectives

After completing this session you should be able to:

1.1 Define key terms used throughout this guide.
1.2 Explain the different types of relationship within the 'relationship spectrum'.
1.3 Define and differentiate between a range of relationships between buyers and sellers.
1.4 Formulate a basic risk management process.
1.5 Apply the risk management process to strategic situations.

Unit content coverage

This study session covers the following topics from the official CIPS unit content document.

Learning objective

1.1 Classify and describe the range of relationships which may exist within supply chains.

Timing

You should set aside about 6 hours to read and complete this session, including learning activities, self-assessment questions, the suggested further reading (if any) and the revision question.

1.1 Key terms used throughout the course book

Managing purchasing and supply relationships leads us right into the commercial arena.

Commercial

The Merriam-Webster Dictionary uses many words to define 'commercial'. However, it is summarised as:

> 'Occupied with or engaged in commerce or work intended for commerce. Suitable, adequate, or prepared for commerce, viewed with regard to profit, designed for a large market, emphasizing skills and subjects useful in business.'

> By permission. From the *Merriam-Webster Online Dictionary* ©2005 by Merriam-Webster, Incorporated (Merriam-Webster: http://www.merriam-webster.com).

It sounds obvious, but let's get it out in the open. Apart from the public and charity sectors, organisations are in business to make a profit. They trade to sell goods and services for more than they buy them for. We need to recognise this driver and the pressures that it creates on organisations, the people who work in them and the relationships that exist between people in the same and different organisations. This pressure influences the tactics that both buyers and sellers use in doing business; it influences the way people behave towards other people and as such it is at the heart of many of the relationships in our working life.

Relationship

The Merriam-Webster Dictionary defines 'relationship' as:

> 'A state of being related or interrelated, the relation connecting or binding participants in a relationship, a state of affairs existing between those having relations or dealings.'

> By permission. From the *Merriam-Webster Online Dictionary* ©2005 by Merriam-Webster, Incorporated (Merriam-Webster: http://www.merriam-webster.com).

Like it or not, we are related to our suppliers, we might even have a close relationship which binds us to them (and them to us) and we certainly have dealings with them on a regular basis. Our suppliers and the people who work for them are, in varying degrees, important to us, and the success of our business depends upon them and, in the context of our relationship with them, what they are and are not prepared to do for us!

Purchasing and supply relationships

It is therefore possible to define a purchasing and supply relationship as 'A business relationship, varying in its degree of closeness, between the people of two or more organisations for the supply of goods, works, materials and services with the objective of benefit for all parties and normally profit for at least one party.'

Unpicking this definition, we can see that:

- there are differences in closeness of relationships
- people are involved

- everyone involved should benefit and
- the profit motive will normally appear somewhere in the relationship.

'Benefit' and 'profit' may not of course mean money in every case. There are cases where suppliers will work for a lower than normal return or no return at all. In these cases we need to understand that the suppliers' motives may include the kudos of working with an organisation, gaining market share or gaining a reference site. These are all 'valuable' to sales organisations and too often purchasing organisations give their advantage away for nothing. An example here might be a supplier providing goods to the royal family.

Supplier

A European buyer once described suppliers thus: 'Suppliers are like dogs, you find them stealing food from your fridge and so you kick them. The dog goes away, but later he will always come back to try and get more things from the fridge.'

What an appalling description! Yet some buyers behave like this towards suppliers. Close your eyes and visualise the suppliers you meet. What do you see, a person or an organisation? When we meet suppliers, do we actually not meet human beings? Do they bleed if they cut themselves? The answer of course is 'yes' to both questions and so let's understand that the people we meet on behalf of the supplying organisations have feelings, in the same way that buyers are people who represent their organisation and, incidentally, have feelings too.

This does not mean the adoption of soft, easy relationships! But it does mean that a relationship with a supplier recognises the human factors in working with other people to get the best out of them and their organisation. We will discuss a range of relationships within a concept called the relationship spectrum later in this study session. However, first let's define a supplier.

The CIPS *Official Dictionary of Purchasing and Supply Terminology* (Compton and Jessop, 2001) defines 'supplier' as:

> 'A general term used by supplies staff for all kinds of providers of goods and services purchased or procured by them.'

This is basic and has some advantages, but it is inadequate. **Supplier** is a general and well-understood term and it does cover a wide range of providers, from a small printer of stationery to a multi-million pound outsourcing contract. It can be useful to help some organisations, who put on airs and graces in their relationships with us, to understand that they are in fact 'suppliers'.

To fully define what is meant by the term 'supplier', the definition must include something about the:

- benefit that is brought to the purchasing organisation by the supplier

- differing relationships that are available
- benefit that the supplier seeks to gain from the relationship with its customers
- different business objectives that the supplier and purchasing organisation have
- resource that the supplier is and can be for the purchasing organisation
- need for quality.

The definition that follows is more complex, yet it holds within it the points identified above:

> 'An independent commercial organisation used as a resource within different relationship types to deliver goods, works, materials and services of an appropriate quality to its customers as requested and specified by the customers in return for payment, benefit and the achievement of its own business goals.'

This definition will need adapting to include suppliers who are in fact different parts of the same organisation and also suppliers of goods and services who are motivated by the concept of 'service' and not the concept of profit; for example public sector organisations set up to supply training or information to the general public or special-interest groups.

Other definitions used in this course book

The following terms appear within this course book . The list below also shows the study session in which the term is primarily focused on.

- adversarial relationship (study session 1)
- agile supply (study session 8)
- arm's-length relationship (study session 1)
- closer tactical relationship (study session 1)
- co-destiny relationship (study session 1)
- corporate social responsibility (study session 7)
- e-procurement (study session 5)
- e-purchasing (study session 5)
- e-sourcing (study session 5)
- lean supply (study session 8)
- market management matrix (study session 4)
- outsourcing relationship (study session 1)
- partnership relationship (study session 1)
- reciprocal trading (study session 12)
- relationship development (study session 19)
- relationship spectrum (study session 1)
- risk management (study session 1)
- risk (study session 1)
- single-sourced relationship (study session 1)
- stakeholder (study session 2)
- strategic alliance relationship (study session 1)
- supplier appraisal (study session 9)
- supplier development (study session 19)
- supplier preferencing (study session 4)
- supplier relationship management (SRM) (study session 19)

- supply positioning (study session 3)
- transactional relationship (study session 1)
- vendor rating (study session 9)

Caveat

Purchasing as a profession enjoys using several words to define the same or similar concepts. Consider 'purchasing' and 'procurement'. In discussing purchasing with other people throughout your career you will be wise to check their use of a term relative to the concept being discussed. This is frustrating to us all, but we have no choice but to get used to it.

1.2 The buyer/seller relationship spectrum

As human beings we meet other people and have relationships with them. Some of these relationships are immensely close, others are more distant and some people we will only meet once in our lives. In the same way, organisations purchasing goods and services will have purchasing and supply relationships with a large number of supplier organisations and their characteristics and objectives will lead them to form stronger and more frequent ties with some supplier organisations than with others. For example, an industrial organisation may rarely need to use a specialist firm of caterers, and their relationship with the caterers will be very much more distant than it is with suppliers of its raw material, yet a racecourse will have a close relationship with the same catering organisation who provide high-quality food for its corporate hospitality clients.

There is therefore a spectrum of relationships between buyers and sellers. Figure 1.1 presents the extremes of the **relationship spectrum** graphically, with closer relationships on the right-hand side of the page and more distant relationships on the left. The diagrams of this concept will be developed throughout study sessions 1 and 2.

Figure 1.1: The extremes of the relationship spectrum

◄─────────────────────────────────────►

Distant relationships   Closer relationships

At this stage of the process four key aspects need to be considered:

1   Given that this programme of study is being initiated from the purchaser's viewpoint, the view of the relationship spectrum in this study session and many others in this guide is being approached from the same viewpoint. Later we will consider the seller's view of relationships.
2   The needs, objectives and aspirations of both organisations in the relationship mean that over time the relationship may move along the spectrum to a new position and even back to its old position.
3   It is fundamental to our dealings with sellers that we have the view that however we see our relationship with them, we are going to behave in a professional and ethical manner throughout the relationship.
4   There is no one 'correct' or 'appropriate' relationship type or style. Buyers need to be able to reflect their organisation and its requirements

1

in one of a number of relationship styles, each of which is managed professionally.

Within the relationship spectrum there are a number of names that are given to relationships and each name is placed on the spectrum (see figure 1.2).

Figure 1.2: The relationship spectrum – diagram 1

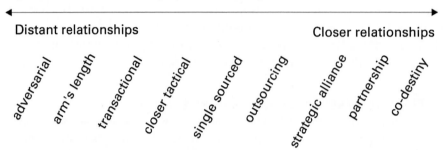

Distant relationships   Closer relationships

adversarial   arm's length   transactional   closer tactical   single sourced   outsourcing   strategic alliance   partnership   co-destiny

Learning activity 1.1

Consider suppliers you work with and how you might classify your relationships with them. Table 1.1 identifies the relationship types and provides space for your notes.

Table 1.1 Your suppliers and the relationship spectrum

Relationship type	Your notes
Adversarial relationship	
Arm's-length relationship	
Transactional relationship	
Closer tactical relationship	
Single-sourced relationship	
Outsourcing relationship	
Strategic alliance	
Partnership relationship	
Co-destiny relationship	

Feedback on page 15

Self-assessment question 1.1

The relationship spectrum definitions are listed below alphabetically. Take a blank piece of paper and *from memory*, draw them in the order they appear in figure 1.2 from right to left:

- adversarial relationship
- arm's-length relationship
- closer tactical relationship
- co-destiny relationship
- outsourcing relationship
- partnership relationship
- single-sourced relationship

(continued on next page)

Self-assessment question 1.1 *(continued)*
- strategic alliance
- transactional relationship.

Feedback on page 16

1.3 Define and differentiate between different relationships

Each of the relationship types is described in table 1.2. In study session 3 we will investigate the characteristics of each relationship in more detail; however, at this early stage of your study, it is important to start to understand the differences in these types of relationships.

Table 1.2 Relationship types

Relationship type or style	Definition
Adversarial relationship	An adversarial relationship is one where both the buyer and the seller seek to maximise their position in any given supply opportunity, even to the detriment of the other party or parties.
	These relationships are characterised by conflict, opposition and a very low level of trust.
Arm's-length relationship	An arm's-length relationship is one where a buyer buys infrequently from a supplier, and does not have high volumes or the need for a closer relationship.
	No matter how good the supplier is, there is no point (for the buyer) in getting into a closer relationship. The supplier is used when needed.
Transactional relationship	A transactional relationship focuses on the successful completion of ordinary transactions which deliver low-value, low-risk goods and services to the buyer from a competent supplier.
	Successful completion of these transactions makes our business tick. Being adversarial here could cause pain for the buyer.
Closer tactical relationship	A closer tactical relationship is one with a competent supplier who focuses on the successful completion of low-risk transactions and coordinates the supply of low-risk goods and services from other (second tier?) suppliers.
	The benefit is worth the investment in time upstream and downstream, but a really 'close' relationship will not meet the buyer's needs.
Single-sourced relationship	A single-sourced relationship is one where a purchasing organisation forms an exclusive agreement with one supplier for the supply of a range of specified items, usually at a fixed unit price and for a specific period.
	This relationship gives economies of scale benefits to both the buyer and the seller.

(continued on next page)

Table 1.2 *(continued)*

Relationship type or style	Definition
Outsourcing relationship	An outsourcing relationship involves the retention of responsibility for services by the purchasing organisation, but the devolution of the day-to-day performance of those services to an external organisation, under a contract with agreed standards, costs and conditions. *This is a strategic decision to utilise the expertise of a supplier rather than perform the services/make the goods ourselves.*
Strategic alliance relationship	A strategic alliance relationship is one between two organisations who work together for the provision of goods or services to their own mutual benefit. The organisations may ally themselves for all or part of their service/product portfolio, a given geographical area, a given market or for defensive reasons. *Buyers may be part of an alliance; however, they may also face an alliance and in some cases may not be aware that they are facing an alliance.*
Partnership relationship	A partnership relationship is a commitment between a buyer and a supplier to a long-term relationship based on trust and clear mutually agreed objectives. Sharing risks and rewards is fundamental through the common goals of: • continuous improvement • an improved competitive position • the elimination of waste • acceleration of innovation • expansion of markets • the growth of profit. *Many organisations 'talk' about partnerships, but living up to the partnership definition is not as easy as defining it.*
Co-destiny relationship	'Co-destiny is a strategic relationship where the organisations involved choose to share common destinies in all aspects of their business for mutual benefit. The relationship relies on total trust and both organisations become fully interdependent and as such, they succeed or fail together' (devised by Ford, Fogg, Ayliffe and Schollar) *Organisations may be supply chain partners, or members of a supplier association. All will invest and all succeed or fail together.*

Learning activity 1.2

This activity is a progression of learning activity 1.1 above. Go to learning activity 1.1 above, look at the names of the suppliers you have assigned to the relationships, and review and refine the list using table 1.2. Use the

(continued on next page)

Learning activity 1.2 *(continued)*

blank rows to write the names of suppliers. Use the space to reflect on why you have pigeonholed a given supplier against a given definition, make a note of that too in the space provided and make notes about whether the relationship is exactly as defined, different or even there in name only.

Feedback on page 16

Self-assessment question 1.2

Match the statements in table 1.3 below to the relationship types within the relationship spectrum. Alphabetically, the relationship types are:

- adversarial relationship
- arm's-length relationship
- closer tactical relationship
- co-destiny relationship
- single-sourced relationship
- outsourcing relationship
- partnership relationship
- strategic alliance
- transactional relationship.

Table 1.3 Relationship types – revision

	Statement	Relationship type
1	This relationship is where the supplier simply delivers the goods.	
2	This relationship is where we work together for specific goals.	
3	This relationship is where we chose this supplier alone above the others.	
4	This relationship is long term, sharing and caring.	
5	This relationship is one where the specialist supplier takes on certain functions for us.	
6	This relationship is one where we can't envisage life without them.	
7	This relationship is one where many of our ordinary requirements are taken care of for us.	
8	This relationship is one where we call the supplier when we need them.	
9	This relationship is characterised by conflict.	

Feedback on page 16

1.4 A basic risk management process

Introduction

The Merriam-Webster Dictionary uses many words to define **risk**; however, it is summarised as:

'The possibility of loss or injury, someone or something that creates or suggests a hazard, the chance of loss or the perils to the subject matter of an insurance contract; *also*: the degree of probability of such loss'

By permission. From the *Merriam-Webster Online Dictionary* ©2005 by Merriam-Webster, Incorporated (Merriam-Webster: http://www.merriam-webster.com).

Purchasing and supply relationships involve risk. A supplier may not deliver on time, the delivery may include broken components or the service may not meet the needs of the people who receive it. Equally, the purchasing organisation may not specify its requirement adequately, may not give the supplier enough time to deliver or may order the wrong service. The risk, if it materialises, may have little or no impact, it may impact profit, or for example the delivery of a service to senior citizens by a government department, or even in an extreme case it may cause loss of life.

In her book *Investment Appraisal for Non-financial Managers* (1997), Kate Moran describes risk as follows:

'The risk of an investment is associated with uncertainty – it is the chance that expected outcomes for tomorrow are not fulfilled – that something else happens instead. One way of looking at a risk is to say that risk occurs when more things can happen than will happen.'

Risk management is the process of recognising the risk and minimising the likelihood of a given risk occurring and the impact to the purchasing organisation if the risk does occur.

A risk management process

Risk management requires the following steps as identified in figure 1.4 and each step in this process is described below.

Figure 1.4: A risk management process

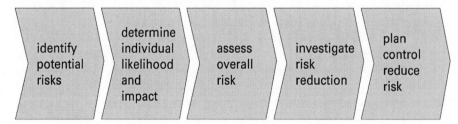

Step 1: Identify sources of risk

Sources of risk can include:

*   Predictable risks: it's cold in winter; vehicles need antifreeze to continue operation, tender plants in a garden may need covering. People in your team go on holiday causing a shortage of staff; a new product will replace an old one, causing a drop in demand for components of the old product. Christmas comes; demand for postal services peaks and some items take longer to reach customers. Note that some of these risks are internal and some external to the purchasing organisation.
*   Unpredictable risks: an organisation may attempt to take over your organisation, a road accident may delay a shipment or a service

provider, demand for your service may exceed your resources, people within your organisation may leave, a new system may cause delays in processing payments within a government department. Again, note that some of these risks are internal and some external to the purchasing organisation.

- Risks may be technical, involving machines and systems, non-technical involving people, or legal involving the risk of being taken to court if for example health and safety legislation is not complied with. Some risks are, by their very nature, easier to identify than others. Ways in which risks can be identified include:
  - the previous experience of the purchasing team, colleagues from internal customer areas and suppliers (where appropriate) working in multidisciplinary teams
  - specific research into situations and scenarios
  - using specialists to advise and investigate potential risks
  - workshops running 'what if' scenarios and analysing and evaluating the outcomes of the various scenarios.

Step 2: Determine individual likelihood and impact

The impact of any one risk is arrived at by considering the likelihood of the risk arising and the consequence to the organisation of the risk arising.

It may be assumed that it is very likely that during a peak holiday season a given motorway will be crowded and deliveries on that route and other routes in the area will require a longer time to be effected.

The consequence of a failure to deliver food to a motorway services area during a peak period in a holiday season may mean that the company running the motorway services misses major sales and many families have no opportunity to buy food. The consequences for people relying on the motorway services are significant, the bad publicity for the motorway services organisation might lead other families to plan their journeys to miss those services.

A failure to deliver wheels to a car production plant may mean that production has to stop, whereas a two-day delay in the receipt of copier paper to the car production plant or the motorway services may not cause any problem at all.

Purchasing organisations must evaluate their purchases and consider the likelihood and impact of any one risk. Where the risk, whatever it is, will affect the delivery of important goods and services then more steps will need to be taken to prevent the materialisation of the risk.

Step 3: Assess overall impact

Several different risks may impinge upon the purchase of any one requirement of goods and services. It is therefore prudent to consider the risks together. One common way of undertaking this analysis is to put the risks into a table and arrive at a common view of their likelihood and impact amongst key stakeholders. For example, consider table 1.5.

- The likelihood of the risk arising is scored on a scale from one to five, with five being a very high risk and one being a very low risk.

- The impact of the risk arising is scored on a scale from one to five, with five being a very high risk and one being a very low risk.
- The scores are multiplied together and the right-hand column is added to give a total. The total is then compared with the worst-case scenario.

Table 1.5 Risk assessment – overall impact

Risk description	Likelihood	Impact	Calc
Late delivery of final specification	3	4	12
Shortage of resources at service provider during installation period due to holidays	2	5	10
Shortage of hardware components	1	5	5
Drop in demand in home market	2	3	6
Problems with new version of software	2	4	8
Total			41

The overall potential impact of the risks identified is therefore 41. On its own this is a meaningless number, it has to be seen in the context of the worst case scenario, which in this case is $5 \times 5 \times 5 = 125$ (5 risks identified × a worst-case likelihood for each of 5 × highest impact for each at 5). Proportionately the final figures are then graded. In this case where the calculations reveal a total risk between:

- 5 and 25 the risk is very low (the bottom 20% with 125 as 100%)
- 26 and 50 the risk is low (the next 20% with 125 as 100%)
- 51 and 75 the risk is medium (the middle 20% with 125 as 100%)
- 76 and 100 the risk is high (the next to highest 20% with 125 as 100%)
- 101 and 125 the risk is very high (the highest 20% with 125 as 100%).

This purchase would therefore be considered a low risk.

Step 4: Investigate risk reduction

Where an overall risk was initially judged to be high, the individual risks need to be assessed and investigated to determine whether they can be reduced before the purchase goes ahead. It may not be welcomed in all quarters, but it is appropriate in some cases to question whether a purchase should go ahead given the high risks that have been identified. In the above example the highest risk is the late delivery of the final specification, and prudent buyers would investigate what could be done to reduce that risk further.

Determining the likelihood can lead to questions about why a risk is important, what can be done to reduce it and how the reduction will be achieved, when it will occur and whether that can be changed, who should be responsible for managing and reducing the risk and finally what the various options are to reduce risk cost. Risk can be avoided by choosing an alternative path or solution in a purchase, deflected to another party under contractual terms or alleviated by a contingency, where resources or money is set aside for the worst case scenarios, should they arise.

Step 5: Plan, control and reduce risk

The challenging and even exciting part of risk identification and management has been discussed above. However, the boring and painstaking part of the process is the planning, the monitoring of the actuals against the plan, the selection of action to alert others to the risk which is materialising and the action necessary to bring matters back to where they should be, if that is possible. Important steps here include the:

- nomination of someone who is responsible for checking actuals against targets
- agreement of the tools that will be used to track the risks
- visibility of checks and the use of the tracking tools
- nomination of a decision maker once risks appear to be materialising
- agreed escalation procedures.

These roles will need to be adopted by people within internal stakeholder areas, purchasing and suppliers, depending upon the purchase in question. Software can be used to diarise checks, and reports from suppliers on progress can be automated, with action only necessary in exceptional circumstances. Simple manual processes like a monthly top risk form circulated to interested parties and forming a discussion aimed at risk reduction are also used as prime monitoring tools.

Learning activity 1.3

You are purchasing an important new item from a supplier you have not dealt with before. Apply the risk management process in this section to that purchase.

Feedback on page 16

Self-assessment question 1.3

Determine whether the following statements are true or false and give reasons for your answers.

1   Risk assessment is best done by purchasing people alone. True or false?
2   All risks must be treated equally. True or false?
3   Risk management is a process that requires individual risks to be identified first. True or false?
4   Some circumstances which lead to a risk are predictable. True or false?
5   Purchases which appear to be a high risk should be stopped. True or false?

Feedback on page 17

1.5   Risk management in strategic situations

The same risk management process outlined in figure 1.4 can be applied to identifying and managing risk in strategic situations.

1

Learning activity 1.4

Reflect upon the strategic relationships that your organisation has and the risks to which you may be exposed.

Feedback on page 17

The difference in strategic situations may be the complexity but will certainly be the consequence of the risk materialising. In strategic situations risk may, on occasion, be about the survival of the organisation or organisations working together in a strategic alliance. The risk may come from various sides:

- Inside one of the organisations. One of the organisations may become financially unstable, people inside the organisation may behave improperly to the people within the other organisation, or there may be a strategic decision to end the alliance and/or seek another partner. All of these circumstances may have serious repercussions for the other organisation within the alliance.
- Inside the alliance and between the allies or partners. The organisations may start to disagree; they may start to be secretive towards each other or one party may be attracted towards a third party. One of the partners could be taken over by a competitor of the other partner. Again, all of these circumstances may have serious repercussions for the other organisation within the alliance.
- Outside the alliance from competitors. Both organisations may suffer if competitors manage to steal their market share, or if their offering is for some reason not favoured by customers.
- Outside the alliance from other sources. Circumstances outside the alliance may make the goods and services offered by it unwanted by the market.

All of these circumstances and others may impact the relationship between the organisations and the criticality of the relationship to the organisations is one reason why risk identification and risk management are activities specified as being undertaken jointly by partners and allies within the closest relationships identified within the relationship spectrum.

Self-assessment question 1.4

Complete the text below, filling in the blank words using the words in the following list:

- alliance
- disagreeing
- existence
- favoured
- fundamental
- management

(continued on next page)

14

Self-assessment question 1.4 *(continued)*
- offering
- outside
- people
- together
- within

Risk identification and risk _____ are _____ activities for allies and partners to conduct _____. Risk in this circumstance can threaten the very _____ of the organisations concerned and can arise from:

- _____ one organisation
- organisations _____
- competitors to the _____
- the behaviour of _____ in one organisation
- _____ forces.

The alliance can also have major problems if their _____ is for some reason not _____ by customers.

Feedback on page 17

Revision question

There is no revision question for this session.

Summary

Purchasing and supply relationships and managing them is vital to all organisations, irrespective of sector. It is important to:

- recognise that no one relationship meets all the needs of a purchasing organisation
- consider the different needs of an organisation and develop and appropriate relationships
- contrast the risk and relative cost of the goods and services bought by organisations in considering a relationship using supply positioning.

Used properly, it facilitates a multifunctional view from the point of view of the purchasing organisation and allows quantification of risk and the development of purchasing strategies and tactics in a number of areas relevant to the management of purchasing and supply relationships.

Suggested further reading

You could read the relevant sections of Compton and Jessop (2001) and Steele and Court (1996).

Feedback on learning activities and self-assessment questions

Feedback on learning activity 1.1

The relationship types are defined in section 1.3.

Now go on and use self-assessment question 1.1 to test your memory of the relationship spectrum.

Feedback on self-assessment question 1.1

Your diagram should appear as in figure 1.3.

Figure 1.3: The relationship spectrum – diagram 1

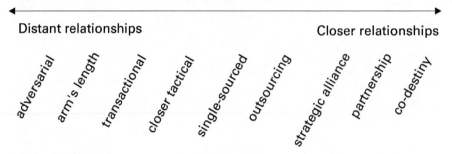

Feedback on learning activity 1.2

You will find that some of your relationships match exactly and some are more or less than those described. You may for example feel that a relationship is best described as a partnership *minus* one or two attributes or that your relationship and the name match, but you feel you would like to nudge the relationship along the spectrum one way or other. That's fine, for the names and their places on the spectrum will not exactly fit all of the relationships of everyone. If the exercise starts to make you think about working and developing with your suppliers then it has achieved its aim.

Feedback on self-assessment question 1.2

Table 1.4 Relationship types – revision

	Relationship type
1	Transactional relationship
2	Strategic alliance/Specific collaboration relationship
3	Single-sourced relationship
4	Partnership relationship
5	Outsourcing relationship
6	Co-destiny relationship
7	Closer tactical relationship
8	Arm's-length relationship
9	Adversarial relationship

Feedback on learning activity 1.3

Identification:

- Ask what could go wrong with the item once it arrived.
- Ask what could prevent the supplier delivering.

Determine likelihood and impact:

- How would its failure impact our organisation? How likely is that?

- Is it likely that the supplier would not be able to deliver? How would that impact us?

Assess overall impact:

- How do we assess the likelihood of all of the risk materialising, with the impact as we assess it in each case, against the worst-case scenario?

Investigate risk reduction:

- Take each risk and understand how we can reduce the likelihood and the impact.
- Investigate the supplier's track record with other customers, look at their accounts, test their offerings.

Plan, control, reduce risk:

- Appoint someone to keep close to the supplier and internal customers during the initial delivery period until the supplier's track record is established.

Feedback on self-assessment question 1.3

1 False. Purchasing people need to be involved, but they need the input of internal stakeholders and suppliers in a number of cases.
2 False. Some risks warrant much more attention from those managing them than others.
3 True. Identify the individual risks, their likelihood and their impact first, then consider all of the risks together.
4 True. Christmas is an annual event, it leads to shortages of some products due to increased demand. Whilst the precise extent of the increase in demand is a risk which needs to be considered, the fact that sales of sticky tape will increase and could lead to shortages is predictable.
5 True and perhaps false as well! Prudence would suggest doing everything possible to avoid high risk situations; however, the risk of a purchase may mean that an opportunity can be grasped by an organisation before its competitors and great rewards may accrue. The Special Air Services motto is 'who dares wins'.

Feedback on learning activity 1.4

Essentially the risks in these situations can cause the organisation's primary processes to stop functioning and even cause the organisation itself to fail. High-street banks believe that without IT for five days they would be out of business.

Feedback on self-assessment question 1.4

Risk identification and risk *management* are *fundamental* activities for allies and partners to conduct *together*. Risk in this circumstance can threaten the very *existence* of the organisations concerned and can arise from:

- *within* one organisation
- organisations *disagreeing*

1

- competitors to the *alliance*
- the behaviour of *people* in one organisation
- *outside* forces.

The alliance can also have major problems if their *offering* is for some reason not *favoured* by customers.

Relationship and process stakeholders

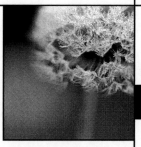

Who has a stake
in the process of
purchasing?

Introduction

This study session defines stakeholders, explores who they are in different circumstances and investigates both their needs and the strains and stresses of working with them in the process of purchasing.

Session learning objectives

After completing this session you should be able to:

2.1 Identify and evaluate stakeholders in the process of purchasing.
2.2 Evaluate typical requirements of external customer stakeholders.
2.3 Evaluate typical requirements of internal customer stakeholders other than technical specialists.
2.4 Evaluate typical requirements of technical specialist stakeholders.
2.5 Evaluate typical requirements of internal supplier stakeholders.
2.6 Evaluate typical requirements of external supplier stakeholders.

Unit content coverage

This study session covers the following topics from the official CIPS unit content document.

Learning objective

1.7 Evaluate the relationship between internal and external stakeholders in the supply chain and propose ways of maintaining objectivity within the relationships.

Prior knowledge

You should have access to an organisation which purchases.

Timing

You should set aside about 6 hours to read and complete this session, including learning activities, self-assessment questions, the suggested further reading (if any) and the revision question.

2

2.1 What are stakeholders?

Definition

Stakeholders are people working in different functions of organisations who have an ongoing interest and influence on the process of purchasing.

To fully evaluate the term 'stakeholder', it is appropriate to include suppliers and customers.

Learning activity 2.1

For your own organisation, or one with which you are familiar, identify all those functions or groups that have an interest in the purchasing function. Try to group them according to whether they are primary functions within the organisation, functions directly related to purchasing, other business support functions, or outside groups.

Feedback on page 36

Who typically are stakeholders?

Different organisations will have different people who have an ongoing interest in the process of purchasing. Three examples are given below:

- a manufacturing organisation
- a service organisation
- a local government body.

Stakeholders in a manufacturing organisation

Figure 2.1 shows typical stakeholders within a manufacturing organisation.

Figure 2.1: Typical stakeholders – manufacturing

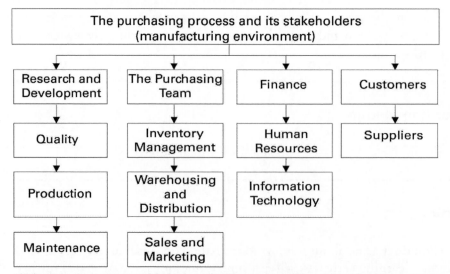

NB: The hierarchical sequence of the business functions in the chart is not meant to give prominence to one function over another, it is simply a convenient way of grouping stakeholders together in this environment.

This diagram demonstrates that many functions within a manufacturing organisation have interest and influence in the process of purchasing. The stakeholders break down into four broad groups:

- Those who are directly involved in the primary business functions of the organisation. Frequently functions like production and maintenance are also called internal customers.
- Those who are aligned with purchasing in supply chain functions.
- Other functions who support the primary business processes and are also internal customers where they influence specific purchases.
- External parties like suppliers and customers.

The requirements of groups of stakeholders is discussed later in this study session; however, consider the influences – which will sometimes conflict – that people in different business areas within this manufacturing organisation will want to have on choice of supplier, choice of item, standards used, timing, quantities ordered and quantities held in stock. Managing a relationship with these different groups is a vital part of purchasing's role.

Stakeholders in a service organisation

Take a look at figure 2.2.

Figure 2.2: Service industry stakeholders

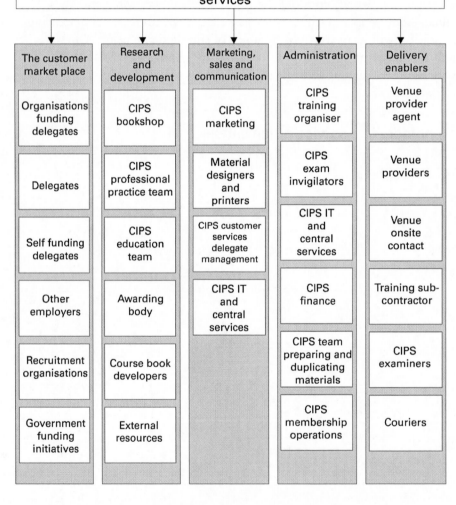

The purchasing process and its stakeholders - service supply
CIPS graduate diploma training
delivered by the CIPS public training

As a chartered institute, CIPS is governed by its members and a
governance structure which is prescribed by
the charter and bye-laws. The charter invests the 'government
and control of the institute and its affairs' in a
council which is its senior governing body. Through the
governance structure these stakeholders have a
formative role to play in the development of all products and
services

The customer market place	Research and development	Marketing, sales and communication	Administration	Delivery enablers
Organisations funding delegates	CIPS bookshop	CIPS marketing	CIPS training organiser	Venue provider agent
Delegates	CIPS professional practice team	Material designers and printers	CIPS exam invigilators	Venue providers
Self funding delegates	CIPS education team	CIPS customer services delegate management	CIPS IT and central services	Venue onsite contact
Other employers	Awarding body	CIPS IT and central services	CIPS finance	Training sub-contractor
Recruitment organisations	Course book developers		CIPS team preparing and duplicating materials	CIPS examiners
Government funding initiatives	External resources		CIPS membership operations	Couriers

NB: The hierarchical sequence of the business functions in the chart is not meant to give prominence to one function over another, it is simply a convenient way of grouping stakeholders together in this environment.

Within the organisation that designs and delivers the Graduate Diploma to the purchasing profession there are many stakeholders. Different views will be expressed about what the syllabus should comprise, how the examinations are structured and how the programmes will be delivered. Bringing the programme together is a complex feat of organisation.

Stakeholders in a local government organisation

Figure 2.3 represents the stakeholders in the process of purchasing in a local authority within the UK.

Figure 2.3: Typical stakeholders – UK County Council

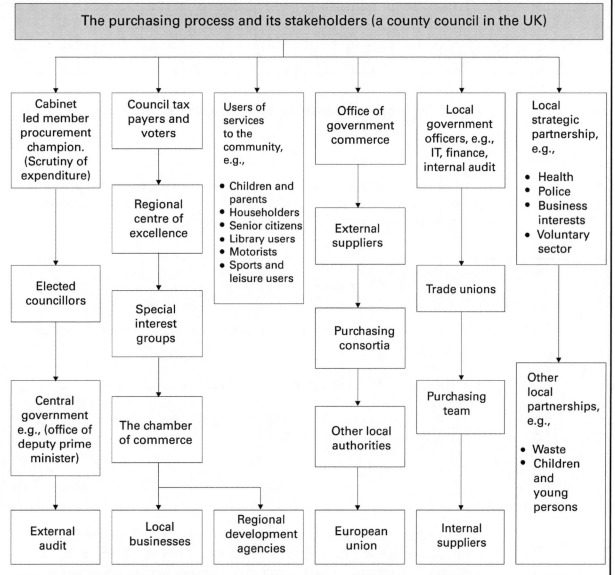

NB: The hierarchical sequence of the business functions in this chart is not meant to give prominence to one function over another, it is simply a convenient way of grouping stakeholders together in this environment. The author would like to thank Fiona Holbourn of Leicestershire county council and Ken May of ESPO for their assistance in refining this diagram

Here we can see that literally hundreds of people have a stake in their community and what is bought by it and for it. For example, a new road scheme may impact residents directly, different political parties may have views, access to a sports centre or school may be impacted and the local chamber of commerce may have a strong view. Special-interest groups may be formed to attempt to halt the development. There may be several options, some costing more and others costing less, with different options impacting different residents. The specification may be changed and changed again as the democratic process takes its course. Suppliers may be asked to quote for several options, which is an additional cost to them. Changes may be made after contracts are signed if an election means that a political party with differing views comes to power.

2

Self-assessment question 2.1

List ten typical stakeholders in the purchasing process.

Feedback on page 37

2.2 Typical requirements of external customer stakeholders

Definition

External customers are 'organisations not part of the buyer's organisation who are prepared to pay for goods, works, materials and services provided by the buyer's organisation'.

Learning activity 2.2

Consider the three most important external customers to your organisation. Name them.

1 Consider the impact that they have within your organisation, its processes and the goods and services that are made and/or delivered.
2 Consider the changes or things you have to do for or because of specific customers with your suppliers.

Feedback on page 37

External customers, often represented by buyers themselves, will focus on areas similar to the ones that we ourselves as buyers will focus on. The buyers at an external customer will of course consider our organisation using the supply positioning model and be more or less interested in our organisation, depending upon their view. However, their view may include:

- delivery, to the right place, on time, undamaged
- cost, lower in absolute terms
- total cost of ownership (TCOO)
- price, if they have not yet moved on to TCOO
- quality, fitness for purpose
- quantity, a full delivery
- service responsiveness
- changes in schedule
- proactivity, early warning of supply problems
- proactivity, offering new products and services
- our organisation carrying stocks for them.

These requirements may impact purchasing processes in a number of ways. Four examples are provided below, you may be able to think of others.

- One obvious impact is changes in demand which cause peaks and troughs, known as the bullwhip effect. This causes excesses and shortages of supply and panics to meet seemingly ever-changing needs. This pressure tests the strength of internal and external relationships to near breaking point.
- A second impact arises when external customers are themselves faced with pressures to reduce cost or add new features for given amounts. This pressure passes down. Again, this pressure on a supply chain means a constant search to take cost out of products and services
- Thirdly, there is an increasing requirement for quality. External customers want exactly what we as buyers want from our suppliers – right first time. This impacts the service we provide, the quality of the goods and services we purchase, the business processes we use and the relationships we need to develop with our own suppliers.
- Fourthly, an external customer may require us as their supplier to use the services or products of another supplier in the delivery of the services to them. This request, which may be expressed as a demand, may mean that our organisation has to include non-standard components or work with different service providers to the normal components or service providers we use. Here, not only have we the additional relationship to manage, but we also have the relationship with an existing supplier or provider to manage as well.

Self-assessment question 2.2

If a given external customer was seen as 'demanding', identify the positive and negative impacts this would have on relationships within your organisation.

Feedback on page 37

2.3 Requirements of internal non-technical stakeholders

Definition

Internal non-technical stakeholders are 'people in other functions who use the goods and services purchased or have a right to be consulted on decisions made about what is purchased and the process used to purchase'.

Typically these people and functions will include:

- business managers responsible for projects or parts of the business
- finance, who may exercise control over budgets and/or project costing
- logistics, who may have to handle, store or move goods and materials
- internal customers or users of the goods and services purchased
- quality and standards people who may have a view on the current purchase and how it fits in with standards used throughout the organisation

2

- production or operations who may rely on the service or product to carry out their fundamental purposes.

Learning activity 2.3

Consider the three most difficult internal customers in your business and how they impact relationships within the supply chain. Note that 'difficulty' here may reflect a difficult technical request, or someone who is being bloody-minded.

Feedback on page 38

Business managers

Managers responsible for projects or parts of the business will be accountable for the success of the areas under their control, and where they view that success as relying upon a purchase, then they may want to be heavily involved, perhaps too heavily. Here, purchasing may find itself confronted with requisitions 'covering' the purchase of items or services already received, or it may be that 'only one supplier will do'. Both of these options place the process of purchasing in a very weak position in negotiation. Solutions to this issue include early involvement, buyers knowing the areas where major purchases are necessary *and* knowing the markets where their customers need to purchase.

Finance

Finance and the people who work within financial teams are much maligned by many people in business for their 'bean counter' attitude. However, there is a genuine role for the finance team within the process of purchasing, in setting and reporting on budgets, financial appraisal of suppliers and acting as a backstop against invoices which are different to what has been expected. The area of cash management is also a key area where finance have a stake in the process of purchasing. Businesses need cash to survive and when cash is low, finance can retain money rather than pay it to suppliers to keep cash in the bank positive or within the overdraft limit.

This stake often reveals itself to buyers in the form of a phone call from a supplier who has not been paid and the supplier usually reminds the buyer of two considerations. The first point is a statement that the given payment terms were agreed and the second one is a question asking the buyer how they would feel if the supplier was late in delivery. There is a genuine conflict of interest between two parts of the organisation here, and one which strongly impacts the relationship between the purchasing organisation and the supplier. To remain credible in a relationship with a supplier, purchasing organisations must pay when they have agreed to. However, for reasons beyond their control, like a customer not paying them, solvency may be more critical than credibility. There is no single correct answer to this situation, but the reputation of a buyer will be enhanced if he or she is able to keep suppliers informed on potential payment delays and this itself will rely on a good relationship with members of the finance team.

Logistics

Logistics and warehousing teams have to handle a variety and volume of unusual loads. Communication from the purchasing process to them must warn them of unusual loads or changes in volumes to enable them to organise their resources accordingly. Integrated systems will do this to an extent; however, the human touch is important and usually welcomed. For example, imagine how you would describe this conversation between the stores manager and the purchasing manager one afternoon. The stores manager had received three generators on the back of a lorry; the generators were too heavy to unload without a crane, which had to be hired in specially. Additionally, the stores manager had just had to explain the situation to a French lorry driver, who having delivered to the UK, had hoped to go home that night and was now not going to be able to complete his journey.

The logistics team must communicate with the purchasing team to make it aware of any difficulties with receipts or issues with packaging or handling items delivered by suppliers.

The end user

Frequently, at the end of a supply chain within the purchasing organisation is someone using the pens and paper, cleaning service, computer system or coffee machine resulting from a purchase. These customers are sometimes not listened to or they are regarded as whingers. Best practice in the purchase of goods and services being used by others within the purchasing organisation is to involve them in the specification or statement of requirements, and to do so frequently, as they know:

- what they want
- what will or will not work
- how things could be improved.

However, the other side of the coin is the situation where these end users are resistant to change and work to make a new situation fail.

Success here can depend upon selecting the right people to be involved in the project.

Functions like quality, standard and production are covered more fully in 2.4 below.

Self-assessment question 2.3

A new contract for vending machines is being considered and as a member of the purchasing team you have been asked to be involved from the start. Assuming that your organisation is a distribution depot, running 24 hours a day, who would you involve in the multidisciplinary team to draft the

(continued on next page)

Self-assessment question 2.3 *(continued)*

requirements specification? What would you look to each area to bring to the discussion? Complete table 2.1.

Table 2.1 Stakeholder functions and areas of interest

Function	Areas of interest

Feedback on page 38

2.4 Requirements of technical specialist stakeholders

Definition

Technical specialists are 'people who have the knowledge to advise on and even design a requirement, be it goods, works, materials or services. In their area they are considered as experts.'

To some, the term 'technical specialist' conjures up men in blue coats with micrometers and technical drawings. In some arenas this may still be true, but specialists with technical knowledge exist in many organisations. Here are just a few:

- architects
- chefs
- design engineers
- education standards specialists
- equipment maintenance engineers
- information technology specialists
- nurses and doctors
- production engineers
- research scientists
- social services care advisers
- software designers
- soldiers.

The common denominator of this diverse group of people is that they have the technical knowledge to advise on and even design the requirement, be it goods, works, materials or services. In their area they may be the experts within the organisation and they may well be perceived as the experts in their field or profession. Technical specialists frequently have a very clear idea about what they want from a given requirement and their clarity can on occasion lead to them wanting to select a supplier. This can cause conflict with others in the purchasing process who would prefer to select a supplier on a wider range of criteria. In other cases the specification and requisition for a requirement may include a brand name or one supplier's model number and in extreme cases the goods or services may have been delivered before 'the paperwork is done'. There is a link here to the relationship life cycle model described in study session 6. A review of that material may help you understand the process which ends with the specification of a brand by a technical specialist.

Learning activity 2.4

Consider the technical experts in your own organisation. Examine their requirements of the purchasing process and the relationships that are currently in place to meet their needs. Are these arrangements appropriate?

Feedback on page 38

What drives technical specialists? Quality is one driver; security is another driver. Quality in the sense that the technical specialist will want what they are designing or influencing – be it the food for the restaurant, the pump for the brewery or the service looking after old people – to be the best it can be. Security in the sense that the technical specialist will want to use goods, services and a source that they know, often from past experience, will perform and not let them down. This means that there can be conflict in a relationship where the technical specialist insists that the goods from the supplier they have nominated are 'the only ones that will do'. This conflict can be difficult to handle, as a buyer may feel that it is appropriate to test the market to achieve best overall value. In the public sector the EUs procurement directives can be used to bring about a competitive situation, in the private sector it may be a matter of negotiation with the technical specialist before negotiation with the supplier(s). One fear that technical specialists have is that 'purchasing' will get three quotes and take the cheapest – irrespective of quality. Purchasing people must ensure that technical specialists understand that where quality matters, it is weighed at an equal or higher level than 'price' and that total cost of ownership and not price is a key focus.

The text on this area so far has presumed that the buyer seeks a competitive solution and it must be remembered that this is not the case every time. Where a partnership exists and the EU procurement directives do not prevail, the most appropriate course of action may be to develop a new product directly with a partner supplier.

Other drivers can include aspects like inventiveness and technological advancement, particularly where the specialist works in a research and development area.

These requirements lead to purchases for strange items in small quantities from unusual sources and once purchased there is no guarantee of further volume. It can be the case that the technical specialist feels that a special component must be made, even when a standard component may be available. 'Special' has additional cost and risk implications, when compared with standard 'off-the-shelf' components.

In obtaining these goods and services buyers will need an agile mind, a resourceful approach and a strong working relationship with technical

2

specialists. One way to build a relationship in these areas is to offer to meet with the specialists at an agreed frequency to understand where their projects are leading and then proactively source requirements.

Lack of time, budgetary pressures, strong personalities and tradition can all also lead to pressure to use given suppliers and their services in preference to an open competition.

Not all technical specialists are, however, attempting to determine the selection of supplier. Many of them work with colleagues in purchasing to produce generic specifications which can be used to test the market's ability to supply. Many other technical specialists collaborate within the partnership arrangements which they, purchasing and suppliers, have developed.

Examples of ways of working effectively with technical specialists can include the following:

- Seconding a specialist to the purchasing team as a resource. The Surrey and Sussex NHS Supply Confederation have seconded two staff nurses to a team of project buyers working across a group of over 20 hospitals in their area. During the planning of purchasing strategies, the staff nurses have played a vital role in assisting the purchasing teams to fully understand the goods and services under consideration and also the drivers of the specialists in the hospitals.
- Developing regular meetings with technical specialists to understand their needs and become aware of projects and plans. For example, early warning of maintenance teams' plans to overhaul equipment could enable the purchase of spares needed in advance.
- Identifying prime contacts in customer and purchasing teams may avoid the necessity for formal meetings and keep communication at an appropriate level.
- Multidisciplinary teams can be set up for projects involving significant purchases.
- Locating a purchasing resource within the team of technical specialists where there is an ongoing requirement for purchasing support.

Self-assessment question 2.4

Identify where there may be conflict in relationships with internal customers and technical specialists.

Feedback on page 38

2.5 Internal supplier stakeholders

Definition

Internal supplier stakeholders are 'parts of the buyer's organisation which produce and supply goods and services which themselves form part of goods and services offered to external customers by your part of your organisation'.

Internal suppliers may be on the same site or on difference sites, even in different countries.

Organisations use different business models to manage internal suppliers and these models impact the relationships that purchasing organisations have with them. The models are described below and there are combinations of 'choice' and 'payment'.

Learning activity 2.5

Consider how flexible and responsive your own internal suppliers are and ask yourself what you could do to work for the greater good of the organisation. Where would you place them on the relationship spectrum?

Feedback on page 39

Choice models

Choice models refer to the freedom of choice or restriction of choice that one part of an organisation has in selecting sources of supply including internal suppliers.

1   It is mandatory that internal customers purchase their requirements of a given nature from the internal supplier. There is no choice.
2   Internal customers must give first refusal to the internal supplier when they need to purchase their requirements of a given nature. If the internal supplier is not able to or does not want to supply the goods or services then the internal customer is free to choose another supplier.
3   Internal customers may only buy from the open market if the internal supplier cannot meet the price of external sources.
4   Internal customers may only buy from the open market if the internal supplier cannot meet the time constraint that the internal customer is facing.
5   There is no obligation to use the internal supplier, who competes with other external suppliers for the work of the internal customer.

Purchasing policies may also allow variation of these five main choice models.

Payment models

1   Internal suppliers may receive no payment; they may be regarded as a cost centre or an overhead which contributes to cost of sales.
2   Internal suppliers may 'transfer' items produced or services delivered at cost.
3   Internal suppliers may 'transfer' items produced or services delivered at cost plus a small margin or contribution to overheads.
4   Internal suppliers may 'transfer' items produced or services delivered at a negotiated transfer price.

5   Internal suppliers may 'sell' items produced or services delivered at a market rate.

There is no one 'correct' model or combination of models when considering these issues. Different organisations find appropriate mechanisms and as time progresses organisations will change from one model to another. Debating whether one model is more appropriate than the other is outside the syllabus, but examining the relationship impacts of these models is germane to this syllabus. The following points need to be considered:

1   The logic often used for mandatory use of an internal supplier is 'that the work should be kept "in house" allowing maximum utilisation of the resources of the organisation, rather than allowing other organisations to make money from us'.
    Against this is the argument that inefficient internal resources may hamper the organisation's ability to sell in competitive markets or, in the case of the public sector, eat more of a given budget than would otherwise be the case.
    Internal suppliers who know that internal customers must use them can take longer to fulfil those needs than would otherwise be the case, supply other external and 'real' customers before internal customers, or load cost onto jobs that they know they will get. These circumstances introduce conflict between parts of the organisation and relationships are often strained, with a lack of trust and a lack of sharing of information. Frustrated buyers may find ways around the mandate.

2   First refusal and time constraint-based selection can be part of the normal make or buy decision. Here a given good or service forming part of the purchasing organisation's processes is subcontracted to outside organisations by choice when internal resources are at or over existing capacity. When this policy operates the conflict described in 1 above does not exist. However, delays in making decisions can lead to delays in the sourcing process and delays for external customers. Indecision and the resulting delay will cause conflict, lack of trust and attempts to create situations which the internal supplier cannot fulfil.

3   Two forces squeeze buyers forced to operate a price comparison system. First, they have the pressure to give the internal supplier as much work as possible, supported by the theory that the more work the supplier has, the lower will be their overhead costs and also their prices. Against this is the buyer's relationship with the external supply market, who will legitimately question why they have not won the work they quoted for. Suppliers will lose interest in quoting and supplying organisations that use their quotations as a stick to beat down the price of internal suppliers. Buyers will lose the trust of suppliers who feel that they are in this situation and internal relationships will be strained by the constraints upon the buyer and the pressure received from external suppliers.

4   Some internal supplier organisations thrive on competition and provide an excellent service to internal and external customers alike. In this sense they almost become external suppliers. Buyers using such a service have no impediment in supplier selection and a close relationship may develop in these cases.

5   Removing the internal supplier as a cost centre can remove one source of conflict.

6   Transfer pricing can lead to cost being double counted within an organisation and where the transfer is not at 'cost' the person selling the eventual product or service to an external customer may not know the true cost of the eventual good or service. In such situations orders may be lost if the sales price is unnecessarily high. The author is aware of one organisation which changed back to transfer at cost because of situations where sales were lost.

7   Internal sales at 'market value' suffer the same potential loss of external sales, unless they are coupled with the freedom of choice option; even here, parts of the same organisation working together ought to be motivated to shave costs to win business if the business is worth winning. Such a situation might be more difficult to manage with an external supplier who is not a partner supplier.

In theory it ought to be possible for people working for the same organisation to work more closely together than people working in different organisations. However, where organisations drive their separate parts or divisions to profit, budget or delivery targets, conflict arises and actions are taken to work towards individual targets rather than a greater good. Two real examples of worst-case scenarios with relationships between internal customers and internal suppliers follow. When you read them you will understand why the organisations are not named.

1   A group of companies decided to cut costs and moved all of their people into the building of one of the group of companies, where there was enough space. In the first week of the new arrangement the buyer of one company seated on the fifth floor had arranged a meeting with a manager from the other group company on the second floor. Consequently, the buyer knocked on the door of the manager's office at the appointed time. The manager expressed surprise, as, 'reception had not called him to tell him his visitors had arrived'. The frustrated buyer was asked to report to reception to receive a badge, whereupon the manager would collect him!

2   Within a large group of companies many goods were bought and sold in the areas where the organisation operated. Group rules were introduced to cover disputes on payment when the legal department at group headquarters became aware that one group company was about to issue a writ against another group company.

Self-assessment question 2.5

An internal supplier makes electrical components used in products made by your division and sold to external customers. Using the supplier is mandatory, yet you have problems with their delivery, quality and the cost they charge. Highlight five points that you would put in a business case to your divisional director to commence sourcing these components on the open market.

Feedback on page 39

2

2.6 External supplier stakeholders

Definition

The definition set out in study session 1 for 'supplier' is:

> 'An independent commercial organisation used as a resource within different relationship types to deliver goods, works, materials and services of an appropriate quality to its customers as requested and specified by the customers in return for payment, benefit and the achievement of its own business goals.'

Learning activity 2.6

Consider three suppliers with whom you have good relationships and examine how they present themselves, advance their cause within your organisation and approach you when they have a problem.

Now consider three suppliers with whom you have difficult relationships and examine how they present themselves, advance their cause within your organisation and approach you when they have a problem.

Ask yourself what makes the difference between the two groups of suppliers

Feedback on page 39

Suppliers do have a stake in the process of purchasing for, after all, they literally have to 'deliver the goods'. In this sense purchasing people must ensure that suppliers:

- are fully informed about what is required of them
- understand what, when and where they are to deliver the requirement
- understand how they will be rewarded for delivery
- have a common understanding of the terms and conditions under which both organisations are to operate
- understand what is required of them in terms of the relationship, whether it exists for a single occasion or is ongoing.

The last point moves us away from ensuring that the purchasing 'rights' are met, particularly where we have an ongoing relationship. Aspects of this will be discussed in more detail in study session 3, but to complete the picture of stakeholders we must consider the basic elements of interest and influence that suppliers have on the process of purchasing. Suppliers are concerned to:

- Be paid by the purchasing organisation, on time and in full. Payment is important and too often purchasing organisations, though not always the purchasing function, have delayed payment and soured relationships.
- Increase their business. It is legitimate for suppliers to seek to do this, though it may not be part of the plan.

- Work with profitable customers. Profitable customers are attractive; again, it is legitimate for suppliers to seek profit, and it is also legitimate for purchasing organisations to purchase at the lowest total cost. Negotiation is often the result of these opposing stakes in the process. Both parties in a relationship must be able to move from the competitive tendering and negotiation processes to collaborate together to effect delivery. Note that this is a valid statement irrespective of where the relationship between buyer and seller sits on the relationship spectrum. However, where long-term collaborative relationships exist, the parties will collaborate from the start of each new development rather than compete.

- Deliver quality products and services fit for the purpose that they are intended for. Suppliers take a pride in what they deliver. What they deliver may only be a low-value, low-risk tactical profit item to the purchasing organisation, yet to the supplier it represents their output and as such we must value it, and the relationship that delivers it, albeit investing in the relationship relative to other relationships.

- Be trusted. People like to be trusted and suppliers are people. Buyers can on occasion harm a relationship by too frequently checking up on suppliers and not allowing them 'space' to perform for them.

- Have a secure tenure with a customer and to avoid being put into competition. This aspiration is one all suppliers have. However, buyers should primarily consider the needs of their organisation in determining the length of a contract. Countering this is the thought that suppliers might move towards the buyer in a number of ways if a longer-term contract was on offer. In this sense a little investment in the relationship might pay dividends.

- Be referred to other customers. This is a source of interest to all suppliers and where appropriate the buyer must be prepared to make a recommendation. Some buyers would argue that the recommendation should only be given for something in return, but this view is too narrow in the context of most relationships.

One final aspect of the supplier's stake in the process of purchasing needs to be considered. That is the supplier's relationship with internal customers. Earlier in this study session the point was made that the technical specialist specified their requirement in a way which selected the supplier. It can be that the supplier's literature, taken from an exhibition, sent in the post or downloaded from the web, has led to this situation. However, suppliers are also known to seek appointments with technical specialists, invite them to their premises and/or invite them to events promoting new products and services. Logic dictates that it is not beyond the bounds of possibility that a technical specialist is so impressed with what he or she sees and is told that they decide that the given supplier's offering is the one for them.

In one case known to the author a technical specialist working in the UK was invited to attend a conference and visit the factory, all expenses paid. Where was the factory and the conference? On the west coast of the USA!

Whilst it is legitimate for suppliers to present to technical specialists, purchasing teams are wise to attempt to work with both of these stakeholders to ensure that purchasing decisions are made taking all of the necessary factors into account.

2

Self-assessment question 2.6

You have just returned from holiday and the sales manager from a supplier phones you and asks for a meeting this week, 'to discuss some issues that have arisen with the business between us in recent weeks'. She won't say what the issues are on the phone, but promises to send an email before the meeting on Friday. You are unaware of any issues. What might the issues be and whom would you go and talk to? Could someone have upset them, have we changed delivery again? Concentrate on five issues. Use table 2.3 to format your answers.

Table 2.3 Issues and who to talk to

No.	Issue	Talk to
1		
2		
3		
4		
5		

Feedback on page 39

Revision question

Now try the revision question for this session on page 321.

Summary

Stakeholders are important to our process because they:

- have differing and contrasting views of their requirements
- need different approaches to allow us to meet their needs
- are not easy to manage
- leave some buyers feeling that they spend more time negotiating with internal stakeholders than suppliers.

Buyers must win the trust and respect of their stakeholders, both in their processes and their own abilities, if they are to succeed in providing an appropriate service to these important people within their organisation. Winning trust and respect will mean attempting to understand the drivers of the functions and individuals who are stakeholders.

Feedback on learning activities and self-assessment questions

Feedback on learning activity 2.1

Humorously, it may be said that internal customers of the purchasing process want their requirements yesterday, for a lower price than they paid last time on the basis that they will send the paperwork through later, at some unspecified future time! Seriously, you should have:

- the primary functions of the organisation, whatever that might be
- functions aligned with purchasing in supply chain functions
- functions who support the primary business processes and are also internal customers where they influence specific purchases
- external parties like suppliers and customers.

Feedback on self-assessment question 2.1

Your answer might include the following:

- customers
- finance
- human resources
- information technology
- inventory management
- legal
- maintenance
- marketing
- planning
- purchasing
- quality assurance
- research and development
- sales
- service delivery
- suppliers.

Feedback on learning activity 2.2

In response to question 1, it may be that the customer requests or demands quality standards, parts per million minimum failure rates, deliveries of services in specific ways that suit them and are different from the norm and deliveries on given days. The number of changes customers make will also impact your business processes.

In response to question 2, it may be that a customer insists on a specific supplier, which puts the supplier in a powerful position, or that the changes the customer makes also impact upon the supplier and their suppliers. Cancellation of orders can impact your suppliers in a major way.

Feedback on self-assessment question 2.2

You might have identified the following positive and negative factors.

Positive:

- Stretching to do better than would be the norm.
- People in different functions would have to work together to meet the needs of this customer. This could be turned into team building to be of use with the requirements of all customers.
- Processes improved to meet the needs of this customer can be applied to all customers.

2

- Understanding this customer will allow us to develop processes and relationships to meet other similar customers.
- We may be able to learn specific techniques from them.
- Kudos of working for them may draw other customers towards us.
- Their success will mean more business from them to us.

Negative:

- Conflict between the customer and our organisation.
- Their requirements and the changing nature of them may create conflict between functions and people within our organisation.
- Many changes in requirement schedules.
- Nit-picking in terms of quality or delivery.
- Cost of servicing this customer in terms of people and resources.
- They may appear to be never satisfied.
- Cost may be felt to be more than the benefit.

Feedback on learning activity 2.3

You should have identified people and functions who are stretching and demanding as well as people who just seem to make life difficult for the sake of it. Remember that they are all customers of the purchasing service we provide.

Feedback on self-assessment question 2.3

Table 2.2 shows how your answer should look.

Table 2.2 Stakeholder functions and areas of interest

Function	Areas of interest
Finance	Cash management and collection or cashless systems. Cost to the organisation.
Human resources	Consideration of subsidy, range of drinks and snacks available. Access to the site by suppliers. Cost to the organisation.
Unions	Cost to employees, choice, available times of use, location of machines.
Drivers	Cost to employees, choice, available times of use, location of machines.
Office staff	Choice, location of machines, cost of drinks to them.
Site management	Cost to the organisation.
Quality	Impact upon processes and employee effectiveness.
Warehouse staff	Cost to employees, choice, available times of use, location of machines.

Feedback on learning activity 2.4

You may find that your communication is not good with these internal customers, not frequent enough and strained by a conflict of requirements and business and personal drivers.

Feedback on self-assessment question 2.4

There may be conflict in relationships with internal customers and technical specialists in the following circumstances:

- selection of suppliers
- selection of goods and services

- traditional use of suppliers
- advance warning of projects
- providing enough time to enact competitive purchasing processes
- cost versus quality issues
- special requirements being specified rather than standard components or services
- goods and services arriving before 'the paperwork'.

Feedback on learning activity 2.5

Frequently, although a close relationship should exist, the relationship can be arm's length or even adversarial. To make this relationship work we need to assess what both parties seek from the relationship and to identify situations where we can turn problems into opportunities for improvement. Nevertheless, these relationships are typically adversarial as you the customer expect real service and they the supplier would rather be dealing with a 'real' customer than you.

Feedback on self-assessment question 2.5

Five points that you could put in a business case to your divisional director to commence sourcing these components on the open market could include:

- Our own customers are suffering due to delivery hold-ups.
- Our production is becoming erratic due to delivery hold-ups.
- We are losing sales as we are forced to buy uncompetitive components.
- We are experiencing failures due to quality problems.
- Loss of orders might wake the supplier up.
- The group as a whole is suffering from the intransigent approach of this one internal supplier.
- Dual sourcing would provide security of supply.

Feedback on learning activity 2.6

Typical signs of a good relationship could include:

- new ideas proposed and discussed
- meetings arranged, confirmed and stuck to
- early warnings provided of opportunities and problems
- solutions proposed when problems arise.

Typical signs of a difficult relationship could include:

- new ideas not offered to us even when they appear in the trade press
- meetings arranged, rearranged and attended late or by more junior people
- problems arise as a surprise to them.

Feedback on self-assessment question 2.6

Examples of issues you may have come up with are shown in table 2.4.

2

Table 2.4 Issues and who to talk to

No.	Issue	Talk to
1	Lack of payment	Finance
2	Unreasonable rejections	Quality
3	Constant changes to delivery schedules	Sales, planning, purchasing
4	Someone in your organisation has indicated to someone from the supplier's organisation that the work they do will be going out to quote again	'Someone' needs to be identified and the truth of the matter established
5	Someone in the organisation has leaked the information that there is the potential for further business to be won, but this supplier is not being considered	'Someone' needs to be identified and the truth of the matter established
6	The supplier has been asked by finance to lengthen payment terms	Finance
7	The supplier has been asked to make components to a different specification	Production or quality

Study session 3

Challenges in purchasing and supply relationships, the buyer's view

Introduction

Study session 1 introduced the relationship spectrum and a basic risk management process and study session 2 considered stakeholders and touched on some of the risks that are caused by their actions, as well as some of the positive aspects of the relationships. This study session firstly links these three topics and then considers the challenges of managing purchasing and supply relationships from the buyer's view, using the vital supply positioning tool. Study session 4 links the three topics and also considers the seller's view of purchasing and supply relationships.

Taking the relationships identified within the relationship spectrum, this study session will first consider the supply positioning tool and then review the relationships identified within the relationship spectrum in more detail.

'Tactical relationships don't count,' said 'old Les' the purchasing manager. This was the week before a £25 item stopped our organisation's production!

Session learning objectives

After completing this session you should be able to:

3.1 Diagrammatically explain the supply positioning model in a supplier relationship context.
3.2 Evaluate the risks run by buyers in tactical purchasing and supply relationships.
3.3 Compare the challenges faced by organisations in different business environments and how they impact tactical relationships.
3.4 Evaluate the risks and challenges for buyers in strategic purchasing and supply relationships.
3.5 Understand how strategic relationships may evolve or how they may be subject to a selection process.

Unit content coverage

This study session covers the following topics from the official CIPS unit content document.

Learning objective

1.2 Evaluate the contribution of appropriate and well-managed relationships in achieving cooperation and collaboration between buyers and suppliers.
1.3 Evaluate or analyse the challenges in managing effectively the relationships between purchasers and suppliers.
2.7 Evaluate or analyse the challenges in managing effectively the relationships between purchasers and suppliers.

Prior knowledge

This study session builds on the work of study sessions 1 and 2.

Timing

You should set aside about 10 hours to read and complete this session, including learning activities, self-assessment questions, the suggested further reading (if any) and the revision question.

3.1   The supply positioning model

Introduction

Supply positioning is a tool used to analyse the goods, works, materials and services used by many organisations in different sectors to determine purchasing strategies and tactics and enable their purchasing teams to work within their organisation and within their supply chain to successfully meet their business objectives. The supply positioning model (figure 3.3) was developed by PT Steele and TI Elliott-Shircore of PMMS Consulting Group Limited, first published in *Purchasing and Supply Management* in 1985. Figure 3.1 shows that supply positioning impacts and is impacted by a number of issues relevant to purchasing and supply relationships.

Figure 3.1: Areas considered in a supply positioning analysis

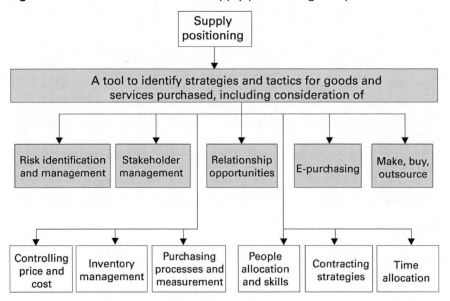

There are a number of important outputs for the purchasing organisation from an analysis using the supply positioning model. They include:

- A clear understanding of the relative importance of items purchased. It therefore follows that the relationships needed to manage and deliver items that are of greater importance are handled differently to the relationships needed to deliver items of lesser importance.
- Identification at item level of the risk involved in purchasing what is needed to fulfil the business objectives. Where there is more risk to the

organisation there are impacts on the relationship needed with internal customers (stakeholders) and the supply market.

- An understanding of the importance of given items to different stakeholders. Again there is an impact upon relationships with stakeholders.
- Consideration of whether the purchasing organisation should make the item or carry out the service itself, use a supplier or outsource a whole area of business. Different relationships are needed here to manage internal and external stakeholders.
- Recognition of purchasing strategies which then leads to the use of different 'e' tools and the development, cessation or amendment of relationships with suppliers to manage the introduction of e-purchasing.
- Impacts upon inventory management, purchasing processes, the allocation of people within the purchasing team to given groups of items and the time spent on items These will also form part of internal and external relationships at a practical level

Understanding and being able to apply this model to the purchasing requirements of your organisation is fundamental in understanding the needs of an organisation in managing and developing purchasing and supply relationships.

Using the supply positioning model

In the first stage of the supply positioning model the supply situation for each good or service purchased is plotted on a graph against two parameters (figure 3.2):

- Risk, vulnerability or supply exposure are shown on the y axis.
- Relative cost to the organisation is shown on the x axis.

Figure 3.2: Plotting purchases against the supply positioning axes

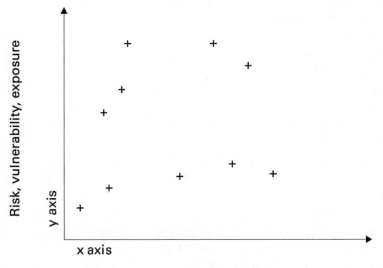

This activity is time-consuming and to be done properly requires the involvement of stakeholders in a multidisciplinary team. Different stakeholders will hold different views of the risk of given items and the purchasing team will input considerations on the state of the supply market.

3

East Sussex Hospitals NHS Trust spent 36 man-hours (two purchasing professionals and a staff nurse assigned to the project) reviewing 350 items to establish a position within the model for each item. Even then, there were questions to be asked of specialists within the hospital and this exercise was only completed based upon a list of the items bought and their annual spend.

Peter Pilgrim, Contracts and Data Manager at East Sussex Hospitals NHS Trust, provides an example:

> 'The provision of loan kits for orthopaedic procedures is an example where risk was not fully understood by everyone within our Trust. These kits include both the tools and implants for an operation and previously the rental of the loan kits for an operation was sourced at the last minute, running a risk of unavailability and a price premium. In future the kits will be purchased and kept for future use, both reducing the lead time risk whilst allowing the replacement of used parts from existing items and resulting in a cost saving for the Trust.'

The y axis is an assessment of the internal and external risks that the purchasing organisation runs in purchasing using a given commodity and its source. These risks may include:

- pace of technological change
- product life cycle
- generic/specific specification
- corporate social responsibility (CSR) in the purchasing process, at the supply source, at customers, in the whole supply chain. CSR issues include:
    - environmental responsibility
    - human rights
    - community involvement
    - impact on society
    - equal opportunities
    - ethics and ethical trading
    - sustainability
    - bio-diversity
    - corporate governance
    - safety
- complexity of specification, process of manufacture
- lead time
    - standard/normal
    - required this time
- the supply market, its capacity, dominant players, competitiveness
- the number of alternative goods and services available
- PESTLE, as it influences us and the supplier
- activity by our competitors
- the supply chain
    - length, complexity, dangers, economic volatility
- our customer requirements
    - external, internal
- our relationship with a given supplier

– level of trust
– their track record
– our track record.

This is a long list and not every consideration will apply in every case. However, the analysis will make everyone involved aware of the risks relevant to the purchase of given goods and services. One simple way to view this axis is to ask the question, 'What potential does this item have to "stop the job"'? Interpret 'job' as the primary business process, reason the organisation exists or needs of a key customer. In the private sector this may be the unavailability of the courier service delivering traveller's cheques needed by the branch of a bank for its customers on a given date and in the public sector it may be the unavailability of documents which are a prerequisite to sending out tax returns. Absence of either of these requirements will prevent the organisation achieving something important.

Once the risk is understood it is then sometimes revealing to consider how inappropriate the relationship that we have or currently seek is to the risks now identified!

The x axis is an assessment of the item's position within the total spend of the organisation on goods, works, materials and services. Hence a £2000 computer may be on the right of the axis for a small sandwich shop, whilst for an international airline it will hardly 'creep' on to the x axis at the left-hand side.

Once items are plotted, the four quadrants of the model are then overlaid onto the graph. The items purchased by the organisation are then identified as being within one of the four quadrants, depending upon where they are on each axis. The four quadrants are titled:

- strategic critical (normally coloured yellow)
- strategic security (normally coloured red)
- tactical profit (normally coloured blue)
- tactical acquisition (normally coloured green).

The supply positioning model

Take a look at figure 3.3.

Figure 3.3: The supply positioning model

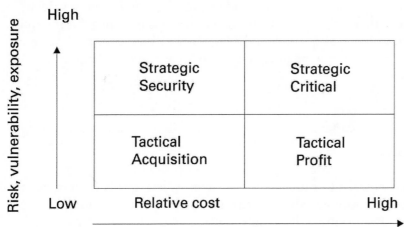

3

The following summarises the typical characteristics and methods of management of goods and services falling into each of the four categories. The analysis refers to the profit motive, which typically exists within the private sector. *Public sector organisations are not normally profit focused; however, the analysis is very relevant for the public sector, where the profit motive is replaced by service considerations, meeting targets and operating within budget.*

Learning activity 3.1

Draw the supply positioning model, name the four quadrants and then list eight items that you purchase. Number the items 1 to 8 and place in them within the supply positioning matrix.

Feedback on page 70

Analysis of each quadrant

Strategic critical

Items in this category are those which are critical to the success of the business, both in terms of their availability and their impact on its competitive edge, cost structure and profitability. In short, they deliver what the business exists to deliver. Availability is constrained by such factors as limited supply sources, long lead times, and technical complexity. Values of individual items are high, and collectively are likely to represent the greatest proportion of an organisation's total expenditure on goods, works, materials and services.

Managing supply arrangements for these items requires considerable skill. The emphasis is on developing and managing long-term, close relationships with suppliers and, through cooperative activities, seeking to optimise the benefits for both parties. Such relationships will involve establishing the business objectives of both parties' programmes of continuous improvement, agreement on relationship values and practices and a framework for managing the business. In terms of items, this group is the smallest; in terms of spend, it is the largest. The theme for this quadrant is checking (we are doing the best we can) and searching (to do better) together.

Strategic security

The basic characteristic of these low-cost items is that they have the greater potential to 'stop the job', whatever the 'job' or core activity is for an organisation. Availability of items in this category is constrained by such

3

factors as limited supply sources, long lead times, or unique or complex technical features, and they offer little opportunity for cost reduction or significant profit contribution. The item value is insignificant compared to the potential cost of disruption to the business through failure of supply. The theme for this quadrant is therefore ensuring security of supply.

The approach to managing supply arrangements for these items is to seek to minimise the constraints that affect their availability. This may be done in a number of ways such as:

- developing alternative supply sources or products
- making a unique item into a generic item
- establishing safety or consignment stocks
- developing closer supplier relationships to provide greater security of supply.

The latter approach may well involve establishing long-term contractual and/or relationship agreements with these suppliers. One of the difficulties associated with these supply arrangements is the relatively weak negotiating position of the buyer versus the supplier. In order to increase the attractiveness of the business to the supplier and increase negotiating leverage, it may be desirable to increase purchase volumes by placing other business with them which is not subject to these supply constraints. In some circumstances an electronic reverse auction can be used in this quadrant.

Tactical profit

These are items which through timely and judicious action in the marketplace provide an opportunity for making significant savings on costs, thus contributing to profit or stretching public sector budgets. Typical characteristics of these items are that they are readily available from a number of alternative sources and do not require any special action in the selection or management of supply sources. They will normally be regarded as 'commodity' products and may be of medium or high value. The theme of this quadrant is therefore 'trade and drive for profit' and this is a major area where electronic reverse auctions can be used successfully.

Management of supply arrangements for these items is based on taking maximum advantage of the competitive nature of the marketplace. Here, there is limited value to be gained from the development of close, long-term relationships with selected suppliers, the pursuit of which may well result in a lost ability to take advantage of short-term market opportunities. The emphasis is therefore on short-term commitments to suppliers and maintaining flexibility to purchase from whichever sources offer the best terms. 'Short-term commitment' does not necessarily mean a short-term relationship. Buyer and seller know of each other and know that when a purchasing need for the requirement arises, the seller will be given an opportunity in the same way that other sellers are. The relationship therefore continues to exist, whilst the supply is dependent on the seller's ability to compete on each occasion.

3

Tactical acquisition

Items falling into this category are the numerous, low-value, low-risk items typically required by most businesses to satisfy their routine requirements. The word 'numerous' is key here, the items in this category probably account for 70% by volume of the number of items purchased and purchasing departments which fail to address this area become quickly swamped by these items. The total value of this area in terms of spend may be no more than 2% of the total spend of the organisation.

Items would normally be available ex-stock or on short lead times from a relatively large number of supply sources and would be to standard designs or specifications not reflecting quality or safety-critical features. The low level of expenditure and risk associated with these items does not justify anything other than the minimum of effort in managing supply arrangements and inventory levels, ensuring that they are available when required with the minimum of attention, inconvenience and cost.

The approach to managing supply arrangements for these items is to simplify the purchasing process in order to reduce costs of acquisition, which are typically disproportionately high relative to the importance of items purchased. Paperwork should be minimised or eliminated through the use of:

- purchasing cards
- web-based catalogues
- the internet
- supplier topping up
- call-off contracts
- systems contracting
- cheque with order
- electronic reverse auctions.

One key feature of many of these options is that purchasing sets up an arrangement for its customer areas to deal direct with the supplier on a day-to-day basis. The theme of this quadrant is therefore 'organise and let go'.

Where possible items should be aggregated to increase negotiating leverage. Long-term contractual commitments are not normally required or desirable, although supply agreements which are operating satisfactorily may be allowed to continue indefinitely.

Low-value, low-risk does not, however, mean that the relationship does not matter. The relationship with suppliers of goods and services in this quadrant does matter, for it is important that they literally 'deliver the goods' without requiring significant involvement of the purchasing team, who are therefore free to concentrate on more important items.

One caveat

Supply Positioning is used successfully as described above by many organisations worldwide to help them form strategies and tactics which bring about changes in the supply situation and relationships with suppliers. *However, it remains the buyer's view and does not and is not intended to fully address the supplier's view of a given supply situation.*

For example, a UK organisation viewed fuel oil as vital (higher cost strategic security), because they needed the fuel oil to run their boilers and key production processes. In the winter, the buyer concerned was advised that the latest delivery had not arrived from the current supplier. His telephone call to the supplier to chase delivery was firstly met by the question, 'Do we supply you, are you sure?' and, once this was established, the buyer was informed that 'Once the hospitals and schools have had their deliveries, you will get yours!' No amount of pressure would make the supplier deliver earlier. Fortunately the fuel oil arrived on time, but the buyer changed supplier within the month.

Another model is used to assess the supplier's view. This is called 'supplier preferencing' and is discussed in study session 4.

Self-assessment question 3.1

(a) What are the themes and colours of the four quadrants?
 (i) strategic critical
 (ii) strategic security
 (iii) tactical profit
 (iv) tactical acquisition.
(b) Assuming you were an NHS Trust, which quadrant would you expect to find the following requirements in?
 (i) A4 inkjet printer paper.
 (ii) A contract to remove clinical waste.
 (iii) An MRI body scanner used to diagnose cancer patients.
 (iv) Laptop computers.

Feedback on page 71

3.2 The risks and challenges of tactical relationships

What determines a purchasing organisation's view of the relationship?

Managing relationships in purchasing and supply presents many challenges to purchasing organisations. One challenge is to work out the relationship type that best reflects the purchasing organisation's business objectives in working with suppliers. Several factors determine the view that a purchasing organisation will have of the relationship they seek and/or are experiencing with a supplier in a given circumstance with a given supplier. These factors are two-way factors, in that both the buyer and the seller will influence them by their behaviour. The relationship sought will influence the factors, which themselves will influence the behaviour of the parties. However, the reverse is true, particularly as the relationship progresses. The behaviour of people will influence the factors, which will influence how the relationship actually functions in practice. The factors include:

- quality of information exchange
- trust
- openness
- commitment
- duration
- risk assessment
- risk management.

Figure 3.5 shows the extreme positions on each of the above factors. The text that follows the diagram considers each of the tactical relationships. This figure is titled 'diagram 2' as it develops diagram 1 (shown in figure 1.2).

Figure 3.5: The relationship spectrum – diagram 2

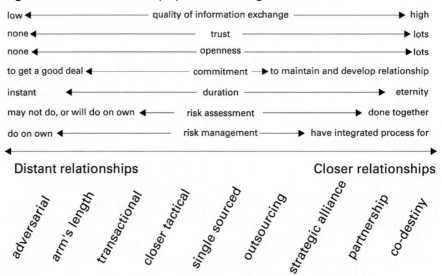

Analysing tactical relationships

This section examines the challenges faced by the buyer adopting a given relationship style. In each case the relationship will be defined, set in the context of supply positioning, the relationship factors evaluated and the challenge for the purchasing organisation described. In the case of the closer tactical relationship, a section on practicalities is included as well to more fully describe this relationship.

Learning activity 3.2

Take figure 3.6 where the supply positioning is matrix flattened and the relationship spectrum drawn above it. Note how the position of adversarial and co-destiny relationships have been placed and then place the following relationships on the chart:

- adversarial relationship
- arm's-length relationship
- transactional relationship

(continued on next page)

Learning activity 3.2 *(continued)*

- closer tactical relationship
- single-sourced relationship.

Figure 3.6: The relationship spectrum and supply positioning

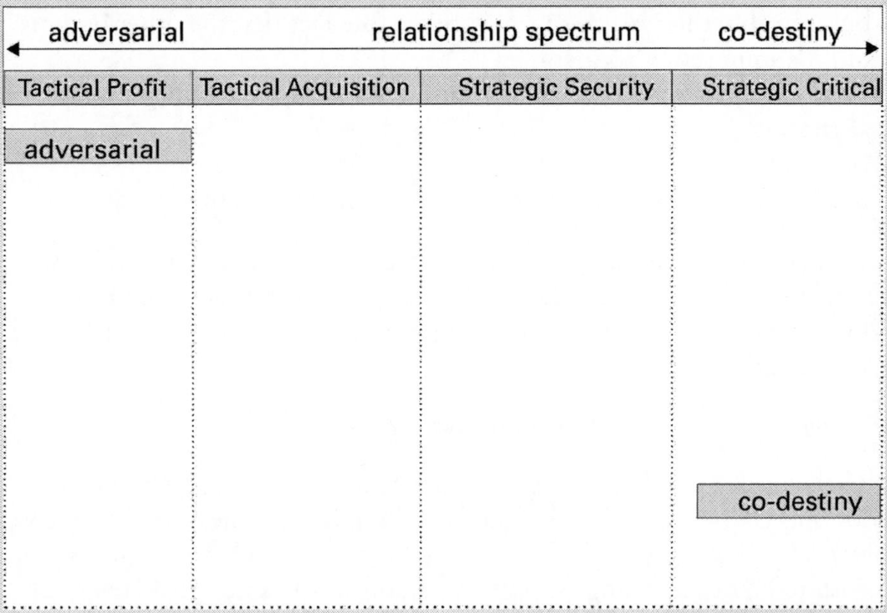

◄ adversarial	relationship spectrum		co-destiny ►
Tactical Profit	Tactical Acquisition	Strategic Security	Strategic Critical
adversarial			
			co-destiny

Feedback on page 71

3

An adversarial relationship

Definition

An **adversarial relationship** is one where both the buyer and the seller seek to maximise their position in any given supply opportunity, even to the detriment of the other party or parties.

In the context of supply positioning

These relationships are normally found in the tactical profit quadrant; where risk is low, the supply market has many potential suppliers, the requirement is standard and the purchasing organisation has a relatively large spend in this area and therefore attempts to leverage its spend and power over the suppliers by using competitive selection methodologies like tenders and electronic reverse auctions. Personal computers (PCs) and their peripherals are typical of these commodity items. Purchasing organisations will seek a short-term duration for the relationship.

Relationship factors

An adversarial relationship is one where any given deal between the parties is much more important than the relationship. Both parties will therefore:

- Supply information on a 'need to know' basis, with minimum warning before the competitive process starts.
- Only do what they 'believe' they have agreed. If their 'belief' is different to the 'belief' of the other party then there will be conflict and use of threat as a negotiation tactic to resolve the situation.

3

- Limit their concern to their own needs. In an extreme situation a buyer may not change a contract even if the supplier could go bankrupt.
- Exhibit inconsistent attitudes/behaviour. The parties may, in conversation, tell each other how important to them the other party is, but in reality their behaviour may betray the fact that the other party is of little importance to them.
- Treat the other with a lack of care and even outright hostility and/or aggression.
- Be unsure as to the extent that trust exists between them and feel the need to check up on what has been promised by the other party.

The standard nature of the goods and services means that risk is minimised as suppliers can be changed; where risk management is undertaken buyers will limit it to basic factors like managing price, delivery, the given quality and the quantity required.

The challenge for the purchasing organisation

The challenge for purchasing organisations here from this short-term relationship is to secure the given goods and services for the lowest total cost of ownership. A long-term deal is not sought, as the purchasing organisation will wish to be free to change supplier to secure a better deal in a changing market, rather than tied in to a long-term contract. Sellers will seek to maximise their revenue and profit from the given deal and they will not be disposed to do anything for nothing.

An arm's-length relationship

Definition

An **arm's-length relationship** is one where a buyer buys infrequently from a supplier, and does not have high volumes or the need for a closer relationship.

In the context of supply positioning

These relationships are normally found in the tactical profit or tactical acquisition quadrants; where risk is low, the supply market has many potential suppliers, the requirement is standard and the purchasing organisation has a significant and perhaps infrequent spend in this area. Purchasing organisations again therefore attempt to leverage their spend and power over the suppliers by using competitive selection methodologies like tenders and electronic reverse auctions, but not in such an extreme way as they would if they felt that they faced an adversarial situation. The low frequency of purchase is a determining factor here, which will limit the power of the buyer in the market, the benefit to be gained from this purchase in terms of cost savings and the need for a closer relationship. Purchasing organisations will seek a short-term duration for the relationship.

Relationship factors

The arm's-length relationship is one where the given deal is, once again, worth more than the relationship and both parties will:

- Retain information to release as needed, with minimum warning before the competitive process starts.

- Only go as far as the agreement they have made with the supplier.
- Limit their concern to their own needs, but want to ensure that the supplier is around for them in the future.
- Treat the other party with respect, but recognise business may be transient.
- Trust each other to keep their side of the bargain, but not expect them to go beyond it.

The challenge for the purchasing organisation

The challenge for the purchasing organisation is to get the goods and services, without being adversarial and without being committed to a long-term relationship for which they see no benefit, whilst being unresponsive and ruining the existing relationship. The purchasing organisation will therefore literally keep suppliers at arm's length away from them until they need them, avoiding regular review meetings yet knowing who to call when needed and perhaps demanding instant attention from the supplier when they feel they need it. Suppliers will attempt to get closer to the purchasing organisation, but realise where they stand and not make special attempts to have resources available to meet the needs of these purchasing organisations.

The standard nature of the goods and services means that risk is minimised as suppliers can be changed; and where risk management is undertaken buyers will limit it to basic factors like managing price, delivery, the given quality and the quantity required.

A transactional relationship

Definition

A **transactional relationship** focuses on the successful completion of ordinary transactions which deliver low-value, low-risk goods and services to the buyer by a competent supplier.

In the context of supply positioning

These relationships are normally found in the tactical acquisition quadrant. Purchasing organisations seek suppliers who will 'deliver the goods' and cause few problems, hence the theme for tactical acquisition, 'organise and let go'. Purchasing organisations will seek a short-term duration for the relationship in some cases, but in others they will be happy to allow a supplier to organise the supply for them, so they may let go of the detail and concentrate on other issues.

Relationship factors

A transactional relationship is one where the deal and the relationship are almost equally important and both parties:

- Will want the supply and the relationship to succeed and be prepared to invest time and effort in achieving this success.
- Exhibit consistent appropriate behaviour. There will be a realisation by the purchasing organisation that suppliers here can take much of the administrative work from them, by the use of processes like purchasing cards and electronic catalogues. Where suppliers can process thousands

of transactions for the purchasing organisation, processing cost is reduced and people released to undertake more strategic actions.

- Invest time in setting up and planning the contract with supplier(s) to be sure it works once implemented.
- Will be happier with a longer-term duration. Normally the competitive nature of the market would lead the purchasing organisation to obtain quotations before awarding a contract. However, if an existing supplier performs well and is considered to be at or around market price it is worth asking the question 'Will we get more from continuing the contract with the existing supplier rather than rebidding it?' Consider the cost of the enquiry process, consider the risk of using the same supplier again, and consider the cost and risk of change. These factors could lead the purchasing organisation to the conclusion that continuing the relationship is on balance the appropriate course of action. NB: Public sector purchasing organisations may not be able to take this course of action. Refer to study session 11.
- Trust each other to keep their side of the bargain.

The challenge for the purchasing organisation

The challenge for the purchasing organisation is to meet a 'selfish' objective, whilst ensuring a continuous supply of goods and services, putting as little effort into the arrangement as possible, without offending the supplier. This challenge steers the purchasing organisation away from using aggression to manage this relationship. Being adversarial here could impact the way the supplier performs, resulting in someone within the purchasing organisation having to spend time and effort sorting the problems out, when their time would be better spent addressing other more critical issues. The purchasing organisation is therefore, within reason, price-insensitive in these relationships. Risk assessment and risk management will be undertaken by the purchasing organisation and reviewed on an exceptional basis.

One risk for the purchasing organisation is that the supplier works very hard to establish itself within the purchasing organisation, and is successful to such an extent that stakeholders fight to keep the supplier and want to avoid the tender process, even when it can be proved that better value for money can be obtained. The supplier has in such a case become indispensable to some areas of the organisation.

Closer tactical relationship

Definition

A **closer tactical relationship** is one with a competent supplier who focuses on the successful completion of low-risk transactions and coordinates the supply of low-risk goods and services from other (second tier?) suppliers.

Practicalities

Practically speaking, the purchasing organisation may select one of its best transactional suppliers, typically one where there is a very good working relationship, and invite them to take over or coordinate the supply of goods and services of another group of say (50) transactional or arm's-length suppliers. This means that the other 50 or so suppliers will supply to the purchasing organisation via or as coordinated by the supplier with whom the purchasing organisation has developed the closer tactical relationship. Examples could include:

- A supplier of standard Microsoft Office training who delivers training programmes to an organisation. The supplier is one of several organisations who deliver standard training to the purchasing organisation and they are asked to coordinate the training of the other five organisations.
- A supplier of electrical components is asked to purchase and supply nuts and bolts, tools and all other workshop consumables.

In each case the purchasing organisation will need to share information about the requirements and their sources with the supplier in question and communicate the new arrangement with all of the suppliers concerned. Two other factors need considering here. First, the selection process for this supply arrangement could be competitive. However, it may be appropriate to simply develop the existing very good relationship towards this status. Second, unless the supplier can by their position in the market purchase these items at a lower cost than the purchasing organisation, it may be appropriate to offer the selected supplier a handling fee. This fee must represent a cost saving to the purchasing organisation, when compared with the total processing and relationship costs of doing business with all of the suppliers.

In one case known to the author a large corporate organisation paid a 10% handling fee to a local ironmongers for coordinating the supply of all of the needs of the several maintenance teams on their several sites within the county. A large volume of small, insignificant items were therefore processed through a trusting relationship at minimum cost to the purchasing organisation. It was an optimised process and it took place well before 'e' was on the horizon.

In the context of supply positioning

These relationships are normally found in an area across the centre of the supply positioning model. The essence of this thought process is that there are situations where relationships are neither below nor above the line which normally differentiates strategic quadrants from the tactical ones. The relationship needed by the purchasing organisation is not partnership or strategic alliance; and single-sourced and outsourcing relationships won't fit either. There would be a clear negative effect if the supplier was treated in an adversarial way and transactional and arm's length cannot describe the closeness that is necessary in the relationship. In a sense this relationship bends the model; however, relationships are not black and white and they are not always capable of being 'put in a box', so this one crosses the boundaries. This is a longer-term arrangement to allow the benefits of the relationship to accrue to both parties.

Relationship factors

The demand for this relationship emanates from the need to reduce the supplier base and the costs associated with maintaining relationships with many suppliers and it moves towards the concept of 'tiering' discussed in study session 18. In the closer tactical relationship, the relationship is more important than the deal. Both parties:

- will be prepared to work hard to make the ongoing supply and the relationship succeed
- invest time and resources together, in the process of developing the relationship to the required status and in implementing it
- exhibit consistent appropriate behaviour which values and respects the other party as a customer or supplier
- develop and deliver 'continuous improvements' during the life of the relationship
- consider risks and risk management together, reflecting these in service level agreements and key performance indicators
- trust each other with information about their own business and how they see it developing.

The challenge for the purchasing organisation

Simply put, the challenge for the purchasing organisation is to get another organisation to do extra for nothing, or extra for as little as possible. The offer of the additional business must be attractive enough for the supplier to bear any additional costs not covered by the additional fee they may receive from the purchasing organisation. In some cases, however, the additional volume of business to relatively small suppliers may enable them to move up the discount structure of the tier two supplier and the momentum from the first purchasing organisation may enable the supplier to offer the same service to other purchasing organisations, therefore making even further economies of scale. Risk is increased in this relationship by putting many eggs in one basket.

Single-sourced relationship

Definition

A **single-sourced relationship** is one where a purchasing organisation forms an exclusive agreement with one supplier for the supply of a range of specified items, usually at a fixed unit price and for a specific period.

In the context of supply positioning

These relationships are normally found in either the strategic security or tactical acquisition quadrants. However, it could be that some higher-risk tactical profit relationships could be single sourced. This is a longer-term arrangement which should allow the benefits of the relationship to accrue to both parties.

Relationship factors

Single sourcing is in itself a risk, as all of the eggs are in the basket of one supplier. The proposition of single sourcing revolves around the view that the relationship with the supplier will involve greater volume, exclusiveness, and cooperation from the purchasing organisation to the supplier, with greater cooperation, lowest cost, and preferential treatment in terms of delivery, excellent service and continuous improvement flowing back from the supplier to the purchasing organisation. That's the theory!

Many European organisations set up these arrangements with suppliers in the 1970s and 1980s in the wake of studies of Japanese vertically integrated relationships, which delivered great benefits to the parties concerned, but were in fact based on a completely different cultural assumption, which was long-term commitment to the members of the supply chain, a cultural assumption which was in many cases invalid in Europe.

Sometimes European single-source relationships succeeded and sometimes the relationships failed. However, in the late 1990s and early twenty-first century some major European manufacturers were dual sourcing again to mitigate the risk of failure to supply and other problems in the relationships. The relationships failed for reasons attributable to both sides.

- 'Buyers felt that suppliers treated them as if they had "gotcha"! The business was won for three years and the customer won't change and so we can give our best resources to other more attractive customers – this business is in the bank!'
- Sellers were sometimes misled about volumes and when their best efforts meant that they could not supply a given item at a cost lower than someone else, the buyer broke the single-source agreement on that item, forgetting the advantages that the purchasing organisation had accrued on the other 99 items.

The single-source relationship is therefore one where the relationship is slightly more important than the deal and both parties:

- will invest time and resources to make the supply and the relationship succeed in meeting the relationship objectives
- exhibit consistent appropriate behaviour(ish)
- give priority to the other party (in theory)
- should trust each other to look out for the needs of the other party.

The challenge for the purchasing organisation

The challenge for the purchasing organisation is to realise the results delivered from the supplier's unique position, which should be greater cooperation, lowest cost and preferential treatment in terms of delivery, excellent service and continuous improvement. The selling organisation will seek the benefits of full resource utilisation and long-term uncontested business.

Self-assessment question 3.2

Contrast the benefits to the purchasing organisation of developing a single-sourced relationship with a supplier, rather than playing the market.

Feedback on page 71

3.3 Challenges faced in tactical relationships

Tactical relationships are often undervalued by purchasing organisations. The items they represent and the relationships that underpin them are

3

not valued as they should be by some organisations, who dismiss items, relationships and the people involved in them, in favour of the glory to be sought from strategic relationships and the buzz of doing multi-million pound deals. It is true that tactical areas represent the humdrum of daily life in the purchasing process, yet they must be given appropriate consideration within the big picture.

Let's remind ourselves that low-value, high-risk purchases are made in the strategic security quadrant and what we are facing here is low-risk, high-value tactical profit items and low-risk, low-value tactical acquisition spend.

The challenge for purchasing organisations is therefore to manage these relationships in a way that delivers the results sought at minimum risk and minimum cost in terms of people and processes, recognising the views and roles of suppliers and stakeholders. Put simply, the challenge is to keep the job going with minimum problems in tactical acquisition and save money or deliver benefit against a given budget in tactical profit.

Learning activity 3.3

Take your own organisation and consider how you purchase the lowest low-value, low-risk items. Is there a more cost-effective way of making these transactions? Do the items receive the same level of sign off, irrespective of unit cost?

Feedback on page 72

Tactical acquisition

One real challenge here for organisations in many sectors is to be price-insensitive! 'Pennywise, pound foolish' is the saying, yet it is foolish to invest resources in processes and people and reduce costs or deliver benefits less than the cost of the resource being applied from within the organisation. Four situations from different sectors are described below.

- One international oil company gave all of the items it bought a risk classification (high risk was one and low risk was nine) and where risk was amongst the lowest categories and cost was below £200 the whole drive was to use simple processes and trust suppliers to deliver. Suppliers who did not perform were simply not used again. Some suppliers view the organisation as cavalier, but they were simply organising and letting go.
- A retailer took the view that a national contract for stationery would take more time to set up and administer that it would save. Their reasoning that, 'just because we are a national organisation we don't have to have a national contract' is one that others could learn from. Staff working on the high street had a credit card to buy stationery and the many other minor items necessary to run the shop and spend was monitored on a quarterly review by the purchasing team at HQ.
- A manufacturer purchased nuts and bolts for their workshops item by item and insisted on signed paperwork for all withdrawals from stores. The process was changed to a two-weekly top-up system by a trusted

local hardware merchant who invoiced once a month and the items were made free issue from the stores. Here the chief accountant was initially reluctant to loosen this control. However, when a test proved that the total cost of an employee filling his pockets with bolts was £22.50, then the risk was accepted and the principle applied to other items bought locally and used in different parts of the business.

- A public sector organisation started to use a purchasing card for low-value, low-risk items. The processes they applied to the card scheme, in recording, multiple checking and signing off the statements – led to an estimated average cost of £70 per transaction. At this stage there was a review of processes and the regime was relaxed somewhat.

One common denominator in these arrangements working towards the purchasing organisations advantage is a trusting relationship with the supplier. Frequently, people working for suppliers will not abuse the trust we place in them in these circumstances and where they do, the market situation is such that we can change supplier without a great cost of change.

Tactical profit

'Hard-nosed, aggressive, ready for a punch-up' is the way one seller described a buyer to me. When questioned, it turned out that the seller was selling standard services to a customer who undoubtedly saw the market as a tactical profit one.

The challenge here is to be hard-nosed, but perhaps assertive and professional rather than aggressive and ready for a punch-up. Buyers must recognise that in some cases the motive of both parties will be the same – to extract maximum benefit from the given deal for their organisation – and that in such circumstances conflict is a likely result. We need not, however, return to the picture of the caveman and the cudgel, for if we transfer the word 'conflict' into the words 'argument and debate' then it is reasonable to argue and debate the issues with a seller to reach a deal which is the best that can be achieved, always retaining the option to go elsewhere if the outcome does not match our aspirations. In this area the time and the effort are worthwhile, as the size of the purchasing organisation's spend can be, in relative terms, a major one. Supplier reactions to our efforts to (say) run an electronic reverse auction will run the full gamut from not interested to desperately keen and this should not surprise us.

Self-assessment question 3.3

Identify the benefits of working with tactical acquisition suppliers to realise 'organise and let go', and contrast this with the benefits of being 'hard nosed' in seeking to 'drive for profit' in tactical profit.

Feedback on page 72

3.4 The risks and challenges of strategic relationships

This section examines the challenges faced by the buyer adopting strategic relationships with suppliers. As with the tactical relationships covered earlier

3

in this session, each relationship will be defined, set in the context of supply positioning, the relationship factors evaluated and the challenge for the purchasing organisation described. The relationships considered here are:

- an outsourcing relationship
- a strategic alliance relationship
- a partnership relationship
- a co-destiny relationship.

These relationships are neither ad hoc nor accidental. The relationships grow and develop, sometimes by design, but frequently the process is one of evolution, as the parties realise that working together brings benefits to both organisations which are greater than the sum of the benefits that would accrue if the organisations remained at the level of a transactional relationship.

Learning activity 3.4

Consider which suppliers are 'strategic' to your organisation. Identify outsourced relationships, partners, strategic alliances and situations where co-destiny is involved. Consider first how easy it is to strictly differentiate your relationships amongst these relationships. Second, consider how easy it is to differentiate between these strategic relationships and the tactical relationships identified in study session 3. Third, consider how the behaviour of both your organisation and the supplier differs from tactical relationships.

Feedback on page 72

An outsourcing relationship

Definition

An **outsourcing relationship** is the retention of responsibility for services by the purchasing organisation, but the devolution of the day-to-day performance of those services to an external organisation, under a contract with agreed standards, costs and conditions.

In the context of supply positioning

The use of outsourcing is clearly a strategic decision for an organisation which is not undertaken lightly, and such relationships can exist in the strategic critical quadrant. However, purchasing organisations must be careful about outsourcing in areas which deliver them competitive advantage. This debate will be explored fully in study sessions 14 and 15 which deal with outsourcing. It is more typical to find that a purchasing organisation has outsourced its canteen, which is a service located within the tactical acquisition quadrant, or that by outsourcing transport, a purchasing organisation moves that commodity into the strategic security quadrant. Outsourcing is not appropriate in the tactical profit quadrant, as purchasing organisations want to take advantage of the market situation and not tie themselves down, but if a purchasing organisation saw advantage in letting the outsourcing organisation at its specialist's get the best out of the market on their behalf, then the relationship could be classified as high tactical profit or low strategic critical.

Relationship factors

An outsourcing relationship is one where a business case demonstrates that the supplier, with their expertise, can do better than the best we as the purchasing organisation can do. 'Better' might for example be interpreted as lower cost, better service or other factors. Outsourcing is much more than 'make or buy'; it frequently reflects the buyer's decision to regard an activity as 'non-core' and one strategic thinker talks of the process as 'insourcing/outsourcing'. Specifically, buyers will seek:

- cost reduction
- service excellence
- freedom from detail
- technical excellence and competence
- future proofing.

Specifically, suppliers will seek:

- profit
- their own economies of scale
- extras within the contract
- standardisation amongst their customers
- a long-term contract, training their human resources, who become more marketable.

The challenge for the purchasing organisation

The challenges for the purchasing organisation include:

- Making a decision on the full facts and full costs. Too often decisions do not involve a fully costed business case.
- Ensuring that the promised benefits are delivered, year after year.
- Ensuring that they are served in a way that best meets their needs, rather than a way that suits the supplier. Trust and openness must be two-way.
- Ensuring that they retain the knowledge to critically assess their service and that suppliers provide information on alternative strategies and their risks.
- Ensuring that the supplier remains 'keen' to deliver the service in the long-term.

One point that buyers debate is this. Is the outsourcer a partner? Certainly outsourcers sell themselves as 'partners'. However, if you read on and review the definition of a partner, you may doubt whether outsourcers you know are truly partners, or simply suppliers who provide a service. One vital test is the extent to which the supplier is prepared to 'do something for nothing'. Doing something for nothing is the hallmark of a partner, a supplier who seeks extras may not be viewed as a partner.

A strategic alliance relationship

Definition

A **strategic alliance relationship** is one between two organisations who work together for the provision of goods or services to their own mutual

3

benefit. The organisations may ally themselves for all or part of their service/product portfolio, a given geographical area, a given market or for defensive reasons.

Buyers may be part of an alliance, but they may also face an alliance and in some cases may not be aware that they are facing an alliance.

In the context of supply positioning

Where a purchasing organisation and one or more suppliers form a strategic alliance the relationship between them must emanate from the strategic critical quadrant. It may be that the purchasing organisation sells hardware and teams up with a software supplier to maximise their business opportunities together.

Relationship factors

As described above the relationship between the parties is worth significantly more than any one deal between them. A customer attempting to prise the parties apart will have difficulty as the organisations have allied themselves for *their own mutual benefit*. Organisations may ally themselves:

- for all or part of their service/product portfolio
- to advance their interests in a given geographical area
- to advance their interests in a given market segment
- for defensive reasons, where another player is entering or has entered the market and they feel that they can fight this competition better together
- to add their 'unique value' to create offerings for existing or new customers.

The challenge for the purchasing organisation

The challenge for the purchasing organisation revolves more around the strategic alliances *it faces from other suppliers*, than the challenges of working together within a strategic alliance.

For example, a purchasing organisation may use a consultancy to advise of its business processes and that consultancy may recommend given software as a solution to the business process needs. The purchasing organisation needs to be sure that the software is being recommended on merit and not because the consultancy:

- receives an introduction fee from the software house
- receives a larger introduction fee from the given software house than others who may meet the purchasing organisation's need
- team recommending the software are only experienced in the given software platform or package.

The innocent purchasing organisation may not realise the nature of the relationship or financial terms between so-called 'independent' parties who present a common, practiced 'front' to steer them towards where they, the alliance, want them to be. Sellers working together in strategic alliances seek to benefit from their alliance for their own legitimate commercial purposes. Working together in a strategic alliance is a common, legitimate business strategy. However, there are occasions when the members of the alliance can be 'economical with the truth'. In these situations the challenge for purchasing organisation is to understand the nature of the relationship between the parties and extract full benefit to them from the relationship. One local authority buyer known to the author inserts a specific clause into invitations to tender to ask the bidders to reveal situations where they benefit from 'alliance partners or subcontractors'.

Having said all of the above, there are circumstances where alliances add real benefit to purchasing organisations.

A partnership relationship

Definition

A **partnership relationship** is a commitment between a buyer and a supplier to a long-term relationship based on trust and clear mutually agreed objectives. Sharing risks and rewards is fundamental through the common goals of:

- continuous improvement
- an improved competitive position
- the elimination of waste
- acceleration of innovation
- expansion of markets
- the growth of profit.

In the context of supply positioning

Partnerships are clearly strategic critical relationships. The logic behind this argument is that the most costly and most risky goods and services the purchasing organisation secures are the vital ones:

- that are used in goods and services that represent its unique selling proposition.
- that represent its greatest opportunity for profit.
- that its most important customers depend upon.
- that the general public relies on them to provide, in the case of a public sector organisation.

In a number of these cases failure to supply the customer with the right quality and service could result in the survival of the organisation being called into question.

Relationship factors

Partnership relationships are ones where the highest level of trust exists and the duration is long-term. The relationship is worth vastly more than any one deal or issue between the parties and other characteristics include the following points:

- the information flow and transactions between parties is optimised
- there is cost transparency, the purchasing organisation being aware of the cost structure of the supplier and the supplier being aware of the proportion of the purchasing organisation's cost that the service or goods they provide accounts for

- 'problems' are highlighted as soon as they arise, solutions are proposed and discussed
- joint project teams tackle problems, technical and market opportunities
- intuitive development can be seen in action
- electronic collaborative development fora are used
- buyers exclude other suppliers and suppliers exclude other buyers, the two parties focus on each other, rather than the supply market
- the relationship feels as if 'we' are in this for the long term! It can be 'for better or worse' to succeed together
- risk identification and risk management are undertaken together.

The challenge for the purchasing organisation

The challenge for the purchasing organisation is to select an appropriate partner and to invest in the relationship to make it work and make it improve and develop.

The word 'select' in this situation may not quite be appropriate, as partnerships may evolve from the chemistry between the people in the organisations concerned over a number of years. In the same way that an advert in a newspaper may not be the best way for human beings to select each other to form a relationship, the invitation to tender process may not be the best way for a purchasing organisation to 'select' a supply partner.

Many organisations 'talk' about partnerships; however, living up to the partnership definition is not as easy as defining it. Temptations exist, which can wreck the relationship.

- Temptation for the purchasing organisation may be in the form of a 'special offer' from another supplier, or to take advantage of a situation which the partner has not realised, or to use another supplier occasionally, 'just in case' they are needed long term.
- Temptation for the supplier may be that another customer is more attractive and by going outside the partnership a new opportunity, short-term gain or higher margin can be made.
- Temptation for both parties together is that they rest on their laurels and don't develop or enhance their offering. Then other partners will seem attractive to their own customers and both parties will suffer.

There can also be a supply chain dimension to consider. Imagine a purchasing organisation undertaking a supplier appraisal on a potential supplier of a key component. The purchasing organisation itself seeks a partnership relationship with the supplier, yet it discovers that this supplier has an adversarial relationship with the supplier of its own key component. Thus the purchasing organisation's relationship, no matter how close it is, will be undermined by the adversarial relationship of its supplier.

A co-destiny relationship

Definition

'**Co-destiny** is a strategic relationship where the organisations involved choose to share common destinies in all aspects of their business for mutual benefit. The relationship relies on total trust and both organisations become fully interdependent and as such, they succeed or fail together.'

Devised by Ford, Fogg, Ayliffe and Schollar

In the context of supply positioning

Once again this relationship must emanate from the strategic critical area. Co-destiny is more than a partnership. However, whilst it is a distinction worth making, it is perhaps the difference of a shade of colour rather than a difference of colour.

Relationship factors

It is possible to argue that a partnership includes all of the factors included as factors in a co-destiny relationship, but it is possible to differentiate the two relationships by indicating that:

- if two or more organisations see a co-destiny between themselves, they cannot consider the existence of their businesses without the other parties
- in a partnership relationship it would, in the worst case scenario, be possible to build a relationship with another partner if the relationship with the initial partner foundered.

To differentiate partnership and co-destiny relationships, the text from the partnership subsection above has been copied down to this section and amended to reflect the change of shade within the same colour that differentiates these close relationships. A co-destiny relationship is one where:

- the highest level of trust exists and the duration is considered eternal
- the relationship is such that the importance of any one deal is not considered by the parties as an issue
- information flow and transactions between parties is optimised, perhaps with shared systems, certainly with integrated systems
- there is cost transparency using shared models
- potential 'problems' are sought out before they arise, solutions are proposed and discussed
- joint project teams tackle problems, technical and market opportunities and long-term strategy
- intuitive development is the norm
- electronic collaborative development fora are widely used
- the question of working with other parties does not arise
- the relationship feels as if 'we' are in this from 'here to eternity'
- risk identification and risk management are processes undertaken together.

The challenge for the purchasing organisation

The challenge for the purchasing organisation is to live up to the ideals of the relationship, to keep refreshing and innovating. The same thoughts expressed above about the selection of a partner relate to a co-destiny relationship, and as the relationship progresses questioners on both sides will raise the issue of a change. However, the long-term, ongoing need of both

3

organisations is recognised and like a human family which may argue and debate, it normally stays together.

The supply chain dimension needs to be considered in this relationship as well. Again, the comments made in the context of the partnership relationship above hold true here, though they are perhaps more vital and the parties concerned will encourage other members of their supply chain to work more closely with them, perhaps to the exclusion of others. When this happens the supply chain itself becomes the competitive force within the market, rather than any one of the members of the chain.

Self-assessment question 3.4

Take figure 3.8 which has the supply positioning matrix flattened and the relationship spectrum drawn above it. Note how the positions of tactical relationships were placed within the chart in learning activity 3.2 above. Your task this time is to position the following relationships on figure 3.8:

- outsourcing relationships
- strategic alliance relationships
- partnership relationships
- co-destiny relationships.

Figure 3.8: The relationship spectrum – tactical relationships

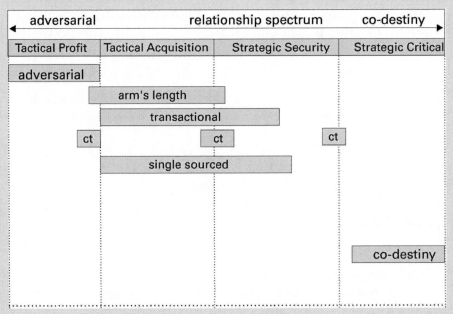

Feedback on page 73

3.5 Selecting strategic suppliers

As a purchasing organisation, how do you select strategic suppliers? Is 'select' the right word? In the sense that there may be a number of providers of the service which we are looking for, then the word 'select' is appropriate, yet if we use the traditional 'three quotes' method to select partners we may not get the result we seek.

3

Learning activity 3.5

Imagine that you are a private sector organisation seeking a new partner. Consider what you would need to know.

Feedback on page 73

There is a sense in which strategic relationships 'evolve' rather than are selected, yet literally the process must involve the choice of one supplier over another and so there must be selection. The process used to 'select' must involve a conscious process, but must be much more than the traditional enquiry or invitation to tender process.

Note that in this text we are assuming that we do not already have a relationship with an organisation that can be developed or evolved into an alliance or a partnership. If such a route were available to us, then less time need be spent on the earlier stages of the process and the later organisational and people aspects may be moved to more quickly. This text also assumes that a business case has been completed and that the business case demonstrates that the project will bring the appropriate rate of return.

The evolution process, in the private sector, often develops over a number of years, almost unconsciously. Consider this situation, based within the private sector.

> A photographer sets up to take wedding photographs and several times she is aware that her clients also need flowers and stationery. In one case she asks a local florist to join with her and it goes well. Over the next two years the two people do seven events together and when the florist repays the compliment and asks the photographer to work on a wedding where she has the flowers to do, the two people sit down together and consider that they might offer a joint service to couples getting married and also talk to a local taxi firm and a stationer to become subcontractors to them. The business grows and prospers and there are now two photographers and a one-stop service being offered by both the florist and the photographer for 120 weddings a year.

Reading this you might say, 'That's fine for a small organisation, but wouldn't work with a large corporate like us'. You might be right, but it could also be argued that it is the business processes that are getting in the way of people in larger organisations developing such relationships. You might also be wrong: look at your suppliers, how many of them offer a 'one stop shop' or an alliance, drawing on the expertise of other organisations to meet your needs? The other consideration is of course, how many of the large businesses started small and worked with others to grow?

Now consider the situation with a large corporate organisation in the private sector, currently delivering services based upon its product range but having identified a market for other services which compliment its current well known and prestigious brand. The skill set required is not within the skill set of the current service employees and it has been decided to seek a 'partner' rather than employ more staff.

The process will involve the specification of the relationship sought, the competencies of the potential partner and a decision to 'buy' rather than 'make'. This will be followed by market research, supplier research and the identification of several possible suppliers. An invitation to tender (ITT) could be used, but a strategic alliance is sought, and making the suppliers compete might not allow them to understand how important the purchasing organisation sees the requirement and might not generate the best ideas from the potential partners. An alternative approach is to use the basic market and supplier analysis tools, including an evaluation of the supplier's accounts, customer base and other partners (if any) to identify and rank the suppliers as potential allies. Next would be an approach to the owners of the organisation to ask them if they are interested in listening to a business proposition. It might be that they are surprised, it might be that they are not interested as they prefer to stay on their own or have other plans. But it might be that they are interested and very keen once they understand that you have selected them first. The discussions start, develop and lead to a formal strategic alliance. Then evolution takes over and the business grows.

Public sector organisations are not, of course, allowed to take the routes identified above and must use the processes specified under the EU Procurement Legislation. Refer to study session 11.

Next it is necessary to review which considerations the purchasing organisation would take when assessing suppliers for strategic capability. This needs to be undertaken first at an organisation and market level and then at a level where we in the purchasing organisation need to feel comfortable with both the supplier itself and the people within the sales organisation.

Organisation and market level analysis

This analysis is undertaken before initial contact is made. Fundamentally, we need to understand whether the potential ally or partner is financially stable, whether they are working with our competitors, whether they have the capability we need, who owns them and where they are located. Once this is established we need to concentrate on synergy issues:

- The complimentary nature of the products and/or services offered. To what extent is there an overlap and how would we cope with (say) a customer asking both organisations to quote for supply?
- The customer bases of the organisations. Will it be possible for both to grow business?
- The new markets open to the alliance, not currently open to the separate organisations.
- The future direction of the organisation. Where is it in its life cycle? Linking with a wilderness organisation or a dying company would be pointless.
- The management team. Who are they? How do they run the business?
- The human resources within the business. Initially here we need a view on the level of expertise available.
- The position in sector or trade. How do they compare with others? Are they leaders or followers?

- Recent press coverage. What is said about them in trade journals or newspapers?
- To what extent are they busy? A busy organisation has many customers. One less busy might not be the one to ally with.

Analysis of these factors will probably lead to the conclusion that one organisation has the strategic fit we seek and is worth courting.

Organisation and people level analysis

The text below is adapted, with permission, from chapters two and three of *The Relationship Manager* by Tony Davis and Richard Pharro (2003). In assessing strategic capability it is appropriate to consider the potential ally or partner in terms of their:

- Unquestionable knowledge of service capability. Here we need to understand that the potential ally or partner has a strategic ability to translate clients' needs into delivery.
- Expert status. In their sector are they considered at least 'one of the' organisations to talk to, if not 'the' one to call upon. Will you, as purchasing a organisation, therefore be harnessing the skill set of the best of breed?
- Authority. Do they have individuals who are the experts, who can speak with authority and can proactively recognise opportunities working with us?
- Visibility. Do we feel that the people we are dealing with will be visible to us and able to get others in their organisation to move for and with us when we need them to?
- Sensitivity. Do we feel that the people and the organisation will be sensitive to our needs and to the needs of our customers?
- Proactivity. To what extent will the organisation and its people seek opportunities for improvement and propose them to us?
- Realism. To what extent do we feel that the organisation and its people have their finger on the pulse and are able to reflect back to us if we propose an unworkable or unsaleable solution?
- Control mechanisms and processes. Do we feel sure that these are adequate to meet our needs?

Remember that the supplier will have exactly the same issue list and questions to ask of the purchasing organisation. Once this activity is complete, the project can move towards the development of a joint offering, contractual arrangements, planning towards launch, launch and commencement of delivery.

Self-assessment question 3.5

Describe an appropriate process for 'selecting' a new partner or ally.

Feedback on page 73

Revision question

Now try the revision question for this session on page 321.

3

Summary

Managing purchasing and supply relationships is a challenge. Buyers need to recognise that:

- the view of the situation and the view of the relationship which a purchasing organisation holds only half of the full picture
- suppliers and their people will have their view of us as a customer
- in some cases the supplier's view, if we truly knew it, would disturb us
- the supplier might well be disturbed to understand how little we valued them.

Supplier preferencing and the market management matrix enable us to:

- understand the view from both sides
- test our assumptions about the relationship
- make plans to correct unfavourable situations.

Risk is also a factor in relationships. Working progressively from supply positioning to the market management matrix will allow us to:

- understand the risks we face
- employ a structured approach to managing risk and moving within the market management matrix to a better situation.

Suggested further reading

You could read the relevant sections in Steele and Court (1996) and Moran (1997).

Review the material in the relationship management and supplier development section and other sections of CIPS knowledge works on the CIPS website.

Feedback on learning activities and self-assessment questions

Feedback on learning activity 3.1

Your drawing should resemble figure 3.4 with your own goods and services allocated a number and placed in a given position within a quadrant.

Figure 3.4: Supply positioning example

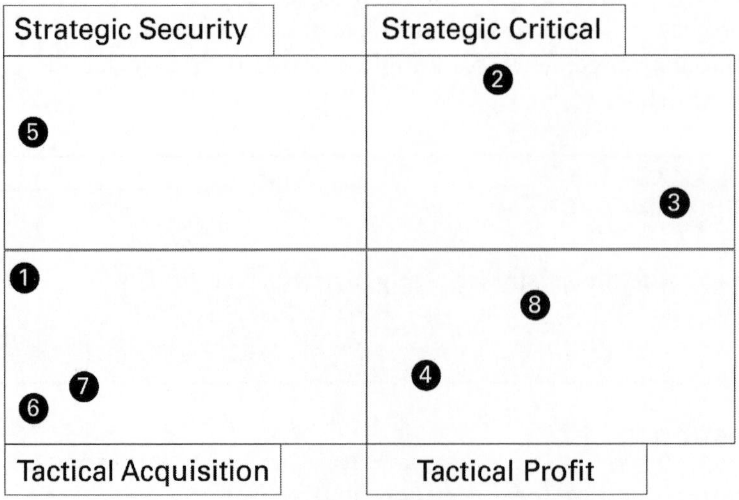

Feedback on self-assessment question 3.1

(a) What are the themes and colours of the four quadrants?
  (i) Strategic critical – checking and searching – yellow.
  (ii) Strategic security – secure supplies – red.
  (iii) Tactical profit – drive for profit – blue.
  (iv) Tactical acquisition – organise and let go – green.
(b) Assuming you were an NHS Trust, which quadrant would you expect to find the following requirements in?
  (i) A4 inkjet printer paper – tactical acquisition.
  (ii) A contract to remove clinical waste – strategic security.
  (iii) An MRI body scanner used to detect cancer patients – strategic critical.
  (iv) Laptop computers – tactical profit.

Feedback on learning activity 3.2

The boxes you have drawn should be in areas like those in figure 3.7. Note that 'ct' refers to closer tactical relationships.

Figure 3.7: The relationship spectrum – tactical relationships

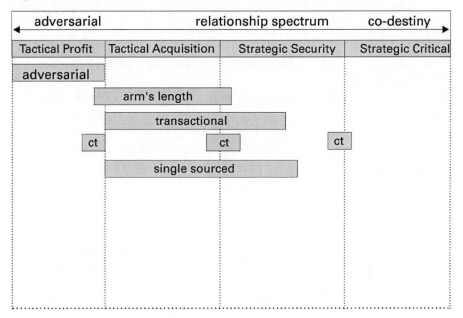

Feedback on self-assessment question 3.2

The benefits of a single-sourced relationship, rather than playing the market include:

- only one relationship to manage
- a closer relationship is possible with the selected supplier
- constant re-bidding is avoided
- long-term cost advantage should be provided from working with a single supplier
- people on both sides will get to know each other better
- the requirements of the purchasing organisation will be better known to the supplier

- at times of shortage the purchasing organisation should receive favourable treatment
- the purchasing organisation should be offered new ideas and enhancements.

The benefits of playing the market, rather than a single-sourced relationship include:

- the purchasing organisation should be able to get the best deal each time
- if anything happens to one supplier we can get help from others
- in a competitive situation suppliers will fight for our business.

Feedback on learning activity 3.3

Consider making a business case for the use of empowered user-driven transactions like electronic catalogues and purchasing cards if you feel your organisation could make these purchases in a more cost-effective way.

Feedback on self-assessment question 3.3

Within the tactical acquisition quadrant of the supply positioning model there must be little emphasis on being adversarial and a more co-operative relationship style. The benefits of this approach will include:

- People in the purchasing organisation being able to focus on more important areas.
- People in the purchasing organisation delivering greater cost savings by addressing situations where proportionately greater cost saving can be achieved.
- Deliveries arriving, goods being fit for purpose without the intervention of people from the purchasing organisation.
- People from supplier's feeling trusted.
- Low cost transactions being used (monthly invoices, purchasing cards, websites).

Within tactical profit the size of the spend warrants the attention of people from the purchasing organisation. The investment of time here can deliver savings because the size of the spend and the standard nature of the goods and services makes competition between sellers much more likely. Being 'hard nosed' will mean that buyers may be involved in adversarial or assertive negotiation and making sellers compete may mean using an electronic reverse auction. Simply put, the savings are there to be made in the tactical profit quadrant, whereas the size of the spend means that the savings can't be made within the tactical acquisition quadrant.

Feedback on learning activity 3.4

You should be able to identify organisations with whom you have strategic relationships sometimes, though it may not be 'easy' to classify and put a firm line down between (say) a strategic alliance, a partnership and co-destiny relationship. Practically, identifying the fine line between the relationship types is less important than recognising that the behaviour of the organisations is appropriate to a strategic relationship.

Feedback on self-assessment question 3.4

Figure 3.9 is the final development of the relationship spectrum; the strategic relationships are added to the tactical ones and placed within the supply positioning quadrants that they relate to. Note that two strategic alliance entries have been made. One entry is the alliance in which the purchasing organisation will choose to participate. Normally this relationship would be sought in the strategic critical quadrant where the joint efforts focus on our key offerings. However, in the strategic security quadrant the alliance could be a solution to reduce our risk. There is also a line across the whole spectrum for strategic alliances *faced* by the purchasing organisation, as suppliers may legitimately unite for their own interests, irrespective of where we as the purchasing organisation see them within the relationship spectrum.

Figure 3.9: The relationship spectrum – all relationship types

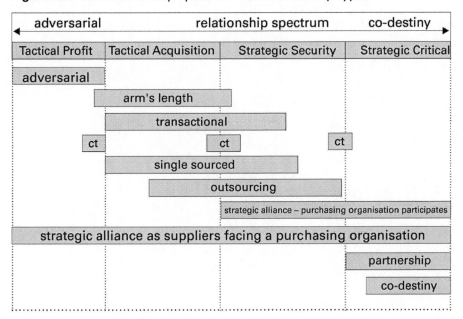

Feedback on learning activity 3.5

You should have indicated that you need to know many details about the supplier, their people and their processes. Now consider whether you feel that the traditional 'three quotes' approach will build the relationship you need.

Feedback on self-assessment question 3.5

1   Specify the relationship sought and the competencies of the potential partner.
2   Investigate any existing relationships which may be developed.
3   Research into the organisations providing the required goods and services.
4   Carry out fundamental analysis. Understand whether the organisations are financially stable, working our with competitors, have the skills, where they are located and who owns them.
5   Organisation and market level analysis.

6   Initial approach.
7   Presentation of proposal.
8   Organisation and people level analysis.
9   Development of joint offering and contractual arrangements.
10   Planning towards launch.
11   Launch and commence delivery.

3

Supplier preferencing and the market management matrix

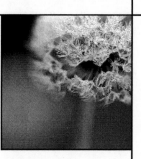

Introduction

Study sessions 1, 2 and 3 have explored purchasing and supply relationships of different types through the relationship spectrum, the needs of stakeholders and the supply positioning model. It's about time we considered how people who work for suppliers see things – isn't it?

For even considering all of **our** wants, needs, theories and strategies, all may be as nought if we do not consider the wants, needs, theories and strategies of people working for our suppliers or potential suppliers!

This study session considers the supplier preferencing model which describes how people working for suppliers see their customers (us – the purchasing organisations), how they may prefer to deal with some customers rather than others and how we may help ourselves be more attractive.

The study session then merges the supply positioning model, remember it as 'supply' not 'supplier' positioning, with the supplier preferencing model to provide a sixteen option market management matrix. This is a complex model – however understanding it is fundamental to managing purchasing and supply relationships effectively. It is used by successful purchasing and supply practitioners on all five continents.

On a flight into Europe the author sat in front of two salesmen going to see a buyer. One salesman said to the other: 'Partnerships are just another buyer's con. They talk nice and then smack you in the face. I tell you what, when we get to his office, I'll say to him, "Don't hit me, I'll hit myself!"'

4

Session learning objectives

After completing this session you should be able to:

4.1 Evaluate the differing views that people who work for suppliers have of purchasing organisations.
4.2 Show diagrammatically the dynamics of differing legitimate objectives of buyers and sellers.
4.3 Describe typical interaction between the purchasing organisation and the selling organisation when a tactical approach is used.
4.4 Describe typical interaction between the purchasing organisation and the selling organisation when a strategic approach is used.
4.5 Define and evaluate the importance of transparent communication in supply relationships.
4.6 Assess the role of people and communication in supply relationships.

Unit content coverage

This study session covers the following topics from the official CIPS unit content document.

Learning objective

1.3 Evaluate or analyse the challenges in managing effectively the relationships between purchasers and suppliers.

4.3 Analyse the role of transparent communications between purchasers and suppliers in the effective management of supply relationships.

Timing

You should set aside about 9 hours to read and complete this session, including learning activities, self-assessment questions, the suggested further reading (if any) and the revision question.

4.1 Seller's views of relationships – supplier preferencing

In study session 3 it was recognised that the supply positioning model had a weakness, that it took no account of the supplier's view of a given situation. Thus, even though a requirement may be vitally important to a purchasing organisation, a supplier may consider either that requirement or that purchasing organisation as unimportant. **Supplier preferencing** is a model which enables purchasing organisations to understand how a seller could see them and their requirement. Originated by Paul Steele and Brian Court of PMMS Consulting Group Limited and published in *Profitable Purchasing Strategies* (Steel and Court, 1996) the model uses two axes, with the y axis reflecting the seller's assessment of the attractiveness of the purchasing organisation and the x axis reflecting the size of the business obtainable by the seller in the term relative value of account. The model is then split into four quadrants reflecting the seller's view, as shown in figure 4.1.

The supplier preferencing model

Figure 4.1: Supplier preferencing

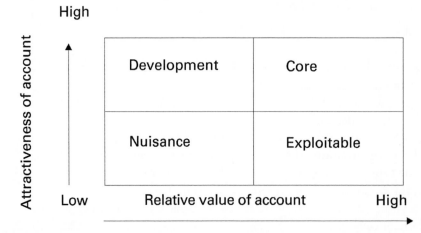

Learning activity 4.1

Where do you feel that the supplier saw the following public sector purchasing organisation?

The purchasing manager had been attempting to understand the supplier's view of his organisation, the sales organisation concerned was normally unhelpful. Because the supplier was a large multinational multidivisional organisation, the spend of the purchasing organisation was miniscule

(continued on next page)

Learning activity 4.1 *(continued)*

compared with the sales organisation's turnover. During a regular meeting, the purchasing manager asked the sales manager what the turnover of the UK division of the sales organisation was, aiming to make an assessment of how large a customer he was. The salesman indicated that he 'did not know' the turnover figure. When pressed, the salesman stuck to this line and, even when asked to phone back or bring the information to the next meeting, did not do so.

Feedback on page 95

Being an attractive customer

George Orwell, in his book *Animal Farm* (1945), wrote: 'All animals are equal, but some animals are more equal than others'. To sales organisations and the people that sell on their behalf, some customers are more attractive than others. 'Attractiveness' is a wide spectrum and before specific factors of attractiveness are considered it is vital to understand that:

- Some factors of attractiveness or unattractiveness result directly from the actions of the purchasing organisation and/or the people in the purchasing organisation who interact with the sales organisation and the people within the sales organisation. For example, late payment will make an organisation more unattractive, whilst early supplier involvement in a new project will make the purchasing organisation more attractive to the sales organisation.
- Some factors of attractiveness or unattractiveness are completely unrelated to the purchasing organisation and there is very little that the purchasing organisation can do to change them. A high-profile organisation in the public eye will be an attractive customer for a supplier to add to their customer list, whilst an organisation spending the same amount of money with a supplier, unknown by name to the general public will be less attractive. An example of a very unattractive organisation at a given moment would be one who it was recognised used child labour in factories in Asia.
- The attractiveness of any purchasing organisation to its suppliers may change over time, due to:
  - the actions of the organisations and their people
  - a change in the need for the requirement at the heart of the relationship
  - the life cycle of the requirement at the heart of the relationship
  - the relationship life cycle
  - the actions and demands of other customers of the supplier.

Table 4.1 lists alphabetically typical aspects of attractiveness and unattractiveness.

Table 4.1

Factors making the purchasing organisation attractive	Factors making the purchasing organisation unattractive
Access to latest technology	Being arrogant
Benefit of association with customer	Being bureaucratic
Business expansion possibilities	Being unreasonably demanding
Consistency of information/demand patterns	Changing delivery schedules frequently

(continued on next page)

Table 4.1 *(continued)*

Factors making the purchasing organisation attractive	Factors making the purchasing organisation unattractive
Ethical behaviour	Changing policy impacting the supplier
Financial soundness	Decision-making unit unclear or complex
Good publicity	Inability to make a decision
Good safe practices	Late payers
Guaranteed payments	Long payment terms
High volume	Never allows the supplier to get things right
Less commercially astute/naïve	Never shows them the 'big picture'
Long contracts	Not keeping their word
Paying on time	Onerous terms and conditions
Prepared to listen	Poor at planning
Prestigious organisation	Re-bid requirements frequently
Professional attitude	Short-term contracts
Profitable contracts	
Rarely go to court	
Will recommend the seller to others	

This list is not a finite one, other factors can be added and existing factors developed and refined for given situations between purchasing organisations and sales organisations.

Relative value of the account

Whilst large accounts are more attractive to sales organisations, the x axis is used by sales organisations to identify the revenue gained from given purchasing organisations and identify them by that factor. Sales organisations recognise, however, that size of revenue is not everything and they may for example be able to generate a profit figure from a small customer equal to that generated by a large customer who uses aggressive negotiation techniques. Equally, the most attractive group of people to supply in the United Kingdom often has small volumes, but sales organisations fall over themselves to supply this organisation. Can you name this very attractive group of people with a relatively low spend? Consider self-assessment question 4.1 below.

Buyers must make an assessment of the size of their business relative to the total size of the business of the supplier. This is not difficult to do. As a buyer you will be aware of the amount of money your organisation spends with the given supplier. Most organisations publish their accounts and for a fee it is possible to obtain a copy of the most recent set of accounts from Companies House (for organisations within the UK). It is then a matter of dividing your spend into the supplier's sales revenue. Where this becomes more complex is if the sales organisation is a multinational and/or multidivisional organisation and the purchasing organisation is similar.

Self-assessment question 4.1

1   At what proportion of a sales organisation's turnover do you become a large customer? Again there is no absolutely right answer to this; however, working with national account sales people the author has

(continued on next page)

4

Self-assessment question 4.1 *(continued)*

been given a figure as a percentage of the sales organisation's business. Take a stab at the figure and look at the answer given and the logic that supports it.

2   Which is the most attractive organisation or group of people to sell to in the United Kingdom? A clue to the answer of this question is that the same question and answer can be applied to The Netherlands and Denmark, but not France or the USA.

Feedback on page 96

Examining the four quadrants in supplier preferencing

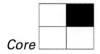

Core

Core customers are purchasing organisations who are critical to the business of the sales organisation. They are the type of organisation which the sales organisation exists to supply. Sellers will fight hard to keep business with these customers if a threat arises, though a core customer will not always get the best price and service. Sellers will seek very close relationships with the purchasing organisation and its people and plan to be aware of and able to divert any potential threat to their position at a very early stage through their relationships at various levels in the business. Here is a sense of 'gotcha', meaning that the sales organisation feels that this purchasing organisation is a secure account and nothing more needs to be offered to maintain the business with that customer. We can also on occasion see the descending core syndrome, where the purchasing organisation's attractiveness is waning, either through the purchasing organisation's actions or the arrival of other customers in the orbit of the supplier. Over time a purchasing organisation can therefore float downward in the core box and even float into the exploitable quadrant.

Development

Development customers are the future potential for the sales organisation and the basic objective of the sales organisation here is to move the purchasing organisation into core. To this end the people in the purchasing organisation will feel that 'nothing is a problem for them' in the eyes of this supplier. Changes in schedule will be accommodated without complaint, non-standard requirements delivered, even at no additional cost, and the purchasing organisation will be first to hear of the new developments that this supplier is making. It might sound like utopia and some buyers reading this description may feel that such situations do not exist. Yet put yourself in the shoes of the sales team approaching a development customer. They have done their homework and research, they realise that this purchasing organisation has a large need for their service and perhaps a sleepy incumbent supplier who is taking the purchasing organisation for granted. There is an opportunity to be grabbed with both hands and the sales organisation will want to benefit from this and the sales people will also see personal rewards for themselves in turning this purchasing organisation into a core customer for them. Simply put, they are going to do everything they ethically can to win the business, in the same way that buyers will do everything ethically that they can to get the best deal for their purchasing organisation.

It must be recognised that some customers will never have the volume to move out of the development quadrant. However, their innate attractiveness places them in development rather than nuisance. For example, the name of a multinational organisation on a sales organisation's customer list is worth something to the sales organisation. The fact that the sales organisation only has a small amount of business with this purchasing organisation is less important than the value of being able to use the name with other purchasing organisations, who probably will not ask about the size of the account.

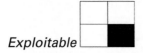

Exploitable

These customers are not very attractive ones for the reasons discussed above, yet they have the virtue of having a large volume of business. Typically, it may be that the purchasing organisation exercises its power over the sales organisation in an aggressive way or that the purchasing organisation is never able to commit to the long-term relationship that the sales organisation seeks. Again, with this view of relationships there are shades of colour and whilst there is black and white in the view of sales people there are lots of shades of grey too. So a large corporate client with a 'macho buyer' may move downwards on the attractiveness axis at one point and the change of buyer to one of a more rounded character may mean that the sales person sees the customer higher on the attractiveness axis. However, the classic exploitable situation is one where the seller wants the business but will not do anything more than just what is necessary to win it and maintain it. In this case any additional requirement that the purchasing organisation has will be considered as an extra, charged at the normal rate. Sellers discussing such situations with buyers will fall back on arguments about price lists and discount levels, the difficulty of doing anything but the norm and other arguments to avoid doing anything for nothing. Contrast this situation with the development situation.

In using this sort of behaviour, the sales organisation will consciously be taking a risk that they might lose the business, but two factors will make the risk worthwhile:

1   The business they are obtaining by their existing behaviour may well be generating what economists would call 'supernormal' profit.
2   Most buyers, they will argue, will give them a warning or an opportunity to improve before the business is awarded to another supplier.

In this situation the sales organisation may well make a decision to continue 'as is', but keep their antennae finely tuned to the purchasing organisation and its people.

Nuisance

This business is low value in terms of the sales organisation's other customers and low attractiveness, it falls into a category where sellers ask themselves 'Why are we doing this?' Calculations about the cost of the business and the revenue generated will be made and a decision may be made to terminate the business. For example, a service division maintaining pumps may conclude that the cost of carrying the spares and training people to maintain photocopiers which one customer continues to use is such a drain on their business that they may write to the customer and indicate that they are terminating the contract. Alternatively, at renewal of contract, they may advise the purchasing organisation that the cost of the service they require will increase by 40% to cover their costs, fully realising that the purchasing organisation may then look elsewhere for its service. Factors like location of site can also influence this decision which is described by sales organisations as 'the cost to serve'.

Supplier preferencing – the challenge for buyers

The challenge for the purchasing organisation and the people who work within it is to work out where they are seen by the sales organisation. Very few sales organisations will openly admit that they see a purchasing organisation in nuisance or exploitable, most will want to indicate how important a given purchasing organisation is for them. These factors may assist you in determining how a given sales organisation sees you within this model:

- Are your telephone calls returned? Are they returned promptly? Does the salesperson make sure you know how to contact them and who to contact if they appear not to be around? This would indicate your purchasing organisation is seen in development or core.
- Telephone calls unreturned and situations where you, as a buyer, never seem able to 'get hold of' your sales contact would indicate that you are a nuisance customer.
- A phone call to the sales team where you, as the buyer, start the conversation with the words, 'Good morning, it's Lucy from XYZ Limited' and the sales team reply 'Who?' or 'Which company? Do we deal with you?' is a clear indication of a nuisance customer. For your information this paragraph is almost word for word the conversation that a well-known UK manufacturer had with another well-known UK supplier. The supplier lost the business later.
- An offer by a supplier to let your purchasing organisation be a 'beta site' to test a new generation of software is a clear indication of you being a valued core customer.
- A request from a supplier for someone from your organisation to participate in a workshop to design the next generation of the product is a clear indication of you being a valued core customer, or an indication that the sales organisation sees your purchasing organisation as a potential core customer in the future.
- A sales organisation which has continued to provide a service or product as it has done for several years, perhaps in the way that the purchasing organisation has always previously requested it, yet the sales organisation

and its competitors have different options available that would be more advantageous or lower cost to the buyer, would indicate an exploitable situation. Sometimes this situation develops because powerful internal customers within the purchasing organisation are perceived as difficult or unresponsive to change. Given this situation, the supplier may simply give up trying to change the individual and carry on as normal.

4

Self-assessment question 4.2

What might a buyer do if, after an investigation, they consider that a supplier sees their purchasing organisation as exploitable and in this situation the buyer would prefer that the supplier saw them as core and changing supplier is not an option?

Feedback on page 96

4.2 The market management matrix

As figure 4.2 demonstrates, the **market management matrix**, originated by Paul Steele and Brian Court of PMMS Consulting Group Limited and published in *Profitable Purchasing Strategies* (Steele and Court, 1996) combines supply positioning with supplier preferencing into a single model which can initially appear to be very complex. However, further analysis will provide a clear focus for situations needing management if risks are to be minimised and opportunities maximised, from the buyer's point of view.

Figure 4.2: The market management matrix

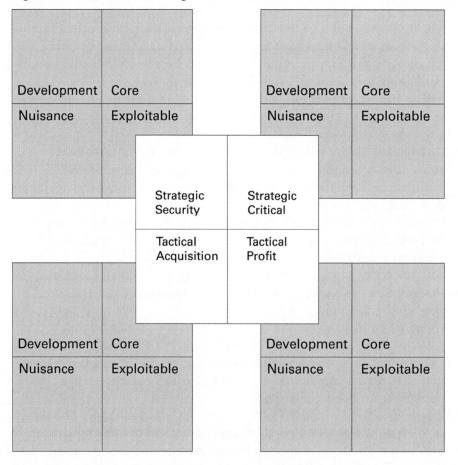

Learning activity 4.2

Look back at the text above and if necessary at the text on supply positioning and supplier preferencing. Of the 16 market situations, which is the:

1 Most risky for the purchasing organisation to be in?
2 One where the purchasing organisation has most power?

The feedback here selects one option for each case. Debate the feedback given and make arguments for other cases.

Feedback on page 96

The dynamics of the supply market can have major impacts upon buyers. For example, some purchasing organisations have embarked on 'partnership' sourcing policies with all the suppliers in their supply positioning 'strategic critical' quadrant, only to be disappointed when the expected benefits did not materialise. What they have failed to recognise is that some of their critical suppliers had a market strategy which simply did not value the business of that particular purchasing organisation.

The market management matrix is a tool which helps buyers to examine and manage the market. It indicates action to:

- create strategic alliances
- identify where additional business could be sourced
- indicate where commercial caution should be exercised in the future
- indicate where a change of supplier may be necessary
- indicate where a change of a relationship rather than change of supplier may be necessary.

For the purchasing organisation, a relationship based on the supply of business-critical requirements would anticipate a relationship with a supplier viewing the purchasing organisation in the 'development' or 'core' quadrant within supplier preferencing, yet this might not be the case and there may be considerable risk attached to the situation where suppliers see the purchasing organisation as nuisance or exploitable.

Be mindful that the views that buyers and suppliers have of each other can and will change over the course of a relationship. For example, you may well start a relationship positioned in the supplier's development quadrant but end up in the nuisance quadrant.

Purchasing organisations must understand the dynamics of this matrix and the 16 situations they may find themselves in. Further discussion of the need to move suppliers who view us as exploitable and nuisance will follow. This study session concentrates on tactical relationships and study session 4 will concentrate on strategic relationships.

Self-assessment question 4.3

The purchasing organisation needs a regular supply of quality paper to print the handouts for the 750 training programmes it runs each year,

(continued on next page)

Self-assessment question 4.3 *(continued)*

plus folders, acetates and cartridges for its printers. It has approached two organisations to meet and discuss its requirements and these are how it described the responses it received:

'Organisation A was keen – they made an appointment the next week and sent the owner's daughter to visit us. Fiona said she was not a sales person, but had spent three years working with dad to learn the business. She brought samples and took away a list of requirements to price up. The next meeting was arranged for two weeks' time at the supplier's show room.'

'Organisation B did respond to our third phone call, asked a few details, including our turnover and said that the "rep" would call us. No one called.'

Questions

1   How does the purchasing organisation see this requirement?
2   How do supplier A and supplier B see this purchasing organisation?

Feedback on page 96

4.3   Improving disadvantageous tactical situations

The bottom half of the market management matrix is reflected in figure 4.3. Disadvantageous situations occur for the purchasing organisation when suppliers see them in nuisance or exploitable, or where on occasion a new idea or development offered by a supplier causes unforeseen problems. The arrows in figure 4.3 show the direction in which the purchasing organisation would like the relationship to move, in an ideal world.

Figure 4.3: Tactical relationships within the market management matrix

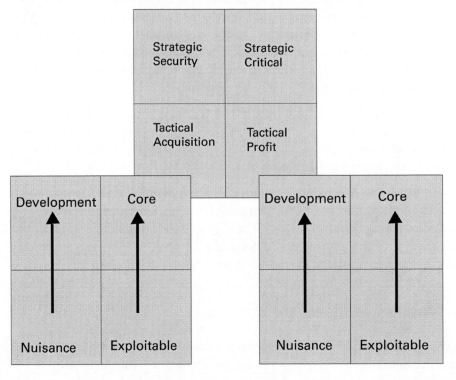

Learning activity 4.3

Think again of three tactical suppliers with whom your purchasing organisation has difficult relationships. Make notes on why you think the relationship is as it is and draw your own version of the market management matrix. Position the relationship as it is now with a cross and then draw an arrow to the position you would like it to be. Now make notes on the actions both parties might need to take in order to move the relationship to where you want it to be.

Feedback on page 97

The purchasing organisation would normally prefer the supplier to see them in the top half of the supplier preferencing model. The text below analyses difficult situations and proposes solutions. As the nature of the goods and services and their importance to any one organisation will vary, you should examine the text below with a challenging mindset, for you may want to debate the answers. If you can debate them then we have succeeded in getting you to understand these vital principles.

Where the purchasing organisation has a tactical acquisition requirement, suppliers who view them as exploitable are not necessarily going to cause a failure to supply problem; there may be a cost issue, but a cost issue in a quadrant that accounts for 2–5% of the total spend; therefore the purchasing organisation may be price-insensitive. At an appropriate time action may therefore include:

- raising the attractiveness of the purchasing organisation (refer back to table 4.1)
- changing supplier, for there will be a number of suppliers in this area.

A purchasing organisation with a tactical acquisition requirement and a supplier with a nuisance view of them are in a position which must be addressed promptly, as it contains the risk that the supplier will for example send goods and services to another customer rather than you. Action may therefore include:

- raising the attractiveness of the purchasing organisation (refer back to table 4.1)
- changing supplier, for there will be a number of suppliers in this area.

A purchasing organisation with a tactical profit requirement and a supplier who views them as exploitable may expect an adversarial relationship. Examine the features of each relationship described in sections 3.1 and 4.4. The objectives of both parties mean that conflict is almost inevitable. Is this a problem? In the sense that no one likes conflict the relationship may be

4

more difficult to handle and at an appropriate time action may therefore include:

1   Raising the attractiveness of the purchasing organisation (refer back to section 4.1).
2   Changing supplier, for there will be a number of suppliers in this area and a short-term relationship is sought by the purchasing organisation.
3   Living with the situation and recognising it for what it is.

The purchasing organisation can use tools like the competitive tender and the electronic reverse auction to force suppliers who are interested in winning business to compete. Remember that although your business may not be the most attractive in the world, both the purchasing organisation and the supplier see a significant amount of business to be awarded and won or lost. Suppliers may choose to bid and negotiate in a very competitive situation rather than miss the opportunity.

Option one may seem a textbook answer; it might also be avoiding the issue. Option two is a real option; however, option three reflects the competitive and challenging nature of purchasing and supply relationships which buyers must manage.

A purchasing organisation with a tactical profit requirement and a supplier with a nuisance view of them are in a situation which must again be addressed promptly, as it contains the risk that the supplier will for example send goods and services to another customer rather than you. Action may therefore include:

- raising the attractiveness of the purchasing organisation (refer back to section 4.1)
- changing supplier, for there will be a number of suppliers in this area and the requirement of the purchasing organisation will be core or development to other organisations.

Self-assessment question 4.4

You have a relationship with a tactical acquisition supplier who you feel is seeing your purchasing organisation as a nuisance. What action would you take? Would the action be a priority, when considered alongside:

1   A tactical acquisition situation where a supplier saw your purchasing organisation as exploitable?
2   A tactical acquisition situation where a supplier saw your purchasing organisation as development?

Feedback on page 97

4.4   Interaction in strategic relationships

In section 4.3 the need to move suppliers from the nuisance and exploitable quadrants was discussed in relation to tactical relationships. Here the same consideration is made. However, if this was an interactive screen-based presentation, rather than a printed document, there would now be a claxon horn sounding and a blue light flashing to alert the participant that these situations had the potential to become a crisis for the purchasing organisation. Sit back and take a moment to reflect on your key purchases, the commodities you place in strategic critical. Now take a moment to reflect on the characteristics of the nuisance quadrant within supplier preferencing. Now put the two together and imagine the likely outcome of that combination. Is the claxon sounding?

Learning activity 4.4

A private sector training services company of 20 trainers relies upon the IT services of a small family firm called Swift IT in the next town five miles away and has a contract and a service level agreement in place. Most of their people are IT-literate and therefore the issues raised with Swift are those that they as advanced users cannot solve and as such they may impact training events and the preparation of the material. Last week three calls were made to Swift which were logged by them and promises were made about return calls with suggested fixes. The current situation is that three laptops are not working well enough to be used on training presentations and trainers have to 'borrow' laptops from each other. Nothing has happened and one of the trainers commented that 'this seems to have become a trend over the last three months. My husband fiddled with the PC for me the last two times and by the time they phoned back it had been fixed.'

Clearly Swift are strategic critical to our business. If you were the owner of the training organisation what would you do?

Feedback on page 97

Take another look at figure 4.2. Look at the priority given to the nuisance and exploitable quadrants linked to the strategic quadrants within supply positioning. Three of those situations are flagged as 'high risk'. Action must be prompt if major calamitous consequences are to be avoided. But what action? Firstly consider what the issues are and whether the purchasing organisation is causing the problem. Then revisit table 4.1 and consider the actions necessary to increase your attraction. Next, consider the factors identified within the relationship spectrum – diagram two; these factors were discussed earlier within this study session.

Figure 4.4: Strategic relationships within the market management matrix

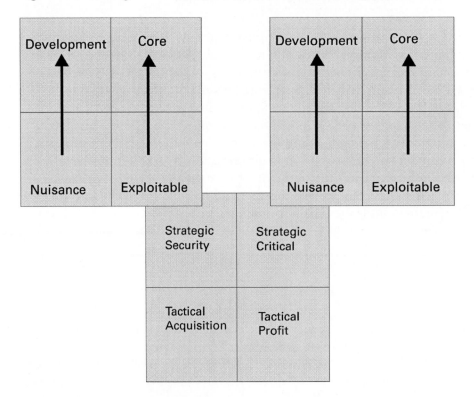

Fundamentals of interaction in strategic relationships

The fundamentals of interaction between buyers and sellers in strategic relationships include:

- What will both parties do?
- What will both parties not do?
- What will both parties give?
- What will both parties expect?
- How much trust exists between the parties?
- The commitment of the parties to each other.
- The duration of the arrangement.
- Joint risk assessment.
- Joint risk management.

The interaction in terms of communication is dealt with during the next subsection and so the following aspects are covered there:

- The extent of transparency and openness.
- The quality of information exchange.
- How will the parties settle their differences?
- How will the parties negotiate?

This is a strategic relationship. What will we, as buyers, be prepared to invest in the relationship? First, the purchasing organisation must be prepared to distinguish this relationship and separate it from other less strategic relationships. This means that senior people within the purchasing team will be involved with senior people in the sales organisation. These discussions will focus on strategy and road maps, they will proactively seek market and product and service development opportunities, and they will share information. Actioning the strategies and plans will be others who will also have frequent discussions on issues that emerge during the relationship, perhaps including forecasts, plans and specific supply chain relationships. Underpinning this level will be the mechanisms which order, confirm delivery, receive and pay. Note that this last sentence talks of 'mechanisms' and not necessarily people, for in a strategic relationship electronic transactions and the reduction of waste in business processes is a norm, meaning that 'people' are involved in the exceptions. Both organisations must be prepared to invest time, people and money in making this relationship work and take opportunities together.

Opportunistic behaviour at the expense of the other party within the relationship is clearly something that must not happen. For example, it cannot be that the buyer hears the seller's idea, indicates to the seller that they feel 'it wouldn't work' and then goes to another supplier to take advantage of the same idea with them. Neither can it be that the seller, privy to the buyer's road map, starts a similar project with another customer. Both parties must look out for each other.

'Giving' may mean time and people as discussed above; however, it may also mean conceding and bearing cost for the sake of the relationship, which is worth far more than the win or loss in any one deal and parties will expect sharing of this nature.

Trust will be high between the parties and sharing of 'secrets' in the form of specifications, marketing and purchasing plans, target customers; road maps and even sales margins will increasingly be shared as the relationship becomes more and more close. In a sense the process of developing a closer and closer relationship is akin to the process of courtship between men and women, moving to the eventual marriage. In purchasing and supply relationships, trust builds as the parties realise that there is more to gain from working together than working with others. This may mean that the purchasing organisation, operating in the private sector, stops using competitive selection processes and works collaboratively with the sales organisation to reduce cost and develop new ideas. Trust here means that the buyer trusts the seller to suggest cost reductions, rather than seeking to increase their margin at the expense of the buyer, and that the seller trusts the buyer to assist with contingent liability when, for example, a joint sales drive underperforms and the seller is left with unsaleable items. Public sector organisations are, of course, required to re-bid work at the end of agreed contractual periods and cannot simply choose to develop with a given supplier. Duration in the private sector can be as long or short as the buyer and seller choose it to be.

The purchasing organisation and the sales organisation have invested so much in the relationship that risk is assessed and managed *together*, because it is the relationship and even the survival of the organisations themselves that is at stake.

4

Learning activity 4.5

Take the bullet points below and make a note against each of how you and a supplier with whom you have a strategic relationship behave towards each other. Be honest!

- What will both parties do?
- What will both parties not do?
- What will both parties give?
- What will both parties expect?
- How much trust exists between the parties?
- The commitment of the parties to each other.
- The duration of the arrangement.
- Joint risk assessment.
- Joint risk management.

Feedback on page 98

Self-assessment question 4.5

Robinsons are the supplier in a strategic alliance relationship with BCA Limited. At a trade fair the Robinsons sales manager hears that Westons, a competitor of BCA, is going to cease production of the product range that competes with BCA's range. What would you expect the sales manager to do?

1 Find out more about the situation and phone Robinsons straight away on her mobile from a quiet corner of the car park.
2 Nothing.
3 Send an email to Robinsons at the end of the week.
4 Talk to Westons with a view to taking over that share of the business for Robinsons.

Feedback on page 98

4.5 The importance of transparent communication in supply relationships

'Communication' is about transmitting, receiving and interpreting information and we communicate by words, symbols and body language. We may in a strategic relationship communicate by cancelling a meeting or not attending it. 'Transparent' means allowing light to pass through, and glass is normally transparent enough to let light through it without distortion. In a strategic relationship we must be prepared to communicate through clear glass rather than glass which is patterned or opaque, which makes it difficult for the sales organisation to understand what we are trying to communicate and vice versa. Specifically, we must consider communication in terms of:

- the extent of transparency and openness
- the quality of information exchange
- how the parties will settle their differences
- how the parties will negotiate.

4

Learning activity 4.6

Consider how you would feel if a large customer asked you to open your books, including your purchasing costs, to them.

Feedback on page 98

Ask yourself: how clear are your intentions as a purchasing organisation to the organisations with which you seek a close relationship? To what extent do the people in the sales organisation attempting to supply to you fully understand your immediate needs, your short-term needs and your long-term business plans? If the answer is 'they do not *fully* understand' to any or all of these needs, then the relationship is not going to reach its full potential. 'Partners', whether we consider the relationship to be a strategic alliance, a partnership or a co-destiny situation, must be fully aware of all of the information necessary to enable them to work with us as if they were fully part of our organisation. This will mean that we share:

- Business strategies, in as far as they relate to the sales organisation and our arrangement with them. Not to be transparent here may mean that the sales organisation is not able to plot a long-term course which dovetails with our strategy.
- Specific plans and road maps. We must share product life cycle information at a very early stage with the partner and be open enough to ask for their suggestions and inputs into the direction of development, the longevity of the given model and the market requirements. This can involve the use of a collaborative development forum where technical specialists exchange ideas and proposals in a secure site within the extranet set up between our organisations.
- Cost, price and margin information. If we are to show our trust and openness there is no greater demonstration than to reveal our costs, prices and margins. Only in rare circumstances do purchasing organisations feel able to take this step, yet they may require a supplier to open the books to them! However, given the appropriate level of trust then the purchasing organisation can only gain by its partner taking a look at and making positive suggestions about these areas. For example the sales organisation may be using a lower-cost packaging process or have a better arrangement with a travel agent than the sales organisation. These circumstances may only come to light if

4

information exchange is transparent. To underline the difference between open book costing and cost transparency it must be understood that 'open book costing' is one way and involves the supplier sharing their breakdown of labour, materials, overheads and profit with the purchasing organisation, while 'cost transparency' means that both parties exchange this information.

- Transactions electronically. Here it can be the case that the purchasing organisation no longer places purchase orders with the sales organisation. Instead they format and send sales order transactions via EDI (electronic data interchange) or using XML (extensible mark-up language) which the sales organisation is able to import into their computer system. Similarly, invoices are not sent to the purchasing organisation by the sales organisation, the purchasing organisation pays once a month on the basis of accepted receipts and is able to remotely interrogate the purchasing organisation's systems to check on the progress of payments. Consider the saving in manpower from eliminating these and other transactions. Consider the benefits from the elimination of errors of transcription. Imagine the benefit to the supply chain if the supplier is able to interrogate the buyer's systems and get up-to-date demand and forecast information. Other examples of the use of 'e-purchasing' will be discussed in study session 5.

The way in which arguments and disputes are settled between the parties will also require transparent communication, an understanding of the other party and a willingness to concede for the sake of the relationship. In these circumstances, conceding may be viewed as a sign of strength and not a sign of weakness. Similarly, negotiation within a very close relationship is not about 'whether we deal with each other' it is about how we share the costs and benefits between us.

Self-assessment question 4.6

Imagine that you are the purchasing manager working for a producer of electrical goods. You have by means of supplier development and negotiation reached a strategic alliance with a manufacturer of circuit boards and are to have a meeting with them next week. They have asked you to give them an idea of how the relationship should work in practice, who should meet whom and about what.

Feedback on page 98

4.6 People and communication in strategic supply relationships

People make or break relationships, companies go to court. Consider your close relationships with a husband, wife, partner, and best friend. Are there things you would share with them and say to them that you wouldn't share and say with a person whom you were with in a queue at a supermarket? The answer is almost certainly 'yes'. Think again: do we feel able to be more openly angry with a husband, wife, partner or best friend? Again, the answer is almost certainly 'yes'.

Learning activity 4.7

Go back to learning activity 4.4 above. Imagine that you are the owner of Swift and that you know that Swift has not performed well to this customer, but what the customer does not know is that your father has just been taken seriously ill and this has inhibited the normal level of service to several customers. You then receive the phone call from the owner of the training organisation. Imaging now that the phone call is:

1   Made in a very aggressive way. How would the relationship develop?
2   Made in a way which seeks to understand the problem. How would the relationship develop?

Feedback on page 99

Now consider the supplying organisations that your purchasing organisation is closest to. Is there:

*   Information that they have about your purchasing organisation which would hurt you if it were to become general knowledge?
*   Information that you have about them which would hurt you if it were to become general knowledge?

Again, the answer is almost certainly 'yes'. Two more questions:

*   Do you feel able to be more open with the people from the organisations who are your strategic suppliers?
*   Do you feel that the people from the organisations who are your strategic suppliers are more open with you?

The answer may not be so clear here. One group of buyers the author worked with indicated that they did not feel able to be more open with even these suppliers and in response to the question, 'Don't you trust them?' they replied, 'No way!' Here the relationship clearly fails the test of the partnership definition and the success of the relationship is going to be limited. Other buyers have indicated that whilst they feel they are being quite open, they feel that the supplier is not open with them. The underlying point here is that the parties in a strategic relationship must have a high level of trust. That trust must manifest itself in the actions described above in this study session if the relationship is to reach its full potential.

A further dimension to the picture is the trust existing between internal stakeholders in the process of purchasing. Ask yourself the four questions above in the context of your relationship with key internal stakeholders.

Now consider the likelihood of success of a strategic alliance where there is little trust and poor communication between the sales team, the service engineers and the purchasing team within the purchasing organisation and then between the purchasing organisation and the sales organisation who make and deliver the parts that the service engineers fit once their sales team have completed a sale. Five words describe this situation and they are: 'a disaster waiting to happen'. The following circumstances can impact communication and the relationships between organisations attempting to operate in a strategic environment:

- Baggage from previous experiences. Here it may be that the people involved in the relationship have a history of mistrust and feelings of being let down. If this is at a high level in one organisation, then the feelings may permeate through the organisation. A 'clear the air session' is needed here.
- Macho behaviour. One person may behave in a way which is more akin to an adversarial relationship, causing someone from the other organisation to be hurt by what is said and/or demanded. It has to be admitted that some buyers are 'one club golfers'; they can only operate in an adversarial way. The same is true of people in some sales organisations and the relationship will soon descend to an adversarial or arm's length one if this situation is not corrected. Changing the people can be one solution.
- Genuine misunderstandings. The English language is a marvel! We can mean to communicate one thing and yet the means we use can communicate another. Here confirmation must be sought as the first step in gaining the true meaning of what has been said and meant.
- Role conflict. The security motive of the IT specialist in demanding one supplier is a genuine point of conflict between one person and a buyer who sees the market as competitive for that requirement.
- Changing the people involved in the relationship. This may be because of an internal move or one person may leave one of the organisations and then the buyer may find that they don't get the help they did before, or the seller feels they are treated dismissively. Again, a 'clear the air session' is needed here and it may be that changing the people back or changing again is necessary. The relationship between the organisations is worth more than the relationship between any two people.
- Difficult business situations. A difficult business situation can lead one organisation to move within the Market Management Matrix and 'demand' things of the other one because they are in need of revenue or lower costs. Here the approach can be the key. An open approach, explaining the situation, may work and deliver the support needed, whereas the confrontation approach may not.

The cost and consequences of letting a strategic relationship deteriorate through poor communication can include:

- loss of customers
- loss of revenue
- higher costs
- missed opportunities
- diminished market share
- additional inventory
- a fractured supply chain.

4

Self-assessment question 4.7

Which options would you consider as the purchasing manager if you felt that a relationship with a key supplier was deteriorating?

Feedback on page 99

Revision question

Now try the revision question for this session on page 321.

Summary

Strategic relationships are vital to organisations in all sectors and of all kinds.

The risk associated with the relationships is such that risk assessment and risk management must be planned and carried out together with partners and allies.

There are differing shades of strategic relationship and buyers need to be less concerned with the definition and shade of the relationship and more concerned that they and everyone within their organisation are acting appropriately towards the highly valued partner or ally.

The view of a relationship as strategic by the purchasing organisation is not, of course, a guarantee of harmony with the other party.

Suppliers are sometimes suspicious about the concept of partnership and have their own view of the customer, which may be exploitable or nuisance.

Buyers must analyse the relationship and attempt to bring all relationships they view as strategic above the horizontal centre line within supplier preferencing, or have plans for handling situations which cannot be brought up to this level.

Suggested further reading

You could read the relevant sections of Steele and Court (1996) and Davis and Pharro (2003).

Review the material in the relationship management and supplier development section and other sections of CIPS knowledge works on the CIPS website.

Feedback on learning activities and self-assessment questions

Feedback on learning activity 4.1

Exploitable, for the salesman was trying to avoid admitting how large a customer the purchasing organisation was and logically following on from this admission would come questions and assertions that 'surely customers of this size would not be treated in the way we feel you have treated us'.

Nuisance is an incorrect answer, as the seller would not attend regular meetings with a nuisance customer.

Feedback on self-assessment question 4.1

1   The figure is one per cent. The logic of these sales professionals is that 'at one per cent of my business I only need 100 more customers like this one to double my business.' Wow!
2   The Royal Family. Imagine the kudos of the Queen being seen wearing a garment made by your organisation. This small group of people are sought after as customers and some sellers will not chase outstanding payments from them in the way they would other customers.

Feedback on self-assessment question 4.2

Opportunities include raising their attractiveness by:

1   Looking at what the purchasing organisation may be doing to make itself unattractive. This may be the way the supplier's people are treated, late and long payment, onerous terms and conditions, being unresponsive to the supplier's suggestions or personality conflicts.
2   Looking at how the sales organisation may see the purchasing organisation. What is the cost to serve? How large a customer are we? Which other customers might the sales organisation see as more attractive?
3   Considering the market, where the purchasing organisation is compared with others.

Following this analysis the first thing to do is address the internal issues in 1 above, even to the extent of arranging special payment terms and changing the people that deal with the supplier, or changing their behaviour. Next, and dependent upon the analysis, will be a 'sales' campaign selling the benefits of dealing with the purchasing organisation to the sales organisation, perhaps realistically admitting the inherent unattractiveness if that exists, stressing how important the sales organisation is to the purchasing organisation and using emotion to persuade the supplier to see the purchasing organisation in a better light.

Feedback on learning activity 4.2

1   Strategic critical to nuisance, as a supplier may not care whether you receive vital requirements on time or at all.
2   Tactical profit to development. The issue here is that the supplier will be prepared to go the extra mile in a situation where the purchasing organisation will find lots of extra miles for them to go.

Feedback on self-assessment question 4.3

1   Strategic critical: if the stationery is not there then the training programmes cannot take place.

2   Organisation A sees the purchasing organisation as development or core, whilst organisation B sees them as a nuisance account which they are not for some reason going to be bothered with.

Feedback on learning activity 4.3

You probably indicated that you would like to move out of the nuisance and exploitable quadrants. Review your comments against the situations described in this section.

Feedback on self-assessment question 4.4

Check that your view of the situation is the correct one, perhaps by making a phone call to the supplier and trying to understand why their view is as it is and then removing any problems existing within your own organisation. Then raising the attractiveness of the purchasing organisation and if necessary changing supplier are appropriate courses of action.

Would the action be a priority? Well, of the three situations, the nuisance situation must be tackled first as there is the possibility of the supplier ceasing to supply. The exploitable situation will only cost money and in the big picture the whole tactical acquisition quadrant is low-value and an area where the purchasing organisation is price-insensitive. New ideas or a development relationship can also be put behind addressing this situation.

Feedback on learning activity 4.4

The following scenario is one of several that could be developed from this situation and within the text in this section there are alternative courses of action. There is no one 'right' path, but there is one 'right' solution. The 'right' solution is the restoration of the relationship to one which is probably a strategic critical to core relationship.

1   Check that the trainers had followed the agreed processes for logging help requests with Swift.
2   Check the responses received from Swift and the trend over the last three months; is it, as we believe, that response has been deteriorating against the service level agreement?
3   Check that there is no other reason for which the purchasing organisation is responsible that would cause Swift to behave outside the SLA. Examples here might be non-payment by us or a deteriorating relationship between the people involved. If there are issues here, rectify them.
4   As the owner of the organisation, phone the owner of Swift. Here we can now consider two of several scenarios:
    (a)   The owner is not there and you leave a message. The message is not returned and so you call the owner's mobile. The owner acknowledges that he 'owes you a call' and promises to phone tomorrow. Tomorrow comes, but the return call does not come. In this scenario you may be a nuisance to Swift and at the back of their queue of customers. This may be nothing you have done but may be the result of:

4

- Swift having won new contracts and having too much business and too few people
- people having left Swift
- problems within the family.

If calls are not returned then a visit by you is called for, given the nearness of Swift, and a 'cards on the table' discussion may be needed. During this discussion it will be necessary to leave Swift in no doubt that their service is impairing your business and, from your point of view, it can't continue. This discussion may then go two ways. One direction would be an apology, prompt action and (say) the immediate loan of laptops from Swift to our people. An alternative route would be a 'take it or leave it' attitude from Swift, whereupon the relationship would end with bad feelings on your part and you would need to source an alternative supplier.

(b) The owner is there and provides a credible reason for the poor performance, apologises for the situation and promises that someone will be with you tomorrow. You emphasise the importance of Swift to your business and the need for prompt action. The technician turns up as promised and over the next two days the laptops and other issues are fixed.

For the next few weeks you ask someone to keep a watching brief on the performance of Swift.

Feedback on learning activity 4.5

Test your answers against the information in this section of the course book and if necessary go back to the text describing supply positioning, supplier preferencing and the market management matrix to check the relationship.

Feedback on self-assessment question 4.5

Option 1 is the preferred one; time may be of the essence, and market share may be there for the taking. Discussions should take place before any action. Discussion with people from Westons on behalf of the alliance might be an option. Option 3 is the lazy option, option 2 is unforgivable in terms of the relationship and option 4 is completely out of the question if the relationship with BCA is of any value at all.

Feedback on learning activity 4.6

You would feel worried, exposed and open to the large customer attempting to reduce their costs by reducing your profit.

Feedback on self-assessment question 4.6

Your answer should have included text along the lines of:

Joint strategy and planning sessions at business, commercial and technical levels with specialists and decision makers working together on:

- risk assessment (business management of both organisations calling on others as necessary)

- risk management (specific teams set up by business management of both organisations as necessary to meet the risk)
- product and service development (technical specialists)
- product life cycles (marketing and project managers)
- market development (marketing, sales and purchasing)
- product development (marketing, project managers, technical specialists, purchasing)
- competitor assessment (marketing, sales and purchasing)
- supply chain development (marketing, sales and purchasing)
- business processes (IT, finance, purchasing, sales, production control).

Setting up business processes for:

- sharing information and getting closer to the supplier and its people
- jointly setting key performance indicators
- sharing of costs and rewards as the relationship progresses
- initial targets in the above areas with an expectation that we would raise the bar and improve things further.

Feedback on learning activity 4.7

Option 1 could lead to a downward spiral and termination of the relationship. Option 2 could lead to understanding and an ongoing relationship.

Feedback on self-assessment question 4.7

Your answer might include the following:

- Get the facts by speaking to people.
- Check that baggage from previous experiences is not impacting the view of internal customers, the supplier or the purchasing team.
- Check for macho behaviour internally or externally.
- Change the people involved if necessary.
- Have an open discussion with those involved
- Check for genuine misunderstandings.
- Check for role conflict.
- Check for conflict between the organisations originating from difficult business situations.

4

'E-purchasing' and its impact upon relationships

5

Introduction

Since the 1980s the development of computer systems, the internet and electronic communication has meant that communication within the supply chain and electronic tools to facilitate purchasing transactions have been more and more widely available to buyers and sellers. These developments have impacted purchasing and supply relationships. One of the problems which has been created for people within our profession is the use of terms to describe this communication and the tools that are on offer. Hence we have 'e-procurement' and 'e-purchasing'. CIPS prefers the term 'e-purchasing' and this term will shortly be defined. This study session provides definitions and then considers the impact on relationships of the tools and techniques now available to our profession by the use of technology to automate business processes.

Session learning objectives

After completing this session you should be able to:

5.1 Define what is meant by e-purchasing.
5.2 Define key e-purchasing tools.
5.3 Link the e-purchasing tools to relationships described in the relationship spectrum and the benefits of the relationships sought.
5.4 Explain how e-purchasing tools can be used to tackle supply situations unfavourable to the purchasing organisation.
5.5 Argue the costs and benefits of e-purchasing from a supplier's point of view.

Unit content coverage

This study session covers the following topics from the official CIPS unit content document.

Learning objective

4.4 Appraise the use of e-purchasing on supply relationships.

Timing

You should set aside about 8 hours to read and complete this session, including learning activities, self-assessment questions, the suggested further reading (if any) and the revision question.

5.1   What is e-purchasing?

Review figure 5.1. This model, now widely accepted, was originally developed by Helen Alder, the Senior Procurement Specialist ('e'/Supply chain) within the CIPS professional practice team to describe the use and application of electronic processes within the purchasing cycle to someone who was having difficulty grasping what 'e' was and how it impacted purchasing, its processes and its relationships. Note that the whole cycle is considered 'e-purchasing'; the right-hand side of the cycle is e-sourcing and the left-hand side is 'e-procurement'.

Figure 5.1: The e-purchasing cycle

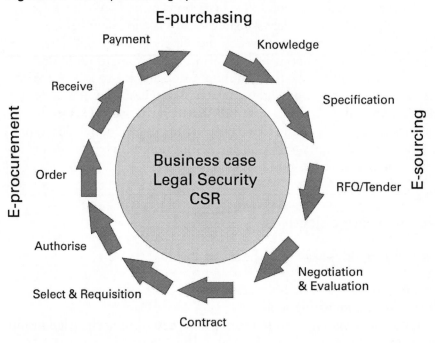

E-purchasing definitions

To provide a wider view of the subject two definitions are provided for each of the terms in table 5.1, one originated by the CIPS professional practice team and the other by the author. The CIPS definitions are deliberately left open, whilst the author's definitions are more specific.

Table 5.1

CIPS definitions	Author's definitions
E-purchasing is the electronic acquisition of goods and services, including all processes from the identification of a need to purchase to the payment for these purchases including post-contract/payment activities such as contract management, supplier management and development.	**E-purchasing** is adopting the use of all relevant electronic technologies to enhance the service provided to internal and external customers through the totality of the purchasing process, recognising that different tools and technologies are relevant in different circumstances.
E-sourcing is using the internet to make decisions and form strategies regarding how and where services or products are obtained.	**E-sourcing** exploits the power of electronic communication during the upstream* processes necessary to identify and secure goods and services and the relationships needed to deliver the requirements of internal and external customers within differential purchasing strategies.

(continued on next page)

Table 5.1 *(continued)*

CIPS definitions	Author's definitions
E-procurement is using the internet to operate the transactional aspects of requisitioning, authorising, ordering, receipting and payment processes for the required services or products.	**E-procurement** harnesses electronic processes to make the downstream* transactional business processes within the purchasing cycle effective and efficient in meeting the needs of internal and external customers and suppliers.

* The use of the terms 'upstream' and 'downstream' in this context is not the normal supply chain usage of the terms. 'Upstream' refers to the value adding part of the purchasing cycle where planning, selection strategy, selection and negotiation arrive at a decision on any one purchase, and 'downstream' refers to the delivery of the service or goods once the agreement is made.

'E-purchasing' is therefore seen as the use of technologies within the whole of the purchasing cycle, 'e-sourcing' the application of technologies to the 'upstream' part of the cycle where suppliers are selected and strategies set, and 'e-procurement' the application of technologies to the part of the process where the supply decision has been made and delivery of goods or services is sought.

The original model was extended in the autumn of 2005 by Helen Alder and the author to reflect where purchasing and supply practitioners are using specific e-purchasing tools and capabilities within the purchasing cycle. Review figure 5.2 and use it to refer to throughout this study session.

Figure 5.2: The e-purchasing cycle – exploded

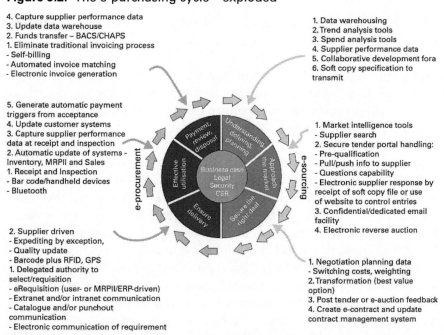

4. Capture supplier performance data
3. Update data warehouse
2. Funds transfer – BACS/CHAPS
1. Eliminate traditional invoicing process
- Self-billing
- Automated invoice matching
- Electronic invoice generation

5. Generate automatic payment triggers from acceptance
4. Update customer systems
3. Capture supplier performance data at receipt and inspection
2. Automatic update of systems - Inventory, MRPII and Sales
1. Receipt and Inspection
- Bar code/handheld devices
- Bluetooth

2. Supplier driven
- Expediting by exception,
- Quality update
- Barcode plus RFID, GPS
1. Delegated authority to select/requisition
- eRequisition (user- or MRPII/ERP-driven)
- Extranet and/or intranet communication
- Catalogue and/or punchout communication
- Electronic communication of requirement

1. Data warehousing
2. Trend analysis tools
3. Spend analysis tools
4. Supplier performance data
5. Collaborative development fora
6. Soft copy specification to transmit

1. Market intelligence tools
- Supplier search
2. Secure tender portal handling:
- Pre-qualification
- Pull/push info to supplier
- Questions capability
- Electronic supplier response by receipt of soft copy file or use of website to control entries
3. Confidential/dedicated email facility
4. Electronic reverse auction

1. Negotiation planning data
- Switching costs, weighting
2. Transformation (best value option)
3. Post tender or e-auction feedback
4. Create e-contract and update contract management system

(diagram labels: Payment, review, disposal / Understanding, defining, planning / Effective utilisation / Business case, Legal, Security, CSR / Approach the market / Ensure delivery / Secure the right deal / e-procurement / e-sourcing)

Learning activity 5.1

How would you define e-purchasing?

Feedback on page 117

5.2 E-purchasing tools

Figure 5.2 identifies a number of e-purchasing tools and capabilities. You must recognise that:

- Different organisations use different names for some of the tools described below.
- Some of the 'tools' and capabilities will reside within the core purchasing software used by the organisation to carry out its business, whilst other 'tools' are external to that software. This will vary from organisation to organisation.
- It is in some cases more appropriate to refer to a 'capability' rather than a 'tool', for example integrated systems are a capability rather than a specific tool, whereas electronic reverse auctions are a tool rather than a capability.
- Email is universally applicable, assuming the parties concerned have it as a capability.
- Electronic data interchange (EDI) or extensible mark-up language (XML) are technical terms to describe communications protocols between organisations. You will not be examined on your understanding of them; however, you need to understand that they are used to facilitate many different transactions between organisations, for example purchase orders and invoices, using the internet. The benefit of using these capabilities is that electronic transactions can replace paper and deliver information faster and more accurately in a format that other computer systems can use.

Each tool identified within figure 5.2 is defined within the context of its use within each of the six purchasing cycle segments.

Within the first segment of the purchasing cycle 'understanding, defining, planning' the requirement to be purchased, data warehousing, trend analysis tools, spend analysis tools, supplier performance data and collaborative development fora are identified.

- A data warehouse is a structured replica of an organisation's transaction data specifically designed to facilitate speedy and accurate enquiry and reporting. Copies of all transaction data are placed within the predetermined structure of the data warehouse and at this stage of the process they can be extracted and analysed to plan a purchase.
- Spend analysis tools are software within the normal purchasing system or external to it which analyse purchasing spend and budget by stakeholder, business unit and other areas as appropriate, within a purchasing organisation on specific goods and services, within groupings and categories, such that commonality can be identified and leverage applied within the supply market.
- Trend analysis tools are software within the normal purchasing system or external to it, which analyse and predict the trends of a purchasing organisation's need for specific goods and services.
- Supplier performance data is information on the performance of existing suppliers on delivering goods and services to the purchasing organisation. This information is used within the purchasing process to develop appropriate specifications, performance criteria and terms

and conditions for future supply arrangements, as well as supplier development plans. Normally this data is within the core purchasing system software.

- A collaborative development forum is a secure website set up between buyers and suppliers for technical stakeholders and others to participate in the design and development of products and services between the organisations concerned, excluding other organisations and even restricting internal access to technically sensitive developments. Technology allows text comments, drawings, charts, spreadsheets, web cams, photographs and other items to be displayed and discussed by participants.
- Soft copy specifications in the form of text, drawings, spreadsheets, charts, web cams, photographs are prepared and transmitted to suppliers as part of the supplier selection process.

Within the second segment of the purchasing cycle, 'approach to the market', market intelligence tools, search engines, secure tender portal handling and a confidential/dedicated email facility are identified.

- General search engines, for example Google and Yahoo!, will allow comprehensive internet searches to identify potential suppliers. Market intelligence tools exist, written specifically for purchasing organisations to identify suppliers and understand their place and performance within given markets. They will search the internet and locate suppliers worldwide, provide reports on given supply markets, profile specific suppliers and review the financial status of the supplier. Many of these tools are on subscription only access and some concentrate on given markets, for example China. Specific reports on the up-to-date status of a market can also be bought.
- Secure tender portals. It is possible to design or licence software which manages the enquiry process, by:
  - setting specification evaluation weightings
  - searching for suppliers, recording selected suppliers, collecting the different documents and files that make up an invitation to tender (ITT)
  - transmitting or inviting suppliers to collect the ITT
  - recording questions and circulating them, with answers, to suppliers
  - receiving responses or providing secure websites in which suppliers can record responses.

Where websites are used password control is also used. Note that this software is also used within the third segment of the model. Software here may be part of an integrated suite or a niche product.

- Confidential/dedicated email facilities using passwords or one-time only addresses can also be used instead of or to complement the above.

Within the third segment of the purchasing cycle, 'securing the right deal', tender portals, electronic reverse auctions, electronic marketplaces, negotiation planning tools and contract creation tools are identified.

- Secure tender portals complete the enquiry process by analysing responses and calculating selection options and including complex calculations on switching costs and lowest cost option against the original evaluation weightings. Feedback to participating suppliers can be generated by the software.

- Electronic reverse auctions, in their various forms, provide an electronic environment for suppliers to bid for one item, a group of items or a whole package of goods and services. The auction takes place over a period of time where suppliers can repeatedly enter new lower bids for the work on offer. One type of electronic reverse auction is a transparent reverse auction. Here, suppliers know which of the several lines on a graph is their line, and they see the lines of the other competing suppliers, but are not told the name of the suppliers. Other forms of e-auction will simply tell the supplier their last bid and their ranking, but not show the lowest bid. Hence the supplier will know they have bid $65,040.00 and they are ranked fifth. Electronic reverse auction software will for example allow buyers to select on price alone, include other factors in addition to price, and may focus on total cost of ownership. Some buyers use them as a precursor to negotiation. Feedback to participants can be provided.

- An electronic marketplace is a website where buyers can place notice of their requirements and sellers can place notice of their capability and capacity. Often the site contains e-auctioning capability and some sites are set up for specific industries and groups of buyers and sellers, who alone have password access.

- Negotiation planning data tools extract information, sometimes into spreadsheets, from suppliers' initial responses to allow buyers to 'play' with the impact of various options prior to and as part of their planning and preparation for negotiation.

- Creation of an electronic contract using electronic signatures can conclude the selection process with the suppliers and software will then update the contract database which will make knowledge of the contract available to all internal stakeholders. Here, software can also manage renewals and collect data for retrospective rebates.

Within the fourth segment of the purchasing cycle, 'ensuring delivery', delegated authority purchasing, electronic requisitions, electronic catalogues, purchasing cards, intranets and extranets are used to place requirements within contracts previously set up, and supplier-driven expediting, bar codes and tracking tools like radio frequency identification and global positioning systems are used to monitor shipments during delivery.

- Delegated authority purchasing may simply mean that authority within the purchasing process is delegated to people up to a given financial limit and transactions are made by them without reference to a purchasing team. Here, software can prompt for discounts previously agreed and collect data for retrospective rebates. Subsequently, a large number of transactions, or frequent multi-person activity might be registered within the trend and spend analysis software based upon entries within the data warehouse and subsequently taken over by the purchasing team. Equally, requirements generated by MRP, MRPII or ERP software may fall within existing contracts and may be delivered electronically to suppliers directly using a pre-agreed electronic data interchange (EDI) or extensible mark up language (XML) format.

- Electronic requisitions generated by stakeholders capture vital information about the requirement and its originator and are transmitted internally to the purchasing team electronically.
- Electronic catalogues can be hosted on the purchasing organisation's hardware. However, the cost of maintenance means that it is preferable for the purchasing organisation to use a catalogue hosted by a supplier, by several suppliers or even a catalogue hosted by a marketplace. Catalogues can also be downloaded from CDs. Here, stakeholders with password access are able to select goods and services from a list normally pre-agreed between the purchasing organisation and the selling organisation during earlier stages of the purchasing process and communicate directly with the supplier to obtain delivery. Requirements are logged against the stakeholder's cost centre, budget (funds) checking can take place and one invoice a month can be provided by suppliers, split by cost centre and/or project. This process may involve a technical and/or financial approval step *if necessary*; however, the essence of the process is to organise the purchase of low-value, low-risk tactical acquisition items and let them go by removing the administration work necessary to effect the purchase.
- Intranets are internal networks within the purchasing organisation, which are used as vehicles to enable internal processes and transactions and catalogues to function. The benefits of accuracy and speed can be put together with systems integration and the use of a single set of data.
- Extranets are networks including external organisations which enable secure transmission of purchasing transactions between the purchasing organisation and the selling organisation. Catalogues, e-auctions and collaborative development fora may all use an extranet. Again, the benefits of accuracy and speed can be put together with systems integration and the use of a shared set of data.
- Bar codes are used to identify items, packages, shipments and the vehicles that are shipping them. This together with radio frequency identification (RFID) and global positioning systems (GPS) facilitates the tracking of, for example, a box of components needed by a purchasing organisation within a container being hauled by a lorry anywhere in the world. Hence suppliers and couriers can proactively inform purchasing organisations where their shipment is. This update can be transmitted electronically to the purchasing organisation and used to update delivery information. On an exceptional basis, triggers can inform the appropriate people within the purchasing organisation that the shipment will be late. Irrespective of shipment issues, a supplier's ERP software can be configured to update the purchasing organisation's software with latest delivery information.

Within the fifth segment of the purchasing cycle, 'effective utilisation', bar codes, blue tooth, software integration and automatic payments triggers are identified.

- On receipt, bar-coded items and packages within shipments are read by handheld or wall- or table-mounted scanning devices, in the same way that items are offered for sale and scanned at supermarkets. Within a computer system this action can move quantities of items from one status to another without keying. For example, goods could move:

- from 'on order with a supplier' to 'received' status
- from 'received' to 'inspected and accepted' status
- from 'received' to 'inspected and rejected' status
- from 'on order with a supplier' to 'in the stores bin' status
- from 'rejected' to 'returned to supplier' status.
- Bar codes can facilitate other transactions including stocktaking, issuing and transfer and, assuming that the bar code is correct, the transaction can be carried out accurately. Bluetooth technology also enables handheld and other devices reading bar codes to communicate with hardware several yards away, thus avoiding additional movement by the person making the transaction.
- Finally within this segment, automatic payment triggers can be made to other parts of an integrated software system to generate self-billing payments (refer to segment six below). Software integration can also update the data warehouse with supplier performance data on receipt timings and quality information.

Within the sixth segment of the purchasing cycle, 'payment, review and disposal', self-billing, automated invoice matching, electronic invoice generation, supplier interrogation, electronic funds transfer (EFT) and systems integration are identified.

- The elimination of the traditional invoicing process involving paper invoices, received in different parts of the organisation, 'signed off' by others, matched in accounts payable and then added to the payment queue is a clear target within the purchasing cycle for process cost saving. This may be achieved by the following means:
    - self-billing. A process where the purchasing organisation generates a supplier payment based upon the quantity received and accepted and uses EFT to send the payment to the supplier's bank account on an agreed day. Here the supplier supplies no invoice and it is necessary to talk to HM Revenue & Customs to ensure they are happy and receiving all of the VAT due to them.
    - automated invoice matching. In this case even if a paper invoice arrives it is matched against the receipt and purchase order within the accounts payable software and if it matches within a tolerance, the item is added to the payment queue. Where suppliers send an invoice electronically the process can even be carried out without human intervention. In both of the above cases exceptions are investigated.
    - electronic invoice generation. Here the purchasing organisation generates the invoice from the receipt and acceptance information, matches it and pays it as described above.
- In some of the above circumstances the supplier loses the control over the request for payment process and some purchasing organisations are therefore providing password-controlled interrogation facilities for suppliers to check on the status of their payments.
- Electronic funds transfer (EFT) using the Bank Automated Clearing System (BACS) and the Clearing House Automated Payment System (CHAPS) for UK payments or via the Society for Worldwide Inter-bank Financial Telecommunications (SWIFT) for international payments means that funds can be transferred to suppliers' bank accounts rather than cheques being written and posted.

- Software integration capabilities can also update the data warehouse with supplier performance data with details of payments.

Learning activity 5.2

Use the terms identified and search the internet for providers of services and the details of what they provide. Consider the services they provide and how and when you would use them.

Feedback on page 117

5

Self-assessment question 5.1

Take the electronic tools and capabilities in table 5.2 below and indicate in which purchasing cycle segment they are used. Some tools and capabilities appear in more than one segment

Table 5.2

No.	Electronic tool or capability	Purchasing cycle segment
1	BACS	
2	Bar coding	
3	Bluetooth	
4	CHAPS	
5	Collaborative development fora	
6	Data warehousing	
7	EFT	
8	Electronic catalogues	
9	Electronic invoicing	
10	Electronic reverse auction	
11	Electronic tendering	
12	Market intelligence tools	
13	Purchasing cards	
14	RFID	
15	Self-billing	
16	Tender portals	
17	Trend analysis	

Feedback on page 117

5.3   E-purchasing tools linked to relationship types

In this part of the study session the learning activity has been placed first and the body of the text forms the feedback for you.

Learning activity 5.3

First re-read part of section 1.2 on the relationship spectrum and supply positioning. Secondly, consider each of the e-purchasing tools and capabilities identified above, select relationships and commodities which

(continued on next page)

Learning activity 5.3 *(continued)*

your organisation purchases and match the tool, the relationship and the commodity together.

Feedback on page 117

In the same way that there is no one 'right' relationship type, it is not possible to apply one single 'e-tool or capability' to all purchasing and supply relationships, with the exceptions of email and search engines. This point is best illustrated using the electronic reverse auction, which is ideal for arm's-length and adversarial relationships and wholly inappropriate as a means of selecting a partner, or organisations with whom to form a strategic alliance or co-destiny relationship. Table 5.4 matches relationships and specific tools. The tools and capabilities are distinguished in terms of supplier selection and operation of working arrangements between the purchasing organisation and the selling organisation. Finally, you will notice that in some cases there are grey areas as the use of tools may overlap the relationship types. There is not always a firm line and the purchasing organisation must do what it feels is most appropriate in a given supplier relationship.

Table 5.4

Relationship type	E-purchasing tool or capability
Adversarial	For selection of supplier an e-auction or electronic tender process would be appropriate. Equally a negotiation and a one-off purchase using a purchasing card by a member of the purchasing team would be adequate. In terms of receipt and payment processes, the short-term nature of the relationship may make electronic receipt and payment processes more costly than the benefit they will deliver; however, if a central email address for invoices is available this can avoid paper invoices (for example, email to accounts-payable@xyzservices, generic accounts payable email address).
Arm's length	For selection of supplier an e-auction or electronic tender process would be appropriate. Equally a negotiation and a one-off purchase using a purchasing card by a member of the purchasing team or an internal customer following up the purchasing team involvement would be adequate. Electronic catalogues may in some cases be appropriate if purchases are frequent enough. In terms of receipt and payment processes, the short-term nature of the relationship may make electronic receipt and payment processes more costly than the benefit they will deliver and again the central email address is a possibility.
Transactional	For selection of supplier an e-auction should be used only if the volume of spend is adequate to cover the cost of the process. A simple electronic tender process would also be an appropriate means of selection and an electronic catalogue a means of effecting delivery of individual requirements once contractual relationships are in place, which in the tactical acquisition quadrant means *organising them and letting them go*! Equally, below a given threshold, a purchasing card activated by an internal customer would be adequate. The greater the number of transactions, the greater the saving from an investment in electronic receipt and payment processes and in addition to the email address, an XML invoice might be appropriate here.
Closer tactical	For selection of supplier, an electronic tender process, or possibly an electronic reverse auction, would be appropriate and one or more electronic catalogues managed by the supplier or purchasing cards used by internal customers a means of effecting delivery of individual requirements once contractual

(continued on next page)

Table 5.4 *(continued)*

Relationship type	E-purchasing tool or capability
	relationships are in place. The greater the number of transactions, the greater the saving from an investment in electronic receipt and payment processes, certainly consolidated invoices and XML or EDI invoices are appropriate here.
Single-sourced	For selection of supplier an e-auction should be used only if the market is competitive enough and the volume of spend is adequate to cover the cost of the process. An electronic tender process would also be an appropriate means of selection and a supplier hosted electronic catalogue a means of effecting delivery of individual requirements once contractual relationships are in place; a purchasing card activated by an internal customer could used to obtain goods and services under the arrangements. The greater the number of transactions, the greater the saving from an investment in electronic receipt and payment processes, certainly consolidated invoices and XML or EDI invoices are appropriate here.
Outsourcing	A comprehensive electronic tender process is required here, or an electronic auction may in some cases be appropriate for less risky situations. The greater the number of transactions, the greater the saving from an investment in electronic receipt and payment processes, however, these processes must not be over-complex in this arrangement, certainly consolidated invoices and XML or EDI invoices are appropriate here.
Strategic alliance, partnership and co-destiny	In selecting and getting to know suppliers, electronic tools like tendering and e-auctions are inappropriate.
	In working together to enhance the service and product offerings and build the joint business, the collaborative development forum is a key tool. In terms of transactions, electronic transfer must be the norm. For example, rather than one organisation sending another a purchase order, the norm could be the purchasing organisation sending the selling organisation a transaction formatted as a sales order, thus enabling the selling organisation to update their MRPII system directly with the requirement, rather than convert the purchase order to a sales order. Equally, if not eliminated by self-billing, the invoice could be formatted as an invoice transaction in the purchasing organisation's software. The organisations would also work together on tenders from other customers and have access to cost and forecasting information within the sphere of their cooperation.

Self-assessment question 5.2

Consider your stakeholders. How can they be involved in the e-tools and capabilities?

Feedback on page 118

5.4 E-purchasing tools and unfavourable situations

In this section, five unfavourable situations are identified and the use of electronic tools and capabilities proposed to assist the purchasing organisation towards a more favourable situation. The situations are:

- a cartel
- a monopoly

- an adversarial relationship where a purchasing organisation seeks a different relationship
- a supplier treating a purchasing organisation as nuisance
- a supplier treating the purchasing organisation as exploitable, yet professing to see the purchasing organisation as core.

A cartel

A cartel is an informal association of suppliers working together to maintain prices at a high level, or create a shortage and control markets for their own benefit. To break the cartel, search engines can be used to identify other suppliers or to identify alternative goods and services, and a ranked e-auction showing the suppliers only their bid and their position, for example, that they have bid £242.98 for a given lot and that they are currently third can induce competition where it has not been seen before, always assuming the suppliers are not talking to each other on the telephone during the auction. Private sector purchasing organisations could also use the tactic of issuing an electronic tender to all of the suppliers bar one, or a tender with items one, two and three to supplier one, items two, three and four to supplier two and items one, three and four to supplier three and so on. Search engines can also be used to work out which of the potential suppliers may be the weak link in the cartel and perhaps a negotiation could be started with them simply to break the cartel.

A monopoly

Again, a search engine can be used to identify other suppliers or to identify alternative goods and services and a competitive tender or e-auction used to introduce competition. If this is not possible, the purchasing organisation may be able to raise their attraction with the monopolist by offering to send electronic transactions in the format preferred by the monopolist. If successful, this may make the supplier behave more ethically towards the purchasing organisation.

An adversarial relationship

An e-auction will make suppliers compete if they feel that the business is interesting to them.

A supplier treating a purchasing organisation as nuisance

Assuming that this relationship is not the one sought, and that the supplier is not a monopolist, then a speedy move by the buyer towards an electronic tender or an e-auction will introduce competition if that is what is sought. Where the purchasing organisation seeks a close strategic relationship then e-tools like a search engine will identify alternatives and face-to-face negotiation with the supplier will be the most appropriate route.

A supplier treating the purchasing organisation as exploitable, yet professing to see the purchasing organisation as core

Here it may be that the purchasing organisation is seeking a partnership and the selling organisation has been indicating, over a number of years, that the purchasing organisation is a core account for them. Despite this, you, as the buyer, feel that the alliance or partnership has become one way and that the supplier really sees you as exploitable. Here there are three choices. Firstly negotiate to resurrect the relationship, secondly use a search engine to establish an alternative partner, or thirdly reclassify the relationship as tactical profit and use an e-auction or an electronic tender.

Learning activity 5.4

Consider difficult supply situations that you face, discuss them with colleagues and consider how you might use e-purchasing to move the situation more towards where you want it to be.

Feedback on page 118

Self-assessment question 5.3

Take figure 5.3 below and sketch horizontally across the figure which e-purchasing tools and capabilities you would use in which of the supply positioning quadrants.

Figure 5.3

adversarial	relationship spectrum		co-destiny
Tactical Profit	Tactical Acquisition	Strategic Security	Strategic Critical

Feedback on page 118

5.5 E-purchasing – the supplier's view

In the same way that relationships involve a buyer's view and a seller's view, there are two views of e-purchasing, its tools and capabilities and its impact upon relationships. Specifically, we need to ask how suppliers and their people seek to benefit from e-purchasing. This is not to *begrudge* suppliers a benefit, rather to be aware:

- of how they *can* benefit and the use of the tools and capabilities available to them during the process of selling, and be able to use that knowledge
- that whilst sellers will moan and wail about the use of tools like electronic reverse auctions, they do benefit from that process even if they do not get the business
- of electronic processes used by sellers to promote their goods and services.

Learning activity 5.5

If you work in a private sector organisation, talk to your sales team and ask them which e-purchasing tools they have met when selling to other customers and which tools they use to sell electronically to customers. If this option is not open to you, evaluate the response of suppliers to your own e-purchasing initiatives.

Feedback on page 118

How do sellers benefit from e-purchasing?

First, the answer to this question is that the answer is the same for them as it is for us as buyers when you consider transaction costs. Electronic purchasing offers fast, accurate and arguably secure transmission of data between organisations, which can be turned into useful information by both parties. Sellers will find that dealing electronically will reduce their transaction costs and even the payment time. Examples of transactions positively impacting suppliers include:

- Invoices no longer need to be printed and posted.
- Payments go straight to the bank.
- Sales orders are received electronically and no longer need to be rekeyed.
- Access to customers' (buyers') websites removes the need for credit control people and phone calls chasing outstanding amounts.
- Forecast information is available to update systems.
- Electronic updates on the latest delivery position are sent to the customer, eliminating the need for the customer to expedite and the need for the sales organisation's people to respond other than in exceptional circumstances.

Second, there is the advantage of the business 'coming to' the supplier without any effort on their part. Here web searches by a customer or a contact from an organisation facilitating an electronic reverse auction for a buyer may mean that the selling organisation is invited to bid for business without having to go through the process of 'selling themselves' to the purchasing organisation. Sales people will tell anyone who will listen how difficult it is to get a foot in the door and directors of sales organisations will tell you how costly it is to keep a sales force on the road making contacts and getting even an opportunity to bid for work. In this case the work comes to them, with little or no effort on their part. The only cost to the sales organisation is perhaps their website.

Do sellers 'like' electronic reverse auctions?

Here we need to separate the incumbent supplier and others taking part. The incumbent supplier is normally not happy when the purchasing organisation suggests an electronic reverse auction; frequently they will offer a substantial reduction or inducement to make the purchasing organisation think again. A buyer faced with this situation must not be tempted to take the reduced offer and will feel a justifiable frustration along the line of 'why could they not have offered that before!'

Other suppliers will normally be interested, particularly if they have an opportunity to oust a competitor from a customer who has previously been difficult for them to 'get into'. In terms of the electronic reverse auction process itself, however, there are several advantages for all participating suppliers. These are:

- Sales organisations see the prices of their competitors if the electronic reverse auction is a transparent one. Where else can they legitimately view this information?
- There is more than one chance to bid. In a sealed tender process or even an ITT process with post-tender negotiation, a limited number of bids can be made. In the electronic reverse auction, as many bids as is necessary can be made.
- The information gained during the process can be used with future sales bids.
- Once the electronic reverse auction process is complete and the business is won, there is empirical evidence from a supplier in the USA that buyers will not re-bid additional small amounts of work like the ones in the original electronic reverse auction; they simply offer the work to the chosen sales organisation. At this stage the supplier is able to recoup some of the margin shaved away in the original electronic reverse auction.

Sales organisations do attempt to condition purchasing organisations that their goods and services should be seen as strategic and not subject to an electronic reverse auction. Sometimes this is correct, but many times it is not and an electronic reverse auction is appropriate.

CIPS and the University of the West of England did some research in 2004 which indicated that suppliers saw five benefits to electronic reverse auctions. These were the ability to react to a competitor's price, visibility of competitor market pricing, a reduced negotiation process, the establishment of a more level playing field and the auction also provided the impetus to improve competitiveness. Five drawbacks recognised by suppliers were that the customer focused on price alone, suppliers felt that they were forced to focus too much on solving cost problems, long-term competitiveness was reduced, prices were driven down below sensible economic levels and the buyer became too dominant.

5

Electronic processes used by sellers to promote their goods and services

CD-ROMs and websites are today key tools in the sales drives of many organisations and technical specialists and internal customers are regular recipients of emails selling goods and services. There is nothing wrong with this legitimate activity, unless it conditions people towards one supplier when there are several to choose from in a competitive market.

Supplier websites and portals also often include an order capture facility to allow customers to conveniently order when they have viewed the specification and pictures or videos of the goods available.

One organisation known to the author has produced a CD-ROM which allows technical specialists to see moving pictures of its equipment, see and download all of the vital statistics and then optionally press an 'order' button, whereupon the CD electronically attempts to find its way out of the customer's network to the selling organisation's website where order capture takes place! Some purchasing organisations will have an intranet, which stops this activity, but some live to regret the fact that they do not block such transactions.

Is there a downside for sellers?

Apart from the more obvious comment about avoiding competition, the following points are what may be considered the downside for sellers:

1 They may be expected to work with many different formats of XML or EDI. This will introduce cost, both to set up and maintain.
2 Some marketplaces and transaction models charge sellers a transaction fee.
3 Where sellers compete on differentiation and not price they may struggle.

Self-assessment question 5.4

List five cost savings accruing to sellers from working with purchasing organisations on e-procurement projects.

Feedback on page 119

Revision question

Now try the revision question for this session on page 321.

Summary

Electronic purchasing is not a panacea for all the ills of the purchasing process. It offers purchasing organisations a number of opportunities to be effective and efficient in their business dealings with internal customers, stakeholders and suppliers. Used well and appropriately, the tools and capabilities available enable relationships to be developed and enhanced, or maintained competitively as needed by the purchasing organisation's strategy.

Suggested further reading

Review the material in the e-business section of CIPS knowledge works on the CIPS website.

Feedback on learning activities and self-assessment questions

Feedback on learning activity 5.1

There are different interpretations but some commonality. One problem, not limited to 'e', is that different organisations use the same word to mean different things. Review the definitions that follow.

Feedback on learning activity 5.2

You should have found many suppliers and services on offer; cross-reference them to figure 5.2.

Feedback on self-assessment question 5.1

Your completed table should look table 5.3.

Table 5.3

No.	Electronic tool or capability	Purchasing cycle segment
1	BACS	6
2	Bar coding	4 and 5
3	Bluetooth	5
4	CHAPS	6
5	Collaborative development fora	1 and arguable throughout the process
6	Data warehousing	1 and updates throughout the process
7	EFT	6
8	Electronic catalogues	4
9	Electronic invoicing	6
10	Electronic reverse auction	3
11	Electronic tendering	2
12	Market intelligence tools	2
13	Purchasing cards	4
14	RFID	4 and 5
15	Self-billing	5 and 6
16	Tender portals	2 and 3
17	Trend analysis	1

Feedback on learning activity 5.3

Now reflect on table 5.4 below, overlaying your commodities and relationships against the tools. You may not find a 100% fit, this is not a black-and-white exercise and you may validly feel able to use the e-tools and concepts identified in a different way to the examples below. The aim of the exercise is to link these concepts from the early chapters of the course book together and form a foundation for future sessions when the themes will be developed and applied in purchasing and supply relationships.

Feedback on self-assessment question 5.2

Consider your stakeholders. How can they be involved in the e-tools and capabilities?

- Ensuring the specification is 'watertight' for an electronic reverse auction.
- Participating in a collaborative development forum.
- Evaluating the technical part of an electronic tender.
- Emailing answers to questions from tenderers.
- Searching for products, services and sources of supply using a search engine.
- Using a purchasing card to order.
- Checking a purchasing card statement.
- Watching an e-auction.

Feedback on learning activity 5.4

None.

Feedback on self-assessment question 5.3

As you will see from figure 5.4 below, some tools can be applied right across the relationship spectrum, whereas others are only applicable in given quadrants.

Figure 5.4

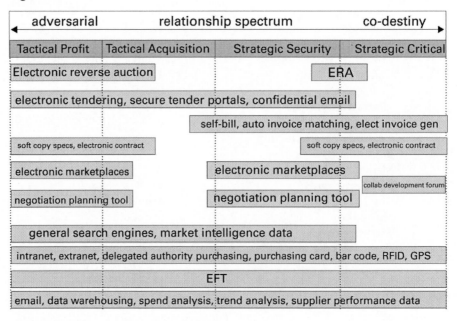

Feedback on learning activity 5.5

None.

Feedback on self-assessment question 5.4

1 Lower transaction costs.
2 Work coming to them.
3 Seeing other suppliers' prices in an electronic reverse auction.
4 Ability to sell to internal customers using CD-ROMs.
5 Ability to bypass purchasing processes by using their website to capture customer orders.

5

The relationship life cycle and managing conflict in relationships

Introduction

An internet search using terms like 'customer+relationship+cycle' will reveal a number of models which describe the relationship cycle from the seller's viewpoint. Most of these models concentrate on getting the sale and a number of them end with the customer, meaning the purchasing organisation, becoming the advocate of the seller to other customers. Interestingly none of the models found by the author have a stage which reflects the termination of the relationship. Purchasing models focus on the purchasing cycle and drive the process from the buyer's point of view.

'It ain't all over until the fat lady sings'. Relationships with suppliers may go on longer than we think they will.

6

Session learning objectives

After completing this session you should be able to:

6.1 Define a relationship life cycle.
6.2 Appraise the position of their organisation in any given relationship life cycle.
6.3 Demonstrate the positive and negative role of conflict within a relationship.
6.4 Assess alternative appropriate courses of action in resolving conflict within relationships.
6.5 Distinguish between different reasons for termination of relationships.

Unit content coverage

This study session covers the following topics from the official CIPS unit content document.

Learning objective

1.4 Define the natural life cycle of supply relationships and analyse the position of specific relationships in their life cycle.
4.1 Identify the causes of conflict in supply relationships and select appropriate methods for their resolution.
4.9 Review the circumstances in which supply relationships end, and select appropriate methods for their termination and, where appropriate, determine ways of retrieving and retaining the relationship.

Timing

You should set aside about 7 hours to read and complete this session, including learning activities, self-assessment questions, the suggested further reading (if any) and the revision question.

6.1 The relationship life cycle

It is necessary to distinguish between the active supply of goods and services between organisations and a business relationship that might exist between them. For over many years purchasing organisations and suppliers will be aware of the existence of each other and may or may not be involved in active supply, but a relationship will exist between the organisations and the people employed by them.

Learning activity 6.1

Consider relationships that you have with suppliers and answer the following questions.

1   How long have you been aware of the supplier's existence?
2   How long have they been delivering goods and services to your organisation?
3   How long will they continue to supply your organisation?
4   How long has the same supplier been aware of your existence?
5   How long have they been delivering goods and services to your organisation?
6   How long will they want to continue to supply your organisation?

Note that the answer to questions 2 and 5 will be the same. However, the question is repeated to create a mirror image of both sides of the relationship.

Feedback on page 136

Figure 6.1 shows the relationship life cycle model. It has three core segments: initiation, agreement and delivery. It progresses clockwise from 12 o'clock.

6

Figure 6.1: The relationship life cycle model

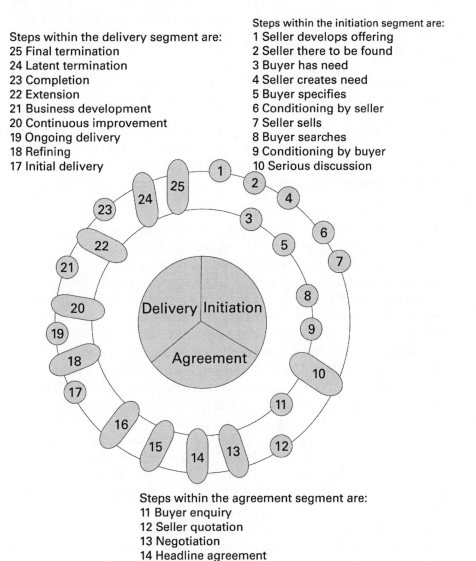

Steps within the delivery segment are:
25 Final termination
24 Latent termination
23 Completion
22 Extension
21 Business development
20 Continuous improvement
19 Ongoing delivery
18 Refining
17 Initial delivery

Steps within the initiation segment are:
1 Seller develops offering
2 Seller there to be found
3 Buyer has need
4 Seller creates need
5 Buyer specifies
6 Conditioning by seller
7 Seller sells
8 Buyer searches
9 Conditioning by buyer
10 Serious discussion

Steps within the agreement segment are:
11 Buyer enquiry
12 Seller quotation
13 Negotiation
14 Headline agreement
15 Detail agreement
16 Implementation

Source: Mike Fogg, PMMS Consulting Group Limited, © Mike Fogg 2006

Outside the three segments are two circles, one representing the activities of the buyer and one the activities of the seller. Attach no importance to the fact that one circle is nearer the centre of the model than the other. Some activities are joint activities and represented by points in both the buyer and seller circles. The model refers to sellers rather than suppliers, but the terms are considered interchangeable.

Initiation is the discovery process where both parties discover each other and their needs and aspirations. *Agreement* is the process where both parties reach agreement relating to a specific deal or requirement. *Delivery* is the process where the supplier delivers the requirement for as long as both parties agree it is needed. Each segment has a number of steps which have been placed in a typical sequence within the cycle, always realising that in some cases steps may be in a different sequence or steps may not be needed at all.

The initiation segment

The initiation segment recognises that in some cases this process will be a development of a previous sale, that there will be a 'fall out' as this segment progresses once:

- sellers identify the most positive prospects for them
- buyers better understand what is available in the market.

Fall out is not 'falling out', it recognises that for both buyers and sellers a greater number of potential prospects exist from which a smaller number of real opportunities will cement. Finally, both parties will legitimately seek to use their own process to control movement around the cycle and this may lead to conflict.

1   *Seller develops offering:* Sellers go through a process of identifying markets and creating goods and services to satisfy the needs which they perceive exist. This will involve market research, design and testing, piloting and then planning a launch. The development may be a redevelopment of a product or service of which the market is already aware, sold in a previous circumstance to the given buyer. Development will be greater at earlier stages of the product or service life cycle, redevelopment will occur at the end of the product life cycle.

2   *Seller there to be found:* Using websites and entries in directories, a seller will passively make their organisation available to be found and make their new and developed goods and services attractive to potential buyers. They may also use tracking devices within the website to discover who has visited them and what they have looked at as part of a process of generating sales leads. This may lead to a sales call. Much space on the internet is currently (early 2006) devoted to services offering to maximise selling opportunities from websites.

3   *Buyer has need:* Purchasing organisations realise that they have a need for goods and services. However, experience has taught them that they need to involve their technical experts in the process of specification as part of an integrated process. 'Buyer' here may mean an internal customer who has been impressed by a seller's presentation and is unconsciously being led towards a solution.

4   *Seller creates need:* Sellers are trained and practiced in the process of creating a need for buyers who were not aware that they had a need. Selling methodologies work at identifying situations and problems which lead towards offering a solution to the need. The unwary buyer may not actually have the need and can be sold products and services which are unnecessary. A particular revenue generation target of sellers is an upgrade or new version of the previous offering which they know that people within customer organisations are using. Within the cycle this activity may follow on from steps 20 and 21.

5   *Buyer specifies:* The technical experts in the organisation specify the need, ideally in generic terms. However, technical experts can be influenced by a seller's website or a slick presentation and specify in a way that leads towards just one supplier. This can lead directly to step 7, then steps 12 and 17. For a large spend a business case represents best practice.

6   *Conditioning by seller:* Conditioning by sellers starts the moment that they consider engaging with a customer. They will undertake

activities to help the buyers understand how rare, difficult or costly the delivery of their offering is. This will be done subtly with buyers, and especially internal customers, from the seller's first interaction with them; conditioning techniques, such as imminent shortage, price lists, discounts and deadlines for the retention of current pricing, will be used as an attempt to move a purchasing organisation to make a decision sooner rather than later. These tactics are legitimate and many buyers are aware of them. However, internal customer decision makers targeted by sellers are not so aware. The process starts early in the relationship cycle to establish the seller's view of the situation as the one which prevails.

7   *Seller sells:* Sellers sell through all of the channels legitimately open to them and make decision makers within target organisations aware of the benefits of the goods and services they offer. Frequently the last function within a purchasing organisation contacted by the seller will be purchasing, as sellers seek to influence the internal customer and/or decision maker, hoping that they will influence or override purchasing processes. Where a buyer is not interested, there is 'fall out'.

8   *Buyer searches:* Following best practice purchasing processes the purchasing organisation searches for suppliers. In the public sector this will include the OJEU notice (refer to study session 11). This process will be carried out against appraisal criteria and will aim to use the buyer's conditions to select a small number of suppliers from a longer list, hence 'fall out'. The search process may include a supplier appraisal process and/or pre-qualification. However, consider how difficult or even pointless the search can be if the seller has conditioned powerful internal stakeholders towards their offering.

9   *Conditioning by buyer:* Like the seller, the purchasing organisation will seek to use conditioning, partially to combat the conditioning by the seller. Buyers will seek to condition sellers that, for example, their initial offer is high, that funds are low, that there are several good offers being made to them and there are processes to go through before a decision is made. Public sector buyers are able to point to the EU procedures as support in this area.

Conditioning by both parties can be viewed as a preliminary skirmish before the battle of negotiation, although in saying this, negotiation in a collaborative relationship is different to negotiation within an adversarial one.

10 *Serious discussion:* For the person within the purchasing team charged with making the purchase, this stage may start with approval of a business case to go ahead, the commitment of a budget holder or the identification of the short list of suppliers. The essence of this step is that several suppliers have been eliminated and serious discussions can take place with the few remaining.

The agreement segment

The agreement segment reflects the fact that both parties must reach agreement relating to a specific requirement and once again fall out will occur. Both parties aim to reach a workable agreement meeting their objectives, exposing them to as little risk as possible.

11 *Buyer enquiry:* 'Good buyers always get three quotes', but they do not in a partnership, where there would be no formal enquiry. In a competitive

purchasing situation the enquiry process seeks to exert control over the selection process and even regain ground lost by asking a given seller to requote against the same information as 'all' others.

12 *Seller quotation:* Sellers will not necessarily wait for buyers to invite them to quote; they will provide a quotation to decision makers, hoping that they may achieve a sale by this route. Bad purchasing practice occurs when this happens, followed by delivery and an invoice, whereupon the buyer may be asked to raise a purchase order. These circumstances may make buyers grind their teeth, yet sellers see this step as a natural follow-on from steps 6 and 7.

13 *Negotiation:* Negotiation starts at the initial contact between the parties. However, this process may be used as an alternative to the enquiry process in the private sector and also in limited circumstances within the public sector. Information gained from earlier skirmishes will be organised, prepared and tested by both parties, who by now are getting to know each other well enough to consider a formal agreement. Both buyers and sellers have 'tricks of the trade' which they put to work within negotiation, but it is important to remember that, whatever relationship (in terms of the relationship spectrum) is sought, the delivery of goods and services will mean that the parties must move to a situation where they are collaborating. Negotiation 'tricks' may win in the short term, but be remembered by the other party in the long term.

14 *Headline agreement:* On occasion the parties may reach a headline agreement, subject to further detailed discussion and planning by a group of specialists. Processes may combine stages 13, 14 and 15 into post-tender negotiation, meaning negotiation on the basis of the supplier's offer. In the public sector the process of clarification is on occasion used (or misused) to achieve the same outcome, when negotiation in the strictest sense is not allowed.

15 *Detail agreement:* Where necessary detail negotiation involving several meetings will be undertaken to finally reach agreement. At the end of this stage a formal agreement will be signed and the process of planning the start of delivery will commence. Fall out here may involve buyers debriefing unsuccessful suppliers on their offers.

16 *Implementation:* Implementation starts with the process of planning the delivery and in complex contracts can involve many people. Actions include notifying internal customers, planning the cessation of business with the incumbent supplier and developing processes and procedures. Fall out has finished.

The delivery segment

Delivery is the process where the supplier delivers the requirement for as long as both parties agree it is needed. In the private sector, the length of the proposed contract may or may not represent the eventual length of the delivery phase. However, in the public sector the eventual length must reflect the length specified within the original OJEU notice. Steps within the delivery segment are:

17 *Initial delivery:* Both parties will make an attempt to make the arrangement succeed. For buyer and seller (now supplier) this may mean using additional resources to ensure that teething problems are minimised as the reality of delivery is encountered. Ideally there should be no surprises for the buyer; the internal customer or the supplier and

the clarity of the negotiated agreement and the quality of the planning at the implementation step will impact the success of initial delivery.

18 *Refining:* Refining may mean 'tinkering' if there has been a clear understanding or it may mean re-negotiation if the understanding was not clear. Refining can also mean that people realise that, working together in a different or developed way, further improvement can quickly be made.

19 *Ongoing delivery:* Ongoing ordering, delivery, receipt and payment are the norm, with payment on time being important to the seller. Literally, the processes for the delivery of goods and services as refined in step 18 are carried out again and again. In some cases this may be the longest step of the whole process, yet in others delivery may be over in a few days following lengthy initiation and agreement phases. Sellers may seek to start the extension steps through regular meetings, progress monitoring and reporting.

20 *Continuous improvement:* In many cases ongoing delivery will mean that, 'what if?' questions arise and in many cases these may involve simple changes. However, the issues of who accommodates the change and at what cost may not be so simple. A seemingly continuous request to give more for the same cost from a purchasing organisation may mean supplier margins are eroded and/or relationships strained. Ideally, a long-term agreement must recognise the need for change and must state how the costs and benefits of improvements will be shared.

21 *Business development:* Sellers will recognise the duration of the agreement and seek to use the personal relationships they have developed within the purchasing organisation to develop further business. Some call this 'deep mining' and seek other sales opportunities within the purchasing organisation for the same or other goods and services, perhaps targeting other sites or divisions. Sellers will also use the name of the purchasing organisation as a reference point for other sales. These tactics may or may not be acceptable to the buyer and acceptability must be related to the purchasing strategy of the organisation for the goods and services in question. Practised bluntly, this technique may find sellers walking around the purchasing organisation seeking business; practised subtly, it links straight into steps 4, 5 and 7 of the initiation segment.

22 *Extension:* Extension is where the agreement between the parties is lengthened as long as both feel they want to participate. Remember supplier preferencing? In some circumstances a supplier may not want to continue working with the purchasing organisation.

23 *Completion:* Literally, completion means that the supply of goods and services from the seller to the buyer is completed and ceases. In many cases completion will occur because the buyer's requirement is complete and there is no need for further supply, whilst in other cases the contractual period may be at an end and the re-bidding process has selected another supplier. Completion may also occur because one party is so unhappy with the current situation that they invoke the termination clause in the agreement. This last option is discussed further throughout the study session.

24 *Latent termination:* When considering termination, it must be remembered that the active supply of goods and services is different from the relationship between the organisations. Latent termination describes the situation where the active supply of goods and services

is complete and the parties remain on good terms, knowing that next time:

- a requirement arises (buyer's view)
- the customer can be persuaded to buy from us (seller's view)
- the parties will pick up from where they left off, by interacting in one of the initiation stages.

25 *Final termination:* Final termination occurs when one or both parties decide that, for whatever reason, they will not deal with the other party again. This can happen, although it is probably a rare occurrence, for over time the people and processes of the organisations involved change and the markets they operate in also change.

The relationship life cycle model and the relationship spectrum

Partnership and a new closer tactical relationship are used as examples here.

An ongoing partnership

Within an ongoing partnership the initiation segment would barely be entered into once the relationship was in progress; the need and specification would be part of an ongoing development programme, which would amount to serious discussion. The agreement segment would involve negotiation around how costs and benefits would be shared and detail agreement and planning within existing frameworks, leading to initial delivery, refining and ongoing delivery within the delivery segment. A key factor in understanding how this model works in practice within this relationship is recognising that the cycle restarts in the delivery segment, with either the continuous improvement step, born out of a realisation that *we* could do better together, or the business development step where *we* realise that there is an opportunity to explore together.

A new closer tactical relationship

This relationship may start at 12 o'clock or it may derive from a business development opportunity within the delivery segment. Whichever party leads the initiative, there will be detailed analysis by that organisation before they speak to the other, or others within the initiation segment. A full enquiry process may not always be necessary here, but much of the work in developing this agreement will take place within the agreement segment. The delivery segment will also see both parties investing time and effort in making the agreed solution work.

Self-assessment question 6.1

1 Purchasers' and sellers' activities always complement each other. True or false?
2 Name the three main segments in the relationship life cycle model.
3 What is the main objective of the buyer during the agreement phase?
4 Which devices do sellers use during step 2 (seller there to be found)?
5 What might a buyer (member of the purchasing team) fear during the seller's business development phase?

(continued on next page)

Self-assessment question 6.1 *(continued)*
6 What is the difference between latent and final termination?

Feedback on page 136

6.2 Understanding your position within a relationship life cycle

As a buyer how do you know where you are in the relationship cycle? Where do you feel you want to move to next? Where does your supplier or potential supplier feel they are at present? Where does your supplier or potential supplier feel they want to move?

Learning activity 6.2

Undertake three short activities here.

1 Consider a supplier you are thinking of dealing with shortly and position them within the relationship life cycle model.
2 Consider a supplier with whom you have a longstanding excellent relationship and position them within the relationship life cycle model.
3 Consider a supplier you would like to replace and position them within the relationship life cycle model.

Feedback on page 136

The learning activity should give you a flavour of the situations you could face and the difficulties and opportunities you may also face.

One of the three unit specification objectives of this study session is to 'recognise the natural life cycle of supply relationships and appraise the position of specific relationships in their life cycle'. An understanding of the relationship life cycle model will identify the natural life cycle and asking yourself, your internal customers and your supplier questions will help you understand more precisely where you are in a relationship at any one time. Let's expand the three situations in the learning activity to highlight this.

1 In situation 1 there is an opportunity; however, there is also a risk and that risk exists for all three parties. The internal customer may be concerned that 'purchasing' will get three quotes, take the lowest price and leave them with a substandard service. To counter this, the technical specialist works with the supplier they prefer and specifies towards their offering. The supplier may not be a passive partner here; they may have 'helped'. By the time we reach step 10 of the model there may be only one party to have serious discussions with, yet the market may be competitive. Where buyers suspect this may be a possibility they need to work on their relationship with the internal customers to ensure they work together through the early steps within the model. In this example a competitive, perhaps tactical profit relationship has been assumed. Action would be different if a partnership relationship was sought. Suppliers may be concerned about the truth of buyer demand

predictions and buyers may be concerned about the supplier's ability to supply.

2 In situation 2 the question is one of fully exploiting the opportunity *together*. Relationships can wither through neglect and, assuming a private sector situation, could we work together with the supplier to ask for their ideas in the form of step 21 and work with them towards step 22? This may mean moving up the risk axis in supply positioning and it may mean developing the relationship towards the closer end of the spectrum.

3 With situation 3 you may have said in your own mind 'never again'. Imagine the meeting to put stage 25 in place and the macho buyer blasts off at the person from the supplier and says 'never again'. Imagine the seller at that same meeting who had realised that they were at step 25 and was about to put their hand up and say: 'Yes, I wouldn't blame you for throwing us out. However, I have prepared a proposal to make things right.' That proposal, which could have benefited the purchasing organisation, stays in the briefcase, when in fact the relationship could have moved back to step 18. An experienced seller known to the author says, 'buyers don't know what goodies I as a seller have in my pocket to give them. If I perceive that I am being treated badly the goodies stay in my pocket'.

To assess where we are within the relationship cycle we must understand the views of all stakeholders in the relationship.

Self-assessment question 6.2

How might a buyer understand that they are perceived by the seller to be within the business development step of the relationship life cycle model?

Feedback on page 136

6.3 The role of conflict within a commercial relationship

How do you see conflict in purchasing and supply relationships? Is it to be avoided? Is it inevitable? Is it both? Does it depend upon the relationship? Let's first examine what we mean by conflict.

Learning activity 6.3

Take an ordinary thesaurus and search for 'conflict'. You should have a long list of words including, for example, discord, dissension, strife, combat, clash, struggle, duel, antagonism, resist, oppose. Now place those words in a continuum, with 'violation' being the most extreme and 'debate' being the least extreme. There is no single correct answer here, you may choose different words from your thesaurus to the ones in the feedback.

Feedback on page 137

From the long list that you found in learning activity 6.3 above, it can be seen there are shades of conflict, ranging perhaps from violence on one end of the spectrum to debate on the other. Consider the vehemence expressed between political parties in the House of Commons, yet at a joint event you might find that the prime minister and the leader of the opposition are sitting and chatting like old friends.

'Old friends' is an inappropriate relationship for buyers and sellers, yet there is a sense where people negotiating must separate the issues from the person they are dealing with and be tough on the issues, yet warm to the human being they are meeting.

In purchasing and supply relationships some conflict is inevitable and can't be avoided. However, it can take different forms.

1   In reality, conflict in an adversarial relationship may in extremis mean the use of bad language (though this is not advocated here). Also, it may mean thumping the table and it will mean withholding information to seek the best deal for one side at the expense of the others. At the end of the negotiation a deal may be struck, but one party may then or later feel cheated by the other and trust can be very low.

2   In a strategic alliance conflict may take the form of a debate about how the parties can together address or exploit a given market or customer. The debate might get heated as people discuss and evaluate ideas and subsequently if the situation does not work as expected, the loser of the argument may say, 'I told you so'. There will, however, be a resolution for the parties view their relationship as more important than any one deal between them.

3   In a partnership the conflict will be a debate about the sharing of cost and benefit, as the relationship is more important than any one deal between the parties. One misconception about partnerships is that there is no conflict. Conflict between people from partners can be like conflict within a family. Within the four walls of a house the members of the family may say things to each other that they would not say to others, simply because they know that they are 'family'. In the same way people from two organisations working together in partnership may feel at liberty to express themselves more freely.

Conflict is therefore natural and occurs across the relationship spectrum and may have different outcomes. However, we must consider the difference between positive and negative conflict. Imagine a situation in a closer tactical relationship where there have been shipment problems on stationery items. Contrast these two approaches.

• A phone call from the buyer to the supplier using emotive language and describing the supplier's 'useless software' as 'not worth the paper it is not written on' and the people that deliver as 'dressed like tramps'.

• A phone call from the buyer to the supplier asking them to 'confirm that the software is not losing our orders, given that our people feel they are keying them in correctly, because I'm not at all happy with things at present'.

The first of these phone calls is likely to ratchet up whatever conflict exists between the parties and the other is likely to keep the conflict within bounds. The first option is unprofessional and not recommended, yet whilst the second option still carries an implied threat it also indicates that some factual evidence has been collected and it leaves the door open for a resolution and the possibility that some part of the problem is being caused by the buyer. Given the second option, a supplier would be keener to fix the problem and resolve the conflict even if it is not 100% their fault.

Self-assessment question 6.3

Imagine that you feel really angry with a tactical supplier of goods. Assume that they have let you down in a big way. How would you approach that person when they came to see you tomorrow?

Feedback on page 137

6.4 Resolving conflict within relationships

This subsection assesses alternative courses of action open to people for resolving conflict within relationships and offers a conflict resolution process set within the context of purchasing and supply relationships.

Learning activity 6.4

Identify five situations which could cause conflict between buyers and sellers in a purchasing and supply relationship. Consider the points irrespective of the type of relationship.

Feedback on page 137

Note the language used in the feedback to learning activity 6.4. The text is impersonal and abrupt in referring to 'the supplier'. We need to remind ourselves again that suppliers are people and that it is people who will probably be responsible for the situation that has caused the conflict.

The second observation you may have made is that all of the situations for potential conflict in the feedback focus on negative actions of *the supplier*. Is it possible that the purchasing organisation could act in ways which might cause conflict? The answer to this question has to be 'yes', so let's examine some of the reasons for conflict originated by the buyer.

1 Deciding not to renew a contract.
2 Inviting an existing supplier, who consider themselves to be a partner, to join an e-auction.
3 Not selecting a supplier who understood they had a given piece of work.
4 Changing schedules.
5 Demanding cost reductions.

Figure 6.2 describes a conflict resolution process, assuming a major conflict has occurred or is about to occur and setting the situation within a purchasing and supply context.

Figure 6.2: A conflict resolution process

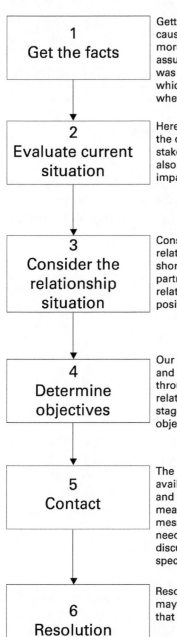

1 Get the facts

Getting the facts is a first vital step as part or all of the problem may have been caused by the purchasing organisation and its people. Secondly, negotiating is much more likely to succeed if it is to succeed if it is based upon facts and not assumptions. At the end of the fact finding phase we need to understand whether it was reasonable for the other party to have been able to avoid causing the situation which has led to the conflict, whether the situation was out of their control or whether we caused the situation. Our response will depend upon this analysis.

2 Evaluate current situation

Here we need to get a broad view of the situation and involve other stakeholders in the discussion. This will be the start of the planning and objective setting process as stakeholders views may lead us to avoid some courses of action. At this stage we may also need to evaluate cost and critically consequences relating to the conflict and its impact upon the supply of goods and services

3 Consider the relationship situation

Consider where the relationship is within the relationship spectrum and the relationship cycle. Here we may tolerate a situation which we will be re-bidding shortly, or be prepared to invest to overcome conflict if the other party is an ally or a partner. We will evaluate the criticality and contractual issues surounding the relationship. Finally, could the action of the other party mean they wish change the position on the relationship spectrum or in the relationship cycle?

4 Determine objectives

Our objectives need to be evaluated in terms of ideal, realistic and fallback positions and include the full range of possibilities from immediate termination at one extreme, through resolution, to using the conflict as a catalyst for developing a long term closer relationship at the other extreme. The involvement of stakeholders is also vital at this stage, as is attempting to understand the situation of the other party and their likely objectives.

5 Contact

The means of communication is important. A wide range of communication media are available to us and these include text messaging, email, faxes and letters, phone calls and video conferencing and well as meetings. In general, the more impersonal the means of communication the less likely is the favourable resolution. Whilst text messaging or email may be a means of alerting the other person to the situation and a need to talk, it will not be the best means of resolving conflict and here face to face discussion is recommended, as it allows the fullest view of the communication spectrum between the people involved.

6 Resolution

Resolution does not always mean that the parties agree and become 'friends' again. It may mean that there is an agreement not to work together in the future, or it may mean that parties disagree to the extent that one party walks out on the other.

To resolve the conflict, our approach can be aggressive where we may threaten; assertive where we may use emotion and logic to persuade; cold where we only use logic to persuade; accommodating where we may bargain or compromise. No one method of persuasion is universally applicable and in the course of resolution it may be necessary to adopt several methods. Acceptance is also a response which may be necessary in the face of a very powerful opponent. Avoiding conflict is a strategy used by some, who agree or attempt to pretend the situation is not as it is. However in avoiding conflict we frequently delay it and may make it worse if the other person feels that we have not even valued them sufficiently to discuss, argue or debate with them.

In purchasing and supply situations the power of one party may mean that the other party has no option but to accede to their demands, or that one party perceives that their best interests are served by giving way. Assertive behaviour and the use of emotion are recommended as ways of persuading someone to move your way in a conflict situation.

Self-assessment question 6.4

Formulate an action plan for resolving a conflict situation when you believe that your colleagues in engineering have caused conflict with a partner by being over-critical of the supplier's design process.

Feedback on page 138

6.5 Reasons for termination of relationships

Termination of a contract, unless the arrangement has run its normal course, is a serious event in a purchasing and supply relationship. Whilst recognising that contract law can advise on when termination is reasonable in any given circumstances, this subsection discusses the subject of termination from the view of how the parties may feel. The relationship life cycle model assumes two different termination situations.

Learning activity 6.5

What reasons could there be for terminating a relationship?

Feedback on page 138

If we were to consider a spectrum of reasons for termination then one end of the spectrum would be normal completion of the contract and violation might be used at the other end of the spectrum. Violation is a dramatic and serious word, it means that someone has acted in a foul way that has infringed, desecrated or transgressed something valued by the other person. In purchasing and supply relationships such events do occur and they result in a major conflict, frequently leading to an irretrievable breakdown of relationships. What sort of event may cause such a situation?

1   A supplier provides a costed proposal to a customer they trust offering an opportunity to expand the customer's market in a way which would benefit them both. The customer evaluates the proposal and declines it, but still works with the supplier. Six months later the supplier sees a press release indicating that the same customer has a joint venture with another organisation working in the way described in the proposal. Assuming that the customer had not started the project with the other organisation prior to their proposal, the supplier may rightly feel violated, conflict may occur and even legal action might be the result. It is also likely that the supplier may stop supplying the customer concerned.

2   A purchasing organisation receives a telephone call from a customer indicating that one of the purchasing organisation's suppliers has solicited business from this customer, indicating that there could be

advantage in 'cutting out the middle man'. The purchasing organisation will feel badly violated by the supplier and wonder how many times the supplier has already done this to them.

There are many reasons why parties in a purchasing and supply relationship may feel violated and the following text provides some examples.

Buyers may feel violated because their supplier:

- selects a more attractive customer
- supplies to other customers rather than them
- lets quality decline and will not improve it
- fundamentally does not deliver as agreed in the contract
- increases price without warning.

Either party may feel violated because:

- of differences of interpretation in the contract
- one poaches the key staff of the other
- of the use of IPR in an unauthorised way
- external factors prevent delivery or communication
- the words and actions of the other party do not match.

Self-assessment question 6.5

In what ways might a supplier feel violated by actions of buyers?

Feedback on page 138

Revision question

Now try the revision question for this session on page 321.

Summary

During the relationship cycle buyers and sellers use different strategies and tactics to attempt to meet their objectives. Relationships exist over time, they:

- develop, mature and die away
- become stronger when there is more trust
- involve people
- involve conflict at different stages of the relationship cycle.

Conflict is a natural occurrence and it:

- exists in a range of forms from discussion to violation
- causes relationships to end
- can be positive or negative
- can be a catalyst for the development of a better relationship

Feedback on learning activities and self-assessment questions

Feedback on learning activity 6.1

If either party is a well-known organisation then the answers to questions 1–4 may be 'a long time'. If your organisation or the supplier is not well known then the answer may be related to your original identification of a need or the supplier's identification of you as a potential target. Questions 2 and 5 represent a statement of fact, but questions 3 and 6 may have very different answers. In extremis, you as the buyer may answer question 3 with a comment like 'as short a time as possible', whilst the supplier may answer question 6 as 'eternity'. The answers of course can be reversed!

Feedback on self-assessment question 6.1

1   False. There are different objectives and activities.
2   Initiation, Agreement, Delivery.
3   To reach a workable agreement, meeting their objectives, exposing them to as little risk as possible.
4   Websites and catalogues.
5   That the seller will create opportunities for further work and that the opportunities may not wholly be justified.
6   With latent termination there is a clear possibility that the buyer and seller may work together again when there is an opportunity or need. With final termination one party feels that they will never work with the other again.

Feedback on learning activity 6.2

The answers here are in the form of more questions!

In case one you may be within the initiation or agreement segments. Which party is driving the process? It could be one of three. It could be purchasing on behalf of your organisation, it could be an internal customer within your business or it could be the supplier. Which is it? Do you want to change things? How will the current situation impact the outcome?

In case two you are probably within the delivery segment, but have you thought where you want the relationship to go? Are you taking the initiative in continuous improvement or extension? If you do nothing will the supplier see you as less attractive within supplier preferencing? Have you asked the people working for the supplier where they would like things to go?

In case three you are probably at stages 24 or 25 of the model. Again, though, have you considered what the supplier would like to do? Are there no advantages to stepping back to stage 22 and considering an extension?

Feedback on self-assessment question 6.2

A buyer might understand that they are perceived by the seller to be within the business development step of the relationship life cycle model if:

1   they are asked for referrals to other parts of the organisation

2   they receive new ideas from the supplier
3   the goods and services are developed by the supplier for or with them
4   they are let into the next-generation development of the product at an early stage, possibly as a beta site
5   the five-year contract has ten months to go and the supplier becomes more attentive
6   colleagues from other areas report that they have been approached by people from the supplier about business 'on the back of' the business currently in place with the supplier.

Feedback on learning activity 6.3

Violation (the most extreme); combat; strife; clash; antagonism; discord; dissension; struggle; duel; resist; oppose; debate (the least extreme).

Feedback on self-assessment question 6.3

Please note that this question was deliberately posed in a vague way to prompt you to consider many options.

This response is one option, other responses exist.

1   Before the meeting:
    1.1 Get the facts as you see them and be sure that you are correct.
    1.2 Consider your alternatives. How many alternative products and suppliers are there? Is there a high cost of change?
2   At the meeting:
    2.1 Welcome them warmly.
    2.2 Ask the supplier how they see the situation and what they intend to do.
    2.3 Make sure that the supplier knows how strongly you feel.
    2.4 If their response is adequate, allow them to repair the situation, perhaps drawing their attention to other options that you might have.
    2.5 If their response in not acceptable to you, thank them for visiting you and indicate that you will be moving your business elsewhere when appropriate.

Some students may feel that this response does not reflect the anger stressed in the question. However, we must realise that there is a difference between *feeling* anger and *showing* it.

Feedback on learning activity 6.4

Situations could include the supplier:

1   Wanting to increase price or any cost component of the total cost of ownership.
2   Not delivering on time.
3   Delivering parts that fail or a service that is not up to what we perceive as a good standard.
4   Not responding to phone calls.
5   Working for a competitor.

Feedback on self-assessment question 6.4

1   Let your contact at the supplier know you understand the situation and will be in contact with them shortly.
2   Get the facts, try to understand what constitutes ' a good design process' and why engineering feel that this supplier is not living up to their expectations.
3   Evaluate the feedback from the supplier and the comments of engineering and other internal stakeholders.
4   Consider the relationship and make sure all internal stakeholders are aware of the importance of the supplier.
5   Work with stakeholders to develop an objective here, which may be sharing knowledge and assisting the supplier to develop their design processes or taking time to understand them as an organisation.
6   Arrange a meeting at the supplier's site, be assertive in reflecting the needs of the engineers for a design process, but accommodating in seeking to assure the people at the supplier that we value them. Offer to set up a joint discussion where the engineers on both sides can develop appropriate processes.

Feedback on learning activity 6.5

Reasons can include:

1   normal completion of the supply of goods and services by the seller as per the contract
2   one party being so unhappy with the current situation that they invoke the termination clause in the agreement. This may be because of failure to perform or failure to pay
3   the buyer's need for the items suddenly ceases or lapses
4   the supplier's source of supply suddenly ceases or lapses
5   the people concerned cannot resolve a conflict.

Feedback on self-assessment question 6.5

Suppliers may feel violated because their customer (buyer):

• has misled them about volumes
• does not pay
• is continually late in paying
• is continually changing the requirement
• misuses supplier's product.

Study session 7
Corporate social responsibility

Introduction

In the first decade of the twenty-first century corporate social responsibility (CSR) has been a big issue for the purchasing community. It has moved the consideration of ethics to a wider and more significant level than the mere question of whether a purchasing manager accepts a ticket to the football cup final. The whole issue of CSR has become more complex and the debate more sophisticated and far-reaching.

No matter what your sector, it is becoming increasingly urgent that risk management strategy – not to mention the creation of opportunities – includes an integrated approach to CSR at board level.'

7

Session learning objectives

After completing this session you should be able to:

7.1 Identify the component parts of 'corporate social responsibility'.
7.2 Argue the cases for and against a position on corporate social responsibility.
7.3 Identify how corporate social responsibility impacts purchasing and supply relationships.

Unit content coverage

This study session covers the following topics from the official CIPS unit content document.

Learning objective

1.6 Analyse and explain corporate social responsibility (CSR) and ethical, technological, legal and environmental constraints on relationship development.

Timing

You should set aside about 7 hours to read and complete this session, including learning activities, self-assessment questions, the suggested further reading (if any) and the revision question.

7.1 What is 'corporate social responsibility?'

Corporate social responsibility (CSR) has become the broadly accepted concept to describe a collection of related issues, all of which combine to represent an organisation's overall ethos, its personality, philosophy and character.

> 'CSR actively manages the economic, social, environmental and human rights impact of its activities across the world, basing these on principles which reflect international values, reaping benefits both for its own operations and reputation as well as for the communities in which it operates.'
>
> (CIPS practice guide on CSR)

Learning activity 7.1

What are the ten component parts of corporate social responsibility?

Feedback on page 152

Additionally, if you are interested in this area, search the CIPS website for CSR and ethics, pull down the documents available and review them.

Ten component parts of CSR were identified above. Let's examine each of them, define their meaning and provide an example.

1 Environmental responsibility

As a purchasing organisation our responsibility here is to the surroundings in which our organisation operates and the impact of our requirements, produced in terms of goods and services by suppliers on surroundings in which they operate, wherever they operate in the world. Hence, we are interested in the waste disposal processes of a supplier producing chemicals for us, even if it's in Malaysia. Are the chemicals simply poured into the nearest stream or are they treated and disposed of in a way which does not harm the local environment?

2 Human rights

The United Nations has a charter of human rights. All people wherever they are in the world have these rights and as a purchasing organisation we must ensure that our employees and the employees of our suppliers have these rights. Immediately, you will think of people working in low-wage far-east economies. Is it ethical for them to be working 16 hours a day for a fraction of a European daily wage to enable a supplier of goods to meet its cost reduction targets? The International Labour Organisation (ILO) has adopted four core 'rights' relating to people at work. These are:

- Freedom of association and the effective recognition of the right to collective bargaining.

- The elimination of all forms of bonded labour and compulsory labour.
- The effective abolition of child labour.
- The elimination of discrimination with respect to employment and occupation.

3 Equal opportunities

Equality considerations include equal pay, equality of selection methods in a competitive environment and the treatment of people in a way which is fair to everyone. The purchasing organisation must therefore ensure that its policies and the policies of its suppliers reflect these issues. It would not be acceptable, or legal within the UK, for a supplier to select the 'best man for the job'.

4 Diversity and supplier diversity

Under this heading we need to consider both diversity per se and supplier diversity.

'Diversity means that individuals and articles are different from one another; perhaps comprising clearly distinct attributes, elements or qualities.'

In their briefing guide CIPS define supplier diversity as, 'Initiatives that aim to increase the number of diverse (eg ethnic-minority owned, women-owned) businesses that supply goods and services to both public and private sector organisations, either directly or as part of a wider emphasis on smaller enterprises in general.' (Ram and Smallbone, 2005)

Primary dimensions are the following: age, ethnicity, gender, physical abilities/qualities, race and sexual orientation. Secondary dimensions of diversity are those that can be changed, and include, but are not limited to: educational background, geographic location, income, marital status, military experience, parental status, religious beliefs and work experiences. Purchasing organisations must therefore ensure that their people and, so far as it is possible to ensure it, people at the suppliers they use, are not discriminated against because of their 'otherness'.

Supplier diversity is a term used to apply the principles of diversity to supplier selection and relationships. This principle goes against the trend of reducing the number of suppliers that the purchasing organisation deals with, for it recommends that organisations consider the 'otherness' that organisations from different backgrounds can contribute. In the USA legislation has forced purchasing organisations to account for and use ethnic minority businesses to promote civil rights and equality through affirmative action. A purchasing organisation having a supplier diversity programme may well therefore choose to make a number of sourcing decisions on the use of suppliers from a given area of the country, or suppliers employing a high proportion of people from ethic minority backgrounds. In the UK and Europe the legislation has focused on equality. However, it is considered possible that in the future there may be a requirement for a supplier diversity programme within the EU legislation, although currently this is not the case.

7

5 Corporate governance

In the UK the Cadbury Committee was set up in 1991 to address the financial aspects of corporate governance and in its 1992 report the committee defined corporate governance as 'the system by which companies are directed and controlled'. The committee made a series of recommendations about best practice for UK companies covering reporting of activity by directors regarding what are called 'hygiene and housekeeping' areas of running a business. The OECD extends the definition to 'a set of relationships between a company's management, its board, its shareholders that provides a structure through which the objectives of the company are set and the means of attaining those objectives and monitoring performance are determined'. Corporate governance is not just about regulations, it is also about relationships. In the light of the Enron failure and other failures in their country, US legislators enacted the Sarbanes Oxley Act in 2002. This Act not only impacts corporate organisations, it impacts the accountants, legal firms, brokers and financial analysts who advise them. The Act provides for heavy fines and lengthy terms of imprisonment for various types of criminal behaviour associated with the corporate environment. These include:

- alteration or destruction of any records with the aim of obstructing a federal investigation
- failure to maintain audits or review work papers for at least five years
- attempting to defraud a purchaser of securities
- any CEO who 'recklessly' violates their certification of the company's financial statements
- two or more persons who together conspire to defraud the federal government or its agencies.

This Act is the most well known of international initiatives. It is, of course, US law and not directly applicable within other countries. However, the UK government, working with professional bodies, has taken initiatives to ensure openness and probity and in 2004 draft regulations on 'operating and financial review' (OFR) were published by the DTI aimed at addressing the same areas as the Sarbanes Oxley Act, applying to all financial years starting on or after 1 April 2005. The Accounting Standards Body (ASB) has constructed a disclosure framework, of which the key elements are the:

1   nature, objectives and strategies of the business
2   development and performance of the business, both in the period under review and in the future
3   resources, principal risks and uncertainties and relationships that may affect the entity's long-term value
4   position of the business including a description of the capital structure, treasury policies and objectives and liquidity of the entity, both in the period under review and the future.

The key point to understand here is that owners and directors of organisations, and their employees, together with their financial, legal and corporate advisers, now have best practice guidelines aimed at ensuring clear reporting and avoiding financial collapses like Enron and Worldcom in the future. Therefore if a relationship with a supplier is such a risk that it could cause serious financial problems for the organisation it must be reported.

Failure to comply with these guidelines can result in very serious consequences for the individuals concerned.

6 Sustainability

In providing customers with services and making and packing products this issue emphasises the use of materials which are either reusable themselves or made from resources which are produced from materials that are recycled or regenerated frequently. Over-fishing, for example, has eliminated fish in many parts of the world, and the use of wood from forests which are not replanted reduces natural resources which will not be available for future generations. The Waste Electrical and Electronic Equipment (WEEE) legislations aims to promote the use of recycled materials and the design of products for reuse. One UK organisation known to the author stores the rainwater from its roof and washes its delivery vehicles with that water.

7 Impact on society

Our organisations and our supply chains do not exist in a vacuum, they exist in our society and they impact society. Imagine the nineteenth-century mill, powered by coal and steam and belching out pollutants from its chimney. The mill impacted the people who lived very near to it by polluting their environment, and the safety record of its operations probably left much to be desired by the standards of today. The products produced may have harmed the people using them. A local or regional monopoly may have restricted choice for the people living in the area. Today, in parts of the world there are still situations akin to the nineteenth-century mill described above.

8 Ethics and ethical trading

Ethics and ethical trading are fundamental to all people in purchasing. Supplier selection must be made on decisions which do not favour one supplier in front of others. Our specifications must honestly reflect our needs; we must not misrepresent our needs by untruthfully leading suppliers to believe that the quantities of goods or services we intend to purchase are higher than we honestly anticipate them to be.

9 Biodiversity

The Merriam-Webster Dictionary defines biodiversity as:

'biological diversity in an environment as indicated by numbers of different species of plants and animals'

By permission. From the *Merriam-Webster Online Dictionary* ©2005 by Merriam-Webster, Incorporated (Merriam-Webster: http://www.merriam-webster.com).

Through its activities, purchasing organisations must proactively avoid reducing the number of interdependent species around us. This means that extraction activities on land or at sea must not reduce the number of species. It could be that the selection of a site for a new freight terminal has an impact on plants and invertebrates unique to a given area of Hong Kong.

A major investment bank funding such a development would commission a study into the impact on wildlife of the new development and in so doing ensure that damage was avoided or minimised.

10 Community involvement

Many organisations support their community in the form of local charities, sporting activities and arts programmes and receive credit for their activities through publicity. However, the issues of closing production sites or moving production to low-wage economies can devastate communities which have depended for many years on single employers. Thus a cost-focused purchasing decision can have an impact upon many, many people. On 30 October 2005 the *Sunday Telegraph* carried a story about the Lego factory in Billund, Denmark. At the time of writing no decision has been made, but it may be possible that in the future the factory employing 2,500 people (it was 3,500) may close and production move elsewhere. Currently 6,000 people live in Billund. Reflect upon the impact of such a closure on the town and its people. During the process of updating this course book in 2008/9 an internet search has revealed how this situation has progressed.

1   The LEGO Billund plant's production unit has only about 1,000 workers to keep the wheels in motion, and by 2012, only 300 to 400 are scheduled to remain.
2   The outsourcing of production to a low cost country has not gone well and production was started again in Billund.
3   Another website viewed in March 2009 indicates that there is low unemployment in Billund and '5000 commuters come to Billund every day to work in its dynamic companies'.

Search the internet using the keywords 'cadbury+csr'. There are case studies on how this organisation sees CSR.

Self-assessment question 7.1

Take table 7.1 and the statements about the ten CSR issues, which have been sorted alphabetically. In the right-hand column indicate whether you believe the issue to be about environmental responsibility, human rights, equal opportunities, diversity, corporate governance, sustainability, impact on society, ethics and ethical trading, biodiversity or community involvement.

Table 7.1 CSR statements

Statement about the CSR issue	CSR issue
Avoid reducing the number of interdependent species	
Impacted the people who lived very near to it by polluting their environment	
Initiatives that aim to increase the number of diverse businesses that supply	
It aims to promote the use of recycled materials and design products for reuse	
Many organisations support their community in the form of local charities	

(continued on next page)

Self-assessment question 7.1 *(continued)*

Statement about the CSR issue	CSR issue
Our responsibility here is to the surroundings in which our organisation operates	
The treatment of people in a way which is fair to everyone	
The United Nations has a charter in this area	
US legislators enacted the Sarbanes Oxley Act in 2002	
We must not misrepresent our needs by untruthfully misleading suppliers about our intentions	

Feedback on page 152

7.2 The cases for and against corporate social responsibility

Take the information in and take information from these documents and play devil's advocate on the need for consideration of CSR.

Learning activity 7.2

Consider a worst-case scenario for one of the CSR areas as it may impact your own organisation.

Feedback on page 153

This text aims to set out the cases for and against CSR. In one sense presenting the case against is at best an academic exercise and at worst improper, as CSR is now accepted as a fundamental aspect of business life. However, as there may still people who would take a short cut, or attempt to negate the rights of others, it is appropriate for purchasing people to marshal arguments they would use to support the case for CSR. A brief scenario is provided for each of the headings identified in section 7.1, which are then evaluated 'for and against' CSR after which a conclusion is drawn. Note that many of the reasons given below against the given CSR issue are invalid and only made in the course book for the sake of this review.

Environmental responsibility

Situation: Recycled paper is not selected as an option by an organisation, or sources of supply are used knowing that the source of supply pollutes the local river with the output of its processes.

- Against CSR: Recycled items can cost more, the world will regenerate itself, it isn't always possible to get recycled items, recycled items are not always the same quality as brand new items. I am a buyer, not an environmentalist. It's not my job to tell suppliers how they do things.
- For CSR: The environment impacts everyone, environmental legislation exists and must be followed, care for the environment today will impact future generations, there are limits beyond which the earth will not regenerate itself. There are many cases when the quality of recycled products is as good as new, other cases when a lower quality

is acceptable and other cases when the purchasing organisations may choose to incur cost to purchase recycled items. Alternatives are available to chemicals that damage the environment, even if they cost more.

- Conclusion: Purchasing organisations should influence their supply chain, using organisations with a good track record on environmental purchases and choosing recycled and environmentally friendly products where appropriate. If the goods and services purchased cost more due to environmental concerns and are within the tactical acquisition quadrant of supply positioning, even a relatively large additional cost will not impact the organisation's spend in a major way. All organisations are stakeholders in our environment and as the interface with the supply market it is appropriate that buyers are intuitively aware of the impact of their actions on the environment and vice versa.

Human rights

Situation: Work is placed with an Asian supplier known to have a dubious record on employee rights.

- Against CSR: It's not always our business to look into these things, anyway the people are pleased to have the jobs even if they don't have the same union rights that we have in the West.
- For CSR: Can you actually argue against human rights for anyone? Our commitment to people extends up the supply chain to staff at suppliers and to people who use the goods and services that we make.
- Conclusion: Human rights are fundamental. No purchasing professional or purchasing organisation should be involved in supply situations that infringe the human rights of others. We may not be able to obtain western wages and benefits for employees in this situation; however, we should work with our suppliers to set minimum acceptable standards based on the four core ILO conventions.

Equal opportunities

Situation: Preferential treatment is given to a person within an organisation. Others who may be suitable are not given a chance.

- Against CSR: The survival of the fittest, it's my decision so I'll decide.
- For CSR: One of the theories of motivation suggests that when people consider that they have a fair chance to achieve they will be more motivated. The theory also says that if the perception is that they can never succeed they will reduce their input to a level which they believe equals their reward. If we were unfairly treated we would complain, so why should we believe that it is appropriate not to treat others equally? Equality is a fundamental human right.
- Conclusion: We are talking about people here. We should not seek to discriminate.

Diversity and supplier diversity

Situation: During a selection process the buyers come to an informal decision that a given supplier will not be selected because the organisation concerned originates from an inner city area of a European capital, in which ethnic minorities tend to live.

- Against CSR: 'We do not want to have to rely on organisations from that sort of area, they will not be sound.'
- For CSR: First, unless the racial mix of the people is audited then the above view is an assumption, and assumptions can be invalid. Second, what is to say that the organisation and its people go about their business in a less effective way than other organisations located in prestigious parts of the country? Indeed the given organisation might have a lower cost base than others. A supplier appraisal seems called for here.
- Conclusion: The temptation to come to a decision-making process with baggage or prejudice must be resisted. The thought process here can be developed to include the fact that the smaller supplier may be keener and may have people who have new ideas and talents that by using a conventional supplier we will miss. One of the roles of a buyer is to stimulate change and growth. Taking input from suppliers here may well bring benefit.

Corporate governance

Situation: It is possible to obtain finance for a project in a way which avoids the finance appearing on the balance sheet (off balance sheet finance) and therefore makes our balance sheet appear to be better than it really is, even though this practice is just outside the corporate governance guidelines.

- Against CSR: Profit is all that matters, not how it's made. We should not be expected to wash our dirty linen in public. If we cut corners no one will know.
- For CSR: Financial responsibility goes beyond short- or long-term 'profit', it relates to the short- and long-term ability of an organisation to demonstrate that it is well managed, financially sound and able to grow and develop. There are standards which govern corporate accounting. Proper corporate governance means that there should be no deliberately dirty linen to wash in public. Where an accidental example occurs, the situation is best admitted voluntarily and action taken to prevent a repetition.
- Conclusion: It is fundamental that all organisations behave properly, are seen to behave properly and account for their behaviour in accordance with accepted standards. 'Off balance sheet' must be disclosed under the new accounting standards and also under the ASB directives.

Sustainability

Situation: We have the choice to use more expensive sustainable products in our end product or lower-cost items which are not obtained from a sustainable source.

- Against CSR: Competitive and budget pressures rule here. It would be nice to buy from a sustainable source, but it's going to cost us.
- For CSR: In many cases there is a finite limit to the amount of resources which can be consumed, it is in the interest of everyone that sustainable resources are used.

- Conclusion: We owe a duty to future generations to leave the world in at least as good a state as we found it.

Impact on society

Situation: A new safer chemical is developed. The cost of using it and replacing the previous more dangerous chemical from a product is high and can only partly be recovered from an increase in the selling price of the end product. The decision has to be taken to use the new, safer or old, more dangerous chemical.

- Against CSR: Who will know that the new chemical exists? It is not possible to consider everyone when we make a decision. People don't have to buy things that they don't want to.
- For CSR: We have a duty of care to people and society at large not to damage them or their environment by producing goods and services which harm others or using processes that harm others.
- Conclusion: Our activities should aim, on balance, to benefit society. They should aim towards improvement and the elimination of dangerous chemicals.

Ethics and ethical trading

Situation: By using a disgruntled employee at a supplier and rewarding the person for their efforts, the purchasing organisation can gain knowledge of the supplier's negotiating position before a meeting.

- Against CSR: We can gain competitive advantage by knowing things like this. It doesn't matter how it gets done, just do it and take all of the advantages and benefits you can from a situation, bear as few of the costs.
- For CSR: There is a position beyond which we should not go and there are activities which we as business people and particularly purchasing people must not be involved in. Ethics is not a movable feast. You are either ethical or not. Other people will respect your ethical behaviour.
- Conclusion: The situation here is clear. Purchasing people must not be involved in activity like this.

Biodiversity

Situation: The new freight terminal needs to be built close to the road network and the railway line, but part of the site is classified as one of special scientific interest as it is the only place in Scotland where three species of birds nest.

- Against CSR: Birds! We are talking of a £50 million investment and lots of jobs for local people. Who cares about birds?
- For CSR: The size of the budget and even additional local jobs must not count as of right in front of a natural resource that could be lost for ever.
- Conclusion: Alternatives such as a nature reserve within the site can be considered as ways of minimising the impact upon the wildlife concerned during both construction and operation.

Community involvement

Situation: An organisation is considering closing a plant in France and moving production to a low wage economy in the far east. The purchasing organisation is the largest employer in the local community and the closure will mean the loss of hundreds of jobs.

- Against CSR: If the people were keen they would be competitive and their factories would not shut. Why should I worry? The firm must stay competitive and in today's world this means doing everything we can to lower costs.
- For CSR: The closure of the factory will devastate the local economy. Is a duty not owed to the employees who are being made redundant? Could the organisation not consider packages for retraining?
- Conclusion: It may be that there is no alternative to closing the factory. However, everything that can be done to lower costs should be done, alternative products should be investigated, to see if they can be switched to this site, and the people concerned should be kept fully informed and given as long a notice as possible. A final consideration here is the one of, 'What would happen to the whole organisation if it retained factories which were uncompetitive?' From a company wide perspective there's an issue here too.

7

Self-assessment question 7.2

In your mind's eye take a leading retailer who you or your family use frequently. If they announced that they were changing and developing practices to fully take on board corporate social responsibility, what benefits and costs would they incur and where would the benefits and costs originate from?

Feedback on page 153

7.3 The impact of CSR on purchasing and supply relationships

Irrespective of the relationship selected within the relationship spectrum, the same standard of CSR must be applied by the purchasing organisation. Literally this means that the standard should be applied to the one-off tactical profit purchase and the co-destiny relationship equally. It is therefore incumbent on purchasing organisations to ask questions and be sure that the answers received are valid, irrespective of the importance of the purchase. Publicity in a national newspaper would not make the distinction between the status of the purchasing relationship in praising or condemning an organisation for its purchasing practices.

OXFAM, Christian Aid and Cafod, all UK charities, ordered thousands of wristbands to support the 'make poverty history' initiative in 2005. Tony Blair, the then prime minister, and celebrities wore the bands made from rubber and fabric. To the great embarrassment of all concerned, it was then discovered that one manufacturer of these bands had fallen below the standards of the Ethical Trading Initiative. Workers were paid below the locally agreed minimum wage; there were concerns about health and safety provisions, long hours, unpaid overtime and the lack of a right to freedom of association. The charities concerned did not simply pull away from the situation; they worked with the supplier, who agreed a timetable to make improvements.

In assessing CSR and a given purchase, it is important to weigh the various issues and risks in the light of the purchase being made, for the significance of the issues will vary with the purchase and the purchasing strategy.

Learning activity 7.3

Look at your organisation's policy in this area. Look at the CIPS website, ask a supplier for their policy.

Feedback on page 153

In study session 1 the topic of risk was discussed and one of the risks highlighted on the y axis of supply positioning was the risk of CSR. Study session 3 considered a risk identification and risk management process and in this study session CSR has been analysed in depth. Putting the three subjects together is one of the basic tasks of a proactive buyer in the twenty-first century. In the context of our purchases and the relationships that underpin them, questions need to be asked to establish the impact of CSR risks on:

- our products and services
- our brand
- the bottom line of our business
- the survival of our business.

At the start of this subsection it was stated that CSR considerations applied irrespective of where the purchasing organisation saw the relationship on the relationship spectrum. This text is repeated to emphasise that CSR applies irrespective of the x axis within supply positioning. We cannot for example say to ourselves, 'the commodity is paperclips so CSR is irrelevant'.

The following steps may be taken by purchasing organisations seeking to understand their suppliers' position on CSR during the lifetime of a relationship. Relate them to the stages of the relationship life cycle model in study session 6. Actions include:

- A questionnaire during the supplier selection process.
- A specific role assigned to a member of the supplier appraisal team during a visit to the supplier.
- Internet searches, reading and searching for information about a supplier in the media in their locality.

- Involvement with non-governmental organisations, for example Traidcraft, who will map supply chains and investigate CSR issues in the developing world. Traidcraft invite interaction with buyers seeking to purchase fair trade items.
- A discussion with suppliers on practices adopted by their own suppliers.
- A visit to production sites in low-wage economies. Staff of the purchasing organisation can do this and it may on occasion be done unannounced.
- Contracting with locally based organisations to check low-wage economy production sites. The advantage of this option is that the contractor will speak the language of the organisation and be able to be less conspicuous than a western face in such an environment.
- An ongoing audit.

The point of this activity is to attempt to ensure that everything possible is done to avoid the purchasing organisation being drawn into any situation which is against its CSR policy and to minimise the risk if, despite all of the precautions, there is a situation where an inappropriate practice is found.

Drivers to improve CSR issues in relationships can come from unlikely places. A local newspaper reported that one chain of shops had instructed its staff to clock off when no customer was in the shop. The policy was reversed within the week, as local people had stopped using the chain of shops completely. A risk analysis by the organisation concerned would almost certainly have prevented the policy leaving the drawing board.

Customers can influence the supply chain and request information on CSR practices from their suppliers. Equally, some customers could pressurise suppliers to take short cuts. Suppliers can influence their customers by drawing issues to their attention, where for example options exist to use recyclable packaging or technologies which eliminate dangerous substances.

The trade unions have a role in promoting health and safety at work, internal stakeholders within our organisation may be able to use technology to automate dangerous processes and lessen the risk of injury to human beings.

The purchasing community has long been aware of the need for an ethical approach to business. There are different views on ethics in different parts of the world. In some societies it is the norm for a buyer to bring a gift, or for a seller to give a gift and here it is acceptable to follow this custom. However, in these situations it is necessary to be cautious and ensure that giving and receiving cannot be construed as more than following local custom. Buyers receiving gifts in this environment may well wish to ensure that they are recorded and perhaps given away to charity once the recipient reaches their home base.

Outside the purchasing organisation's supply chain, government may legislate and competitors may also influence our approach in some ways if they are able to make advances.

Working with suppliers it may be possible in the form of a supplier development project to develop solutions and options which are more environmentally friendly.

Self-assessment question 7.3

If you were about to make a visit to a supplier and had been asked to review their status on corporate social responsibility, identify a number of items that you would want to investigate.

Feedback on page 154

Revision question

Now try the revision question for this session on page 321.

Summary

CSR is not an option. It is a challenge to purchasing people who must influence internal and external stakeholders to work with them to improve the position of their organisation in this vital area.

Suggested further reading

Review the material in the responsible/sustainable procurement and knowledge insight sectons of CIPS knowledge works on the CIPS website.

Feedback on learning activities and self-assessment questions

Feedback on learning activity 7.1

Among the increasing number of issues raised under the overall banner of CSR, the following are perhaps the most common within the supply chain:

- environmental responsibility
- human rights
- equal opportunities
- diversity
- corporate governance
- sustainability
- impact on society
- ethics and ethical trading
- biodiversity
- community involvement.

These aspects of CSR relate to, and recognise the importance of, the various stakeholders concerned (employees, customers, suppliers, the community, the environment, and shareholders, where appropriate).

Feedback on self-assessment question 7.1

The completed table is shown in table 7.2.

Table 7.2 CSR statements – specimen answers

Statement about the CSR issue	CSR issue
Avoid reducing the number of interdependent species	Biodiversity
Impacted the people who lived very near to it by polluting their environment	Impact on society
Initiatives that aim to increase the number of diverse businesses that supply	Diversity
It aims to promote the use of recycled materials and design products for reuse	Sustainability
Many organisations support their community in the form of local charities	Community involvement
Our responsibility here is to the surroundings in which our organisation operates	Environmental responsibility
The treatment of people in a way which is fair to everyone	Equal opportunities
The United Nations has a charter in this area	Human rights
US legislators enacted the Sarbanes Oxley Act in 2002	Corporate governance
We must not misrepresent our needs by untruthfully misleading suppliers about our intentions	Ethics and ethical trading

Feedback on learning activity 7.2

You should have considered where failure to be aware of the tenets of CSR could cause your organisations a major problem, for example if the national television news carried an item about one of your suppliers using sweat-shop labour. The impact is that customers might stop buying your products and services.

Feedback on self-assessment question 7.2

Benefits

- New customers from people who saw CSR as an important issue.
- Good publicity.
- Publicity in the form of articles in the press.
- Motivated employees.
- Greater respect from the community at large.
- Greater respect from their suppliers.
- Customers possibly prepared to pay more for some goods ethically purchased.
- Potential new supply markets.
- Lower life cycle costs from better product knowledge.

Costs

- Higher unit costs of some goods and services.
- Greater process costs involved in assessing and maintaining CSR standards.
- Loss of customers who did not believe in CSR.

Feedback on learning activity 7.3

Consider how you may wish to change things in the light of this study session. Note any risks you may run.

7

Feedback on self-assessment question 7.3

1   Are my colleagues aware of what we seek in terms of CSR?
2   What does their CSR policy contain and how up to date is it?
3   Are people aware of the CSR policy?
4   Is the CSR policy followed? Do you feel the people you talk to at the supplier's site know and buy into the policy or just pay lip service to it?
5   How well does the CSR policy match our own policy?
6   Which aspects of CSR are key to our relationship with this supplier?
7   On those aspects that matter most in this case how do they and their suppliers perform?
8   Can I learn anything from them in this area?
9   What does the organisation know about their suppliers' CSR policy?
10 What are the specific items of praise or improvement we would want to feed back at the end of the supplier appraisal?

7

Lean and agile relationships

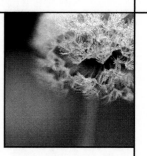

'Lean thinking is "lean" because it does more with less, compared with traditional manufacturing.'
Lysons and Gillingham (2003)

Introduction

This study session considers different approaches to manufacturing and the way they impact upon relationships. It is argued that the principles can be used in services and the public sector, and whilst that is true, the prime use of these approaches is within the manufacturing sector.

Session learning objectives

After completing this session you should be able to:

8.1 Distinguish traditional manufacturing supply philosophies from both lean and agile supply philosophies.
8.2 Assess the lean supply philosophy.
8.3 Assess the agile supply philosophy.

Unit content coverage

This study session covers the following topics from the official CIPS unit content document.

Learning objective

1.5 Differentiate between lean and agile supply philosophies on supplier relationships.

Timing

You should set aside about 5 hours to read and complete this session, including learning activities, self-assessment questions, the suggested further reading (if any) and the revision question.

8.1 Traditional manufacturing compared with lean and agile philosophies

It is probable that there are very few organisations still following 'traditional' manufacturing principles within the UK in the twenty-first century. The logic behind this statement is the author's belief that those organisations which did not change towards a lean philosophy in the last two decades of the twentieth century are no longer with us! Equally, it can be argued that there are very few truly 'lean' organisations operating in the UK today.

How can this contradiction be explained, for what the above text amounts to is a view that industry is neither traditional nor lean? Additionally, there are examples of the 'lean' and 'traditional' approaches in other parts of the world. Some nations, notably the Japanese with their scarcity of physical resources, originated many of the features now recognised as lean thinking to a state of excellence. Other nations with very low-wage economies and questionable ethical practices are able to compete at a lower cost than western economies using traditional approaches to manufacturing. Yet other organisations, protected by trade barriers, continue traditional practices to supply their markets but are unable to compete on world markets. At this stage let's differentiate each term with a short description.

- By **traditional manufacturing** it is meant that all of the resources used to manufacture goods designed by the manufacturer for the market are optimised by focusing on the economies of scale derived from maximising the output of the physical, material and human resources available to produce at the lowest cost of sale possible.
- By **lean manufacturing** it is meant that goods are produced firstly only when a customer needs them and secondly to a standard where the value perceived by the customer governs quality in terms of goods and process. Processes and parts of the product that do not add what is perceived as value are considered waste and eliminated.
- By **agile manufacturing** it is meant that finished goods are not produced. What are produced are goods that are at a high common level and they are subsequently customised to one of several options when a customer places an order.

Clearly these philosophies are different and the adoption of one or other of the philosophies will impact both internal and external stakeholders in purchasing and supply relationships.

Learning activity 8.1

Consider the definitions above. Search on the internet using these terms and see what is returned by your search engine for 'lean+purchasing', 'lean +manufacturing', 'lean+supply', 'agile+purchasing', 'agile+manufacturing', 'agile+supply'.

Feedback on page 167

Traditional manufacturing processes

Traditional manufacturing processes, when and where they exist, involve:

- Finished goods produced to forecasts with options minimised but still available. This tenet works towards the view that 'you can have any colour you like as long as it's black'. Production produced things it thought that people would want to buy and sales sold them to customers. Sometimes they were correct, other times, even with market research, they were wrong.
- Machines and facilities run to economically produce batch quantities in long production runs. Production was the god of the organisation. The author worked with an organisation where the machine shop manager determined the batch quantities produced. He was heard to

say, 'I am not setting that machine up for four hours to produce less than 500 components, it's just not economical!' The point was that the organisation concerned used between 80 and 120 of the components a year and was vastly overstocked. In this environment machines standing idle were considered unacceptable. This approach meant that manufacturing organisations produced at 'optimal' costs even though they had no customers for their products.

- Stock is seen as an essential part of the production process. To allow the machines to run at optimum capacity it was necessary to have buffer stock in between machines and a safety stock of raw materials in the stores. This approach incurred the cost of stocks which spent many hours waiting to be moved through the production processes.

- Stock held just in case it is needed. Many buyers have heard of JIT, meaning 'just in time' in terms of an inventory management philosophy. However, the traditional manufacturing approach held stock 'JIC', meaning just in case it was needed. This not only applied to direct production materials, but spares for maintenance as well. JIC increased the cost of operations and their supporting processes.

- Production processes planned and run by production teams, other processes seen as supporting processes. As a trainee buyer the author was informed that 'if the production manager says jump, we ask how high'. In this approach being a slave to production economics cost many businesses and their suppliers much in other areas like change, expediting and urgent delivery costs.

- Business processes focused on doing everything possible to reduce production process cost. Taking a small order from a customer would therefore not be considered economic due to the set up time and cost, which would be fully applied to the customers' job.

Lean manufacturing is assessed within section 8.2 and can be contrasted with the above approach by featuring:

- the elimination of waste, including stock
- producing only when customers order goods
- a focus on customer value
- removing layers within organisations
- continuous improvements
- batch quantities as low as one
- quality and right first time approaches.

Agile production is assessed within section 8.3 and can be contrasted with the above approach by featuring:

- customer focus
- meeting customer's need quickly
- repositioning the organisation and its products as customer need develops
- the ability to respond to changing volumes and product mix quickly.

8.2 Assess the lean supply philosophy

Lean supply was defined within the *CIPS Position on Practice* as 'developing a value stream to eliminate all waste (including time), promote innovation and enable a level schedule'.

The *CIPS Position on Practice* document identifies five key principles to lean thinking. They are to:

1   specify what creates value as seen from the customer's perspective
2   identify all steps across the value stream
3   make those actions that create that value flow
4   only make what is pulled by the customer just in time
5   strive for perfection by *continually* removing waste.

1 Specify value as seen from the customer's perspective

This means engaging with customers and even the customer's customer to understand what they want, what they don't want and how their perception of value might differ from the purchasing organisation's perception. It may be the case that packaging used by the purchasing organisation is produced to what they consider the 'right' quality. Yet this perception may not be valued by the end customer, who considers:

*   another form of packaging as of value for this product, or
*   the packaging a source of problem when opening consignments
*   the packaging to be of too high a standard, thus adding unnecessary cost.

The purchasing organisation must therefore have a relationship downstream in the supply chain which accesses information on what the end customer perceives as value.

2 Identify all steps across the value stream

Advocates of lean supply indicate that it is next necessary to identify all of the steps that make up the value stream. The use of the term 'value stream' is a development of the term 'supply chain'. The supply chain becomes the value chain when waste is removed from it and the term 'stream' is an alternative to the term 'chain', hence 'value stream'. Frequently organisations assume that they know all of the steps in the supply chain and frequently they are not aware of processes necessary at, for example, a supplier's supplier. The process only comes to light when there is a delay and then its criticality may become apparent. Mapping the full process is an extensive activity. A previous CIPS course book on introduction to supply and materials management had a process map of 24 process steps over 319 cumulative days. The value-adding activity within the process was three hours, meaning that 318 days and 21 hours was non-value adding activity! The source of the example was Womack and Jones (1996).

3 Make those actions that create that value flow

Having identified the value adding activities, it is necessary to consider the linkages and the time taken within the process to ensure that the flow is as smooth as possible and eliminates as much waste as possible. The elimination of waste is discussed below.

4 Only make what is pulled by the customer just in time

It can be argued that inventory is the greatest waste; hence making products for stock is seen as a waste. Lean philosophy will only make what customers need, just before they need it. One purchasing manager described this concept as starting planning and manufacturing for customers' needs when the customer was prepared to 'put money into the piggy bank', meaning when the customer ordered them, not before. Travelling around the UK in the 1990s and very early twenty-first century, it was possible to see disused airfields near car manufacturing plants where thousands of new cars were parked awaiting customer orders. Lean philosophy sees this as a crime and would stop production if there were no customer orders.

5 Strive for perfection by continually removing waste

Two concepts are implicit in this principle. Firstly, there is continuous improvement or 'kaizen' and secondly there is 'muda' or waste.

Continuous improvement means what it says; that we strive on an ongoing basis to improve whatever it is we are doing. Practically, this means that the people involved in the processes delivering goods to customers are searching to improve in areas they can influence to add value to the customer. This can excite, frustrate and cause problems and opportunities in internal and external relationships. An internal team who have reduced the cost of a CD player cost by 7% in a year may be frustrated to be asked to reduce cost further the next year. People may have personally invested a huge amount in a key component and delivered what they consider to be a brilliant design, only to have the design challenged as 'waste' six months later. Another person, however, may see that an improvement to the same key component on the CD player could be used to deliver another 5% reduction to six additional products. This opportunity may excite one person, but upset the originator of the previous 'brilliant' design. Handled improperly, relationships with people in both our supplier's and our own organisation can deteriorate. Consider how the cost of electrical consumer goods has fallen and how to compete with each other organisations producing these goods must continue to improve and reduce cost.

E-purchasing

E-purchasing offers opportunities for reducing waste in transactions processed between organisations driving for lean supply, through use of capabilities like extranets, EDI, XML and through tools like a collaborative development forum, supplier performance data management and reportage, bar codes, RFID, self-billing, systems integration and trend and spend analysis.

Learning activity 8.2

Take the five principles of lean thinking discussed above, re-read the text on the traditional manufacturing organisation in section 8.1 and make notes on how the lean philosophy would change the way the traditional manufacturing organisation would operate.

Feedback on page 167

Waste

'Muda' is a Japanese term for waste. Taiichi Ohno, a Toyota engineer, identified seven wastes. These wastes are the targets for elimination in the supply chain. To the seven original wastes the waste of unsafe practices has been added. These wastes are identified and described below. Waste is defined as 'anything that does not contribute to the creation of value for the customer'. The eight wastes are:

1 over-production
2 waiting
3 transportation
4 inappropriate processing
5 stock
6 unnecessary/excess motion
7 making defective products
8 unsafe practices (added much later after the original seven were identified).

1 Over-production

Simply put, over-production is manufacturing an item before it is actually required. An example of over-produced cars was provided earlier. A lean organisation will not commence production until a customer orders the goods.

2 Waiting

Whenever goods are not moving or being processed, the waste of waiting occurs. In the traditional environment products can spend a large amount of time waiting to be processed. Waiting can be dramatically reduced by linking processes internally and within the supply chain so that one process feeds directly into the next one without delay.

3 Transporting

Transporting a product between processes and/or organisations risks damage, incurs cost, takes time and therefore adds no value. It is, however, inevitable that some transportation is necessary, as production locations are not always located near extractive locations and the need to have specialist areas within an organisation to paint or electroplate products means that transportation is necessary. However, conscious thought, planning of routing and the identification of all steps within a supply chain can mean that transportation can be greatly reduced in a lean supply situation.

4 Inappropriate processing

The consideration here is the use of the right equipment and the right process for the goods being produced. It may be that advanced equipment is used to produce simple goods, thus increasing set-up time and unit cost; or that the equipment is not advanced enough and causes quality problems as it can't meet the specification. The goal here is a combination of flexible equipment, allowing change when necessary, and also high asset utilisation. Also appropriate here is the consideration that a process used may not be

8

valued by the customer. How many of us, as consumers, are frustrated with the vacuum packing of products which take minutes to open when seconds is the opening time we seek? Lean organisations seek to identify and eliminate processes that do not meet their customer's view of value.

5 Stock

Stock, in the form of work in progress or buffer stocks, is a waste linked directly to over-production and waiting. In a traditional manufacturing situation buffer stock is frequently found between machines and processes and is the result of one machine or process finishing its stage of production before the next one is ready to take the goods a step further. In addition, organisations had safety stock in case suppliers did not deliver. Goods therefore waited and in doing so they increased lead times and used productive and storage floor space. The just in time concept, where suppliers and processes only requested items from the previous process when they were ready to process their stage of production aims to eliminate these wastes, both on internal processes and between organisations. Hence, in a lean organisation, suppliers deliver 15 minutes before components are needed and batch sizes are reduced, even to one, to eliminate stock.

6 Unnecessary/excess motion

This waste is related to ergonomics and is seen in all instances where human beings bend, stretch, walk, lift and reach. These issues are also related to the health and safety of human beings. For example, it was understood that a piece of equipment used in hospitals was causing backache for nurses and analysis revealed that the control panel was too high for many nurses to reach comfortably. The manufacturer was contacted and it was discovered that the person who designed the equipment was very tall and had placed the control panel at a convenient height for him. It had never occurred to him that most of the users of the equipment would be of a smaller stature. In this case a remedy was promptly made and the consideration built into future models. Products and processes must be designed to eliminate unnecessary motions. Lean organisations use automation to bring the work to the person rather than the person having to get up and collect the work.

7 Making defective products

Directly impacting profit, defects resulting in the need to rework or scrap items are a real burden to producers. To cover up for a high defect rate it is necessary to hold more stock and have additional processes to rework or inspect items and even reschedule production. Over time it may also be necessary to regain production time and meet customer schedules. Lean organisations seek to identify potential problems in products and processes from the design stage onwards, to eliminate as many defects as possible.

8 Unsafe practices

There are legal requirements imposed on employers and employees in terms of health and safety. Even selfish employers realise that safe practices mean less absenteeism and more productive days. Caring employers also consider the people that work for them and want a safe and motivated workforce. One CIPS student told a group being led by the author that a given operation within their organisation could not be carried out effectively with the safety guard in place on the machine. Special dispensation was gained to remove the guard and special procedures put in place for the employee concerned. However, it was later decided to buy the component from another organisation with specialist equipment at additional unit cost, rather than make it in an unsafe way internally. Lean organisations strive to create safe working environments.

Impact upon relationships

In a sense much of the above text is analytical and it might be possible to fail to understand the impact upon the relationships with stakeholders and suppliers. To understand the impact, consider how a supplier feels when:

- they are again advised that the 'cost down' target for the next year is 'x %'
- the number of acceptable parts per million failures is again reduced
- their customer seeks a further lead time reduction
- their customer wants to pay for stock when it is used, rather than received.

All of these changes will have a cost impact upon the supplier, who may well ask, 'What is the benefit for me in this relationship?'

Now consider the designers within the purchasing organisation or the supplier faced with a requirement from the marketing function to reduce cost by 10%. Do they cut quality? How do they feel when asked to redesign each year to reduce cost and, as they perceive it, reduce value? Consider the feelings of the production manager asked to produce in smaller batches to fulfil the edicts of the lean philosophy. Smaller batches means more changes and set-ups. It probably represents the opposite of what was perceived as best practice when the production manager was trained.

Purchasing professionals may also be faced with cost reduction targets in this type of environment and it can be their approach to the suppliers which makes or breaks the target. Imagine the approach which autocratically tells a supplier by email that '10% is the target for next year'. How will the supplier feel? How motivated will the supplier feel to deliver the 10%? Examine even the words used in the last two sentences, for I have talked of 'the supplier' rather than the people involved. How much better would it be to organise a meeting between the people within the purchasing organisation and the people within the sales organisation and discuss the cost reduction target and the opportunities? In reality, with a large number of suppliers this will be difficult. However, the need may well justify the difficulty and the cost. One fundamental consideration here is the question of the people working for the supplier: 'What's in it for us?' Ask yourself this. If the benefits of cost reduction and the elimination of waste go to the purchasing organisation, how likely are the people at the supplier to offer further reductions? Is it possible that the people involved at the supplier, faced with the demand for a 10% cost reduction, can actually deliver a 12.5% cost reduction, but decide to keep the remaining 2.5% for next year?

What is necessary is a close relationship, perhaps a single-sourced relationship, strategic alliance, partnership or co-destiny relationship, even a closer tactical relationship, but adversarial relationships are not ones where the lean philosophy will work. The process of taking waste out of the product, services and the business processes which underpin them, must share the benefits accruing to both parties and the answer to the supplier's question 'what's in it for me?' is therefore 'a share of the savings'. Some buyers have difficulty with this concept. They cannot countenance the sharing of benefit with suppliers and when they exhibit behaviour which confirms their difficulty they invite people at their suppliers to hide potential benefits and savings.

How would the people feel if we proposed a scheme which offered this? 'Any saving arrived at will accrue to the party proposing the saving in the proportion 60:40.' This means that where the team at the supplier propose an action which results in a £10 reduction in the unit cost of their item to the purchasing organisation, they keep 60% or £6.00 of the saving. If the part previously cost £120 and the reduction would take it to £110, then the supplier would invoice the purchasing organisation at £116. If the idea originated within the purchasing organisation then the supplier would invoice £114. People at suppliers will be keener to eliminate waste and save cost if a share of the benefit accrues to them; relationships between the organisations will improve if the efforts of all organisations are recognised. The percentages between the organisations are, of course, negotiable.

Two final thoughts

Working in a lean way can deliver many benefits to purchasing organisations and sales organisations alike. However, participants in these programmes must realise that continuous means continuous, in terms of improvement! There is rightly a tendency to feel a sense of achievement after a success, yet the lean philosophy insists that another elimination of waste must be sought, and after that, yet another one.

Waste can also be said to reflect the way an organisation is designed. How many layers are there in the organisation? Are all of the layers necessary? Could people in a lower part of the organisation make decisions and could a layer of staff be removed? Many organisations have de-layered and removed managers who were perhaps seen as bureaucrats.

Self-assessment question 8.1

1   The benefits resulting from the lean philosophy are not shared with suppliers by all buyers.
    True/False.
2   Continuous improvement is a major part of the lean philosophy.
    True/False.
3   In a lean philosophy, suppliers have little role to play.
    True/False.
4   In lean systems items are produced and pushed through from manufacturer to customers.

(continued on next page)

Self-assessment question 8.1 *(continued)*

True/False.

5 Lean supply identifies what customers value and strives to eliminate all wasteful activities.
True/False.

6 Lean supply is a philosophy used in banks and building societies.
True/False.

7 Time is one of the seven wastes.
True/False.

Feedback on page 167

8.3 Assess the agile supply philosophy

Learning activity 8.3

Look up 'agile' in a dictionary. Compare it with 'lean'.

Feedback on page 168

The *CIPS Position on Practice* describes **agile supply** as 'using market knowledge and a responsive supply network to exploit profitable opportunities in the marketplace'.

At the start of this study session agile manufacturing was described as not producing finished goods, but producing goods that are at a high common level and are then customised to one of several options when a customer orders the given option.

For example, a remanufacturer of refrigeration compressors may produce over 20 different models, used by customers in supermarkets to chill and refrigerate food dependent on the cubic size of the area to be refrigerated, amongst other considerations. There are three ways of wiring each compressor into the supermarket refrigeration system and it is not possible to predict which one will be chosen until the compressor is ordered. To compete in the market it is vital to be able to despatch compressors ordered by 4 pm on day of order. Is it therefore necessary to hold at least one of 60 different compressor variations in stock to meet the market expectation? No, this is not the case. The compressors are finished and tested, mechanically, then tested on one of three standard wiring test rigs. If they pass the test, the wiring is removed and the compressor without wiring is stored until ordered. Once the wiring configuration is known, a pre-prepared wiring kit is inserted in to the empty wiring box and the compressor is retested, after which it is despatched to the customer.

In this case the customer service is maintained by holding stock of an 'almost finished' compressor and customising it at the last moment, but significantly, the stock needed to provide this service is one-third of the level needed if one of each compressor was held in stock. With compressors costing an average of £1,000 each, it is possible to provide a £60,000 service with £20,000 of stock!

The process described above is also known as 'late customisation' or 'postponement' and many organisations successfully use it within their goods and services. Choices of colour, left-hand and right-hand options and plugs to meet the electrical systems of different countries are other examples. In services, the choice of programme at a car wash or the modular nature of a training package can also allow late customisation.

Agility not only applies to inventory management and final production, it can apply to the design process and the ability to work within a changing market.

In the design process standards, standard components and modules can be agreed at an early stage, capacities stated and accepted and a number of components identified and even ordered from suppliers. Yet the final design of the item is not completed because it is dependent on another major factor. In a changing market the ability to change production on a frequent basis will meet customers' needs and mean that it is possible to take opportunities which other organisations cannot take. This may be achieved by a combination of excellent information on the markets and their movements, good relationships with customers, flexible internal processes, flexible people and good relationships with suppliers. If the market is not a changing one, then the agile philosophy might not be appropriate.

One of the drivers of agile supply is the ever-shortening lifecycle of products. A computer printer bought six months ago will have been replaced by a new model by now. This means that business and production processes must plan for the new model almost as soon as it has commenced production on this one. A second driver is the need for the agile supply chain to be sensitive to changes in the market and to respond to them. Imagine that the computer printer manufacturer senses that the market in a given country would be attracted by an eco-friendly printer which switches itself off if not in use. Do they wait to till the next model before introducing the feature? Or do they adapt an existing model to a new variant for that country and have it in the market very quickly? Knowing what customers want is not necessarily an easy thing to establish, but information shared within a supply chain or supply chain grouping for the benefit of all participants can enable different manufacturers to produce complementary products to meet customers' needs in a short time.

Underpinning these drivers is trust and the integration of systems and processes across normal boundaries to reduce time to market and normal delivery times as a consequence. It could be said that the agile processes are 'cemented', although 'cemented' might be the wrong word! But is it? For what is cemented are the business processes that see change, proactivity, innovation, quality, customer focus and collaboration with suppliers as the norm. Rather than reducing the number of suppliers to a minimum and seeking to continuously reduce waste in product and process, the agile approach will maintain relationships with a wider range of suppliers and potential suppliers so that when there is an urgent customer need for something different, their relationship with a supplier is already in place, trust exists and the time needed to select suppliers is eliminated from the time taken to get the goods to market.

8

When considering the traditional manufacturing approach and the lean philosophy, the role of stock was discussed. Where an agile supply philosophy is used, stock is not a 'crime' per se and it is also not found in abundance as it is in the traditional process. Stock is:

- frequently held as work in progress requiring customisation, rather than finished goods
- deliberately planned to be held
- held at a few stages within the bill of materials hierarchy of the finished item, perhaps at the stage of major modules
- pulled through to higher levels in the bill of materials hierarchy based upon customers' orders
- planned together with customers and suppliers to allow everyone to react as quickly as possible.

Holding stock is therefore valued by people working in an agile supply chain, when it is held at the appropriate level in the bill of materials hierarchy, as a vital asset in meeting customers' needs.

E-purchasing

E-purchasing offers opportunities for agile organisations, through use of capabilities like extranets, EDI, XML and through tools like a collaborative development forum, market intelligence tools, self-billing, systems integration and trend and spend analysis.

Self-assessment question 8.2

Using table 8.1, identify which of the nine statements relate to traditional manufacturing, the lean philosophy or the agile philosophy. Each statement only relates to one of the three.

Table 8.1

No.	Question	Answer
1	As a by-product of poor processes, stock is always around.	
2	Business processes that see change, proactivity, innovation, quality, customer focus and collaboration with suppliers as the norm.	
3	Held at the appropriate level within the bill of materials, stock is seen as an asset.	
4	Late customisation or postponement is used successfully by many organisations here.	
5	Manufacturing organisations produced at 'optimal' costs even though they had no customers for their products.	
6	Production people are king.	
7	Stock is seen as a crime. It is eliminated at all costs between processes and between supply chain organisations.	
8	The ideal is to achieve a seamless flow between processes and significantly reduce the cost of production.	
9	This philosophy considers ergonomics.	

Feedback on page 168

Revision question

Now try the revision question for this session on page 322.

Summary

The lean and agile approaches are not necessarily alternatives. The product ranges of purchasing organisations may or may not lend themselves to agility or lean supply in its strictest sense. However, to operate in the twenty-first century in most situations it is clear that the traditional approach is no longer appropriate and many organisations have adopted features of both lean and agile approaches as common-sense roads to survival, greater market share and better meeting of customers' needs.

Suggested further reading

Review the material in the knowledge summary section of CIPS knowledge works on the CIPS website.

Feedback on learning activities and self-assessment questions

Feedback on learning activity 8.1

You should find academic papers on these approaches, articles to download and references to training programmes identifying the essentials of the approaches. Use these sources to expand your understanding of what is meant by 'lean and agile'.

Feedback on learning activity 8.2

Your notes should include text on issues like:

- Traditional organisations concentrated on their output and not customers needs.
- Goods were produced even if their was no customer for them.
- Stock was essential within the organisation which probably did not know the full extent of its supply chain.
- The concept of 'value' was unknown and there was much waste within supply chain processes.
- There was no focus on ongoing cost reduction, the focus was on process optimisation.
- Organisations operated in isolation, not in a supply or value chain.

Feedback on self-assessment question 8.1

1   True. Some buyers cannot countenance this; however, their suppliers probably don't offer all the reductions in waste that they could do.
2   True.
3   Absolutely not! Amongst other things, lean supply relies upon the innovation and elimination of waste from suppliers. They have a fundamental role.

4   No. Lean is a pull system. Only when customers order is production commenced.

5   True.

6   No. These are service sector organisations; lean supply is typically a manufacturing philosophy.

7   No. There are eight wastes; time is not one of them.

Feedback on learning activity 8.3

Agile means 'marked by ready ability to move with quick easy grace, having a quick resourceful and adaptable character'. Lean means 'lacking or deficient in flesh, containing little or no fat'. (By permission. From the *Merriam-Webster Online Dictionary* ©2005 by Merriam-Webster, Incorporated (Merriam-Webster: http://www.merriam-webster.com).)

Feedback on self-assessment question 8.2

1   Traditional
2   Agile
3   Agile
4   Agile
5   Traditional
6   Traditional
7   Lean
8   Lean
9   Lean

Supplier appraisal

Introduction

This area of the syllabus is one where purchasing as a profession uses several names to describe the same activity. First we will clarify our use of terms and then look at the objectives and a typical process before considering the internal supplier.

Session learning objectives

After completing this session you should be able to:

9.1 Define and distinguish between terms commonly used in different supplier assessments.
9.2 Explain the objectives of supplier appraisal.
9.3 Design a supplier appraisal process.
9.4 Explain the impact of internal suppliers on the supplier selection and appraisal process.

9

Unit content coverage

This study session covers the following topics from the official CIPS unit content document.

Learning objective

2.1 Formulate objectives for relationships with suppliers.
2.2 Evaluate and apply techniques for supplier appraisal and selection.

Timing

You should set aside about 4 hours to read and complete this session, including learning activities, self-assessment questions, the suggested further reading (if any) and the revision question.

9.1 Terms and definitions

Different organisations use different terms to mean the same thing, hence some will talk of supplier assessment when meaning a pre-contract assessment whilst others will use the same two words to describe the post-contract evaluation. The most common and widely understood terms are those used in figure 9.1.

Figure 9.1

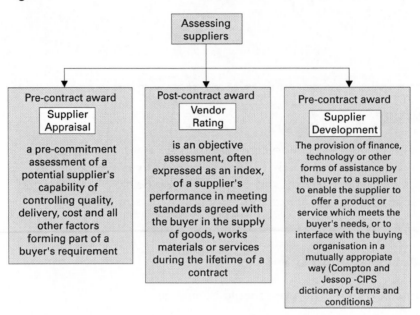

From figure 9.1 it can be seen that supplier appraisal is activity undertaken by the purchasing organisation before a contract is placed with a supplier, whilst vendor rating (vendor being an alternative word for supplier) takes place once the contract is in place; supplier development is entirely different, taking place before and during the lifetime of a contract.

Learning activity 9.1

Consider supplier appraisal, as defined in figure 9.1. What does this process involve? Who does it involve?

Feedback on page 178

The objectives and process of supplier appraisal will be discussed later, but the key point of this section is to get the message over that supplier appraisal is a process which takes place as part of the selection process, well before contracts are signed. 'Vendor rating' is the term used for measuring suppliers' performance once they are delivering goods, works, materials and services for a purchasing organisation.

Self-assessment question 9.1

Take the four quadrants of the supply positioning model and indicate why you would undertake a supplier appraisal in that quadrant. You might conclude that supplier appraisal is inappropriate in some cases.

Feedback on page 178

9.2 The objectives of supplier appraisal

Supplier appraisal is a process which takes time and resources, in fact it can in some cases soak up huge amounts of time and resources for purchasing people and others.

Learning activity 9.2

Consider what your objectives might be and what activities you would undertake on a supplier appraisal of a new organisation supplying training services to your organisation.

Feedback on page 179

In its simplest form, the objectives of supplier appraisal are to understand whether the supplier(s) can meet the requirements of the purchasing organisation. However, it is appropriate to expand the objective to include the following considerations. We need to understand:

1 what the total cost of meeting our requirements is likely to be
2 what the benefits of working with this given supplier will be
3 the extent to which both parties will be able to develop solutions together, where an ongoing relationship is sought
4 the extent to which both parties, as people, can work together really well.

In the early stages of the purchasing cycle the needs and wants of internal customers and stakeholders will be developed into a specification which will form part of an enquiry process, if that process is used. The specification will form the requirement against which the supplier will be appraised.

It is vital to assess the supplier against total cost of ownership, to ensure that costs are not forgotten or deferred, only to arise later. In this case it may be that one supplier will include an element of cost within their offer and another exclude it. Whilst this is basic good purchasing practice, in complex situations the appraisal and its discussions will bring out different options for consideration.

In the case of a major once-only purchase, a long-term developmental relationship may not be sought. However, in other cases it will be appropriate to establish whether it is felt that both organisations can develop together.

Finally we have to ask ourselves this question: can we as people work with them as people?

Note that we are talking about feelings here. In an appraisal there are going to be areas that we can score with certainty. However, there will be other areas which will require a more subjective assessment of both the supplier's and our abilities.

9

Self-assessment question 9.2

A colleague of the author once had this as an objective for a supplier appraisal.

> 'Our objective in this appraisal is to work out where we can squeeze cost out of this supplier and reduce the price of the goods paid by us. I am sure that they are hiding cost in their initial quote.'

Take this objective and:

1 identify what you believe to be the faults in it and
2 indicate where you believe the relationship between the buyer and the seller might develop, given the buyer's attitude.

Feedback on page 179

9.3 A supplier appraisal process

Figure 9.2 identifies a ten-step process for supplier appraisal. It may surprise you that the actual onsite activity does not occur until step nine. This reflects the importance of planning in a successful supplier appraisal process. The process also requires a multidisciplinary team. This process may be a replacement for an enquiry process or two or three enquiry and pre-qualification stages may be placed within this process. The process is adapted to suit the needs of the situation, no one process will suit all situations.

Figure 9.2

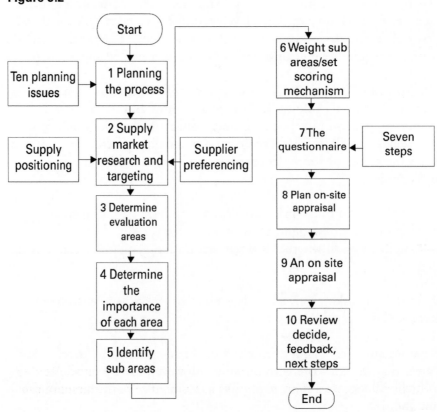

Learning activity 9.3

Review figure 9.2 and consider who you would want to meet during an onsite appraisal for an office cleaning service provider, assuming that you were to visit both the organisation's premises and a site cleaned by them.

Feedback on page 179

Each of the process steps identified in figure 9.2 will be briefly discussed below.

1 Planning the process

It is vital to plan any important process and supplier appraisal is no exception. Figure 9.2 indicates that there are ten planning issues. These issues are presented below in the form of questions.

- What's the objective of *this* appraisal? This appraisal may differ from other appraisals.
- How many suppliers should/must we appraise? The more suppliers, the more time and cost.
- What will be the scale of the appraisals? The greater the scale, the more time and cost.
- What are our resources? Are they adequate? Do we have enough people to complete the process effectively? If not, perhaps we need to change the scale or the number of suppliers.
- Do we have senior management support? If senior management do not support us then funds and people may not be available to us and the process may fail.
- What is our experience of appraising suppliers? The less experience we have the more carefully we need to prepare.
- What is the time required and the time available? If we do not have enough time to do the job properly, then scale it down or fight for other resources.
- What is the current status of our relationships with suppliers? Where we have a close relationship the process may be accepted more easily and we may not need to undertake such a large amount of investigation because we know and trust the organisation and the people. Where this is not the case then we will need to spend more time making a relationship with the supplier.
- Where are the suppliers located? This has clear cost, time and risk impacts. The cost of evaluating a Taiwanese supplier may be much more than evaluating a local supplier. However, the risk involved with a supplier so far away may mean that the evaluation is necessary.
- Will the benefit of the process be greater than the cost? This is a common-sense check.

2 Supply market research and targeting

Here we undertake the supply positioning and supplier preferencing analyses previously discussed to understand which suppliers we should target in this process.

9

3 Determine evaluation areas

In this step of the process it is important to determine the areas of the supplier's business that we wish to investigate, based upon the requirement as we have specified it. Typical areas can include the supplier's:

- basic data
- business systems and processes
- cost structure
- customer support/marketing
- delivery performance
- financial standing
- logistics
- management capability
- manufacturing
- potential to develop opportunities with us
- quality systems
- service provision capability
- standing in business community
- supply chain
- technical/process capability.

Other evaluation areas may be appropriate depending upon the requirement. The extent to which each area is evaluated will depend upon the commodity being purchased, what is known about the supplier and what it may be reasonable to assume. For example, it may be reasonable to assume that Microsoft are financially sound and not attempt to evaluate their accounts in detail for that purpose.

4 Determine importance of each area

In any given supplier appraisal some areas will be more important than others and the multidisciplinary team working on the appraisal will need to argue and debate which areas are most important and weight the areas out of 100%. Criteria need to be identified and described in a sentence that can be understood by everyone in the team and the supplier's people. Hence a criterion for measuring a maintenance service provider's knowledge of the type of equipment we use could be simply stated as 'knowledge of our equipment', but would be better expressed as 'has up-to-date experience in the maintenance of XYZ Series 200 equipment'.

5 Identify sub areas

In a complex appraisal it may be necessary to identify sub areas within the main area. In the maintenance example above it may be appropriate to appraise the number of people who have experience, their qualification, their availability and their location in relationship to the sites where the equipment is to be maintained. In using sub areas there is a trade-off between getting to the bottom of the supplier's capability and the time and complexity introduced.

6 Weight sub areas/Set scoring mechanism

Each of the sub areas is weighted within the main area and then the scoring mechanism is determined. Scoring mechanisms must be designed to be as objective and consistent as possible.

7 The questionnaire

Having reached this stage of the process the multidisciplinary team should have a complete understanding of the requirement being purchased and what is important about that requirement to the purchasing organisation. This last point cannot be underestimated; many purchasing organisations rush into appraisals without doing all of the background work which is necessary to make the process successful. Asking suppliers to complete a questionnaire is a useful way of understanding important aspects of a supplier's business before a visit to the site. Good questionnaires are notoriously difficult to construct. Figure 9.2 identifies seven steps in the process of developing a questionnaire and they are discussed below:

1 Agree clear objectives. Be sure you know what you want the questionnaire to deliver.
2 Design the questionnaire from a standard template, change it to make it relevant to the requirement and the priorities identified in previous steps – don't use one questionnaire for everything. Set evaluation criteria.
3 Prototype and amend. Ask someone in another department to complete the questionnaire with sample answers. Note their comments and amend the questionnaire.
4 Issue the questionnaire and handle supplier questions.
5 Receive and process responses.
6 Evaluate responses against the predetermined criteria.
7 Next, the steps. This includes communication to internal stakeholders, probably a review meeting of the multidisciplinary team and suppliers. It is vital that suppliers are thanked for their participation and kept fully informed.

8 Plan on-site appraisal

Given the priorities and the feedback from the questionnaire, now consider which:

- suppliers will receive an appraisal visit, assuming one is necessary
- suppliers will be dropped from the process at this stage
- members of our multidisciplinary team need to be involved in the visits
- areas of the supplier's operation we wish to investigate in more detail.

Communicate the decisions and requirements to the people you are in contact with at the suppliers. Arrange suitable times for the visits and as a minimum have a telephone conversation with the main contact at the supplier to talk the person through the appraisal you intend to make. Further detailed preparation for some members of the team may include cost analysis.

9 An on-site appraisal

The objectives of an on-site appraisal are to:

- gather information about the supplier, their people and their ability to meet our needs
- assess the supplier's specific capabilities in relation to our requirement
- understand potential problem areas in the processes and approaches of both organisations

- investigate opportunities for improvement and development
- enable comparisons between suppliers to be made
- learn
- develop performance measures with the supplier
- commence the process of building a relationship.

The first activity of the multidisciplinary team when they arrive at a supplier's site is to offer to meet the most senior person present at that time and express their thanks for the time the supplier is taking on the purchasing organisation's requirement and also take this person through the approach and process that will be used.

At the end of the visit a second appointment with the most senior person in the organisation is appropriate and again thanks must be expressed. An interim summary of the finding can then be discussed and a timetable given for a more formal report back to the people involved at the supplier must be presented.

10 Review, decide, feedback, next steps

It is vital to plan time for a feedback session with the multidisciplinary team as soon as possible on their return to the purchasing organisation. Scoring must then take place based upon the predetermined criteria and once all suppliers have been visited, a decision made and communicated to the suppliers. After a major appraisal a meeting with each supplier will be appropriate. The decision may lead to further discussions and negotiations with selected suppliers.

Self-assessment question 9.3

You are involved in a supplier appraisal project for your manufacturing organisation. You are going to appraise three suppliers within your country in their ability to supply turned metal components. Which areas of the business would you want to appraise and what would you want to see?

Feedback on page 179

9.4 The impact of internal suppliers on the supplier selection and appraisal process

Study session 2 discussed the role of internal suppliers and their relationships with the purchasing process and the purchasing team. In this section the impact of internal suppliers on the selection and appraisal process where other commercial suppliers are part of the selection process is discussed.

Learning activity 9.4

Put a supplier's hat on. Imagine that you are bidding for work from a customer who has an internal supplier or a division of their own

(continued on next page)

Learning activity 9.4 *(continued)*

organisation fully capable of doing this work. What reservations might you have?

Feedback on page 180

The presence of an internal supplier will by its very existence be a concern to other suppliers. There will be a suspicion that the purchasing organisation is only asking them to quote for this work for comparison purposes and that once the comparison is made, the internal organisation will be instructed to lower its cost to the internal customer. In this situation the external supplier will have undertaken the work to prepare the quotation with no chance of obtaining the work. Where suppliers suspect this to be the situation, they may refuse to bid or supply a bid and their trust of the person asking them to bid will fall like a stone.

To avoid these situations buyers must invest time in developing a relationship with a supplier likely to face this situation. This may involve meeting them and visiting them to convince them that the purchasing organisation's interest in them as suppliers is genuine. There is of course no better proof of this than awarding work to an external supplier and making sure that other external suppliers know that this has happened.

Where the suppliers are being used to 'test the market' then the purchasing organisation should be honest about this situation and even offer to pay a token amount for the work of the supplier.

The fear of cost and specialist technical information leaking via one part of a purchasing organisation to their internal supplier is a real one and more relevant to supplier appraisals than just an enquiry process. Will a supplier be keen to host an in-depth evaluation of their organisation by people who work for an organisation that has a division competing with them for other customers' work? In a competitive market a supplier would be most unlikely to entertain such a proposal.

Finally, a reversal of the supplier appraisal situation needs to be considered. How welcome will the purchasing team and their specialists be at an internal supplier being made to compete within the open market for business? Consider the pressures which may be brought to bear on the purchasing team to drop the whole process, favour the internal supplier or even pass information from the external suppliers to the internal supplier.

These situations are difficult to manage without clear policies and guidelines which can be communicated to all people in the process.

Self-assessment question 9.4

Your organisation has a division which develops software solutions. In this case the internal stakeholders have obtained management approval to ask external suppliers to offer solutions to the current business requirement

(continued on next page)

Self-assessment question 9.4 *(continued)*
in addition to the internal supplier. As the purchasing professional on the team, how would you communicate this to all suppliers?

Feedback on page 180

Revision question

Now try the revision question for this session on page 322.

Summary

In this study session we covered the following points:

- Supplier appraisal, vendor rating and supplier development are different and take place at different stages of the purchasing cycle.
- The extent to which supplier appraisal is carried out relies upon the purchasing organisation's view of the item within the supply positioning model.
- Supplier appraisal is a positive process.
- The objective of supplier appraisal is to understand whether suppliers can meet the needs of the purchasing organisation and what:
  - the total cost might be
  - benefits will accrue
  - the possibility of working together may be.
- Supplier appraisal is a process which forms part of the wider process involved in selecting suppliers.

Suggested further reading

Review the material in the relationship management and supplier development section of CIPS knowledge works on the CIPS website.

Feedback on learning activities and self-assessment questions

Feedback on learning activity 9.1

You should have noted that supplier appraisal involves asking suppliers questions, visiting suppliers and talking to their people and making an assessment of different suppliers' capabilities. It should involve a range of internal stakeholders who will use their expertise to assess the suppliers' capabilities.

Feedback on self-assessment question 9.1

- *Strategic Critical:* A major supplier appraisal would be appropriate because of the risk and the importance of the commodity to the business of the purchasing organisation.
- *Strategic Security:* Supplier appraisal is a means of identifying or qualifying new sources where monopolies are faced.

- *Tactical Profit:* In this quadrant no appraisal at all might take place due to the standard nature of the products and services, unless the value was extremely high and/or the risk was perceived to be almost enough to push the requirement into the Strategic Critical quadrant.
- *Tactical Acquisition:* Normally no appraisal, the cost of the activity might be more than the benefit incurred. However, if a closer tactical relationship is sought then an appraisal is appropriate.

Feedback on learning activity 9.2

The objectives would include understanding the ethos of the training organisation, their capabilities, their trainers and the experience of the trainers, and the results of their training. As people are the key to this service, it would be appropriate to see a training programme delivered, have samples of material and talk to the trainers to assess their enthusiasm.

Feedback on self-assessment question 9.2

1   *Faults in the objective.* The buyer is adversarial in their approach to a process which is not an adversarial process if undertaken properly. The focus is on price and not total cost of ownership.
2   *Where is the relationship going?* In a word, nowhere. Some suppliers do hide cost and the appraisal is one way of exposing that. However, it is in working together collaboratively that people identify and jointly exploit opportunities to reduce total cost, and price is, of course, a component of total cost.

Feedback on learning activity 9.3

It would be appropriate to meet:

- the owner of the company
- managers and supervisors
- cleaners
- customers at a site cleaned by the organisation
- human resources managers
- the health and safety at work manager.

Feedback on self-assessment question 9.3

It would be appropriate to plan to meet people from the following areas of each supplier.

- *Production:* to understand their production capabilities and capacities.
- *Quality:* to understand the quality processes they have in place and their normal success rates.
- *Operatives:* to assess the motivation and capability of production people.
- *HR:* to understand the way the workforce are treated and the staff turn over rates.
- *Purchasing:* to understand the relationships with the suppliers and their purchasing policies, including CSR.
- *Maintenance:* to understand their maintenance policies and processes.

9

- *Business systems:* to understand their business processes and their ability to engage with us in e-purchasing opportunities. Business systems would also include planning and finance.

Feedback on learning activity 9.4

It would be reasonable to have reservations about:

- cost information leaking to a potential competitor
- confidentiality of technical information
- only being used as a benchmark with no serious intent to place work with you.

Feedback on self-assessment question 9.4

Communication should include:

1   setting up a project team of internal stakeholders excluding the internal supplier
2   a meeting with key people from the internal supplier, including the key stakeholder
3   separate meetings with people from the external suppliers, including the same key internal stakeholder
4   communication of a process to all potential suppliers, including supplier appraisal if appropriate, indicating that the supplier selection decision will be made on merit
5   communication to all stakeholders and team members, and the internal supplier insisting that information will not pass either way between suppliers via the project team.

Evaluating the effectiveness of supplier appraisal

Introduction

Study session 9 defined supplier appraisal and distinguished it from other terms, considered its objectives and the process. All of this is fine, but as they would say in Yorkshire, 'where's the brass' from supplier appraisal? What will it buy me? In this study session we consider the deliverables from both points of view and the impact upon relationship development.

Session learning objectives

After completing this session you should be able to:

10.1 Analyse the deliverables of supplier appraisal for the purchasing organisation.

10.2 Consider a supplier's view of supplier appraisal.

10.3 Assess the impact of supplier appraisal upon relationship development.

Unit content coverage

This study session covers the following topics from the official CIPS unit content document.

Learning objective

2.3 Evaluate the effectiveness of the assessment process.

Timing

You should set aside about 4 hours to read and complete this session, including learning activities, self-assessment questions, the suggested further reading (if any) and the revision question.

10.1 Deliverables of supplier appraisal for the purchasing organisation

So where is the brass from supplier appraisal? Or is it a nice trip out of the office for buyers and others visiting suppliers' premises and being taken to lunch? There is the apocryphal story of the supplier who, upon being asked to participate in an appraisal of the sports centres that they ran by a local authority, offered three locations for possible appraisal, one in the next town, one in London and one in Bermuda. The local authority team selected the third of these locations as the most appropriate to their needs!

10

The process of supplier appraisal does deliver benefits and those benefits or deliverables can be measured in hard evidence, in feelings relating to current performance and in feelings about future performance possibilities. Some professionals will scoff at two of these deliverables being expressed in terms of 'feelings'. However, to say that some of the deliverables from the process are more than an 'indication' of likely performance is optimistic. This does not diminish the importance or the need for the supplier appraisal process where, for example, the purchasing organisation's 'expert' toolmaker reviews the processes and the equipment at a supplier against a structured set of criteria and arrives at an informed view that one supplier is more likely to make tools to manufacture our goods better than another supplier.

Assume that a multidisciplinary team assesses a new supplier which may manufacture metal components for the purchasing organisation. In some areas like finance and quality, factual evidence of the existing performance of the supplier can be obtained. However, this is performance of the company as it is and performance of the goods delivered to other organisations now and in the past. Whilst the performance in terms of quality is most likely to form a good indicator of how the supplier will perform on our parts once they commence manufacture, it remains a feeling, not a certainty. In terms of our future, which at this stage we may not yet have shared with the supplier, it is our feeling, based upon the evidence of the people and processes which we have evaluated, that the supplier will perform in a certain way which leads us to believe that they are the best of the ones we have appraised. Nothing is absolutely certain.

Learning activity 10.1

Take a supplier you use and consider which areas of their performance you could get hard evidence on and in which areas you might have to rely on feelings.

Feedback on page 190

Let's go on to consider the three areas identified:

- hard evidence
- feelings relating to current performance
- feelings relating to future performance possibilities.

Hard evidence

Hard statistical evidence of existing performance is the best indication that a supplier is likely to repeat that performance on the goods and services delivered to your purchasing organisation. The following areas are examples of where it should be possible to obtain hard evidence of a supplier's performance.

1   A supplier manufacturing components ought to be able to provide statistics of their ability to manufacture to the specification provided by their customers. This can be demonstrated through statistical process

control, defect rates and in measures like parts per million (PPM) failures .

2   A supplier providing computer hardware can provide statistics on the number of pieces of equipment that are dead on arrival (DOA) at customers' sites.

3   An outsourced service provider ought to be able to provide statistics relating to ongoing cost reduction at the sites of existing clients.

4   A consultancy specialising in purchasing ought to be able to provide examples of situations where, working with clients, they have saved money on purchases.

5   Suppliers ought to be able to provide statistics on their financial performance, including areas like turnover, profit, stock turn and return on capital employed. This information is in the public domain for public limited companies and purchasing organisations must analyse it and seek to understand trends. What may not be in the public domain is the statistics relating to a division of a Plc. This information may be appropriate to a supplier appraisal and may be requested, although a supplier may not be keen to disclose it.

6   Electronic technology allows couriers to provide accurate statistics on the time of arrival of their shipments and using RFID and satellite tracking technology they can demonstrate where a given package is at any time.

7   Stock availability and stock turn are measurable.

8   The use by a supplier of an EDI standard or the configuration of software used to interface with existing customers is a factual demonstration that they can interface with your organisation in the same way, if you use the appropriate protocols.

You may be able to think of other examples of actual performance relating to your own suppliers.

Feelings relating to current performance

The following areas are examples of where a reliable assessment of current performance can be made even though it is not possible to obtain hard evidence.

1   Suppliers of services, be it catering, cleaning, training or travel agency, can be assessed against a set of structured criteria essential to the purchasing organisation to understand whether they provide a suitable service to existing clients. Given that the criteria are relevant to the needs of the purchasing organisation and given that a suitable contractual arrangement can be arrived at, it is logical to assume that the supplier will perform similarly in serving our organisation.

2   During a supplier appraisal *people* from the purchasing organisation meet *people* from the supplier. As human beings we will feel that we can work with one group of people better than others and no matter how much emphasis we place on structured questionnaires and onsite evaluations, the human element will still be present.

3   Whilst within an organisation for a supplier appraisal it will be possible to understand the internal relationships of those who have a stake in the process of delivering goods and services to us and the way in which they are led by their management team.

10

4   In examining the purchasing processes and purchasing team of the supplier during an appraisal we will form a view of the relationships that the supplier has with their suppliers. Hard evidence may be available in some cases, but the understanding taken from conversations and answers to questions will allow the appraisers to form an opinion on the relationship strategy of the organisation. Remember that our organisation will depend upon those relationships.

5   The state of the equipment and the maintenance policy of a supplier will provide an indication of reliability in manufacturing and service organisations alike.

6   It is a fact that the supplier supplies other customers, some whom are prepared to comment favourably on them. Is it your feeling that the comments from the customers indicate that the supplier will perform well for you?

Feelings relating to future performance possibilities

During the initial supplier appraisal when, for example, two suppliers are being closely appraised, the purchasing organisation may not want to reveal much about its road map and future direction, in case it chooses not to work with this supplier. This may lead to questions which may seem strange to the supplier who asks clarification questions which the buyer is not keen to answer. This can spark a cycle of mistrust. However, the following areas are examples of where a reliable assessment of future performance possibilities can be made even though it is not possible to obtain hard evidence.

1   A supplier can be asked about their investment programme and past programmes used as a yardstick to understand future investment and its impact upon the business and even, for example when related to a specific machine, the possible future impact upon unit price.

2   Questions on the training and development of people, including succession planning, can allow a judgement to be made about a service supplier's ability to meet ongoing needs from a pool of individual providers.

3   The consideration of the attitude of the people in the supplier organisation is quite a subjective measure. Yet the feeling that some people will respond to a change and a challenge better than others can be an important part of a supplier appraisal where the purchasing organisation acknowledges that it will face those changes and challenges itself and seeks to work with people of a similar mind.

4   Suppliers may have a road map of where they expect their goods and services to develop in coming years. At an initial stage of the relationship this may only be available for the purchasing organisation at a high level. However, its existence is an indication of a developing organisation.

Self-assessment question 10.1

'Old Les' the purchasing manager, is very sceptical about the value of supplier appraisal. Argue a case to convince him that an appraisal of a

(continued on next page)

Self-assessment question 10.1 *(continued)*

potential supplier of catering services to your office complex of 240 people is worthwhile.

Feedback on page 190

10.2 A supplier's view of supplier appraisal

Do suppliers feel happy about being appraised? On the one hand it is an opportunity to gain additional business, but on the other hand some buyers use the process solely as a means to reduce suppliers' profits.

Learning activity 10.2

Imagine that you are a provider of IT maintenance and you receive a letter from a large and prestigious bank asking to come and undertake a three-day supplier appraisal with a team of four of their people. How would you feel? What would worry you?

Feedback on page 190

10

Factors conditioning a supplier's view of supplier appraisal

Much will depend upon the way that the buyer approaches the supplier. The supplier's view of the prospective appraisal can be coloured by:

*   their interest in winning the business
*   the information they are given on the whole supplier selection process
*   the information they are given on supplier appraisal process
*   their knowledge of the purchasing organisation and the people concerned
*   their experience of previous supplier appraisals
*   the time they are given to prepare for the appraisal
*   the timing of the appraisal visit
*   the buyer's reaction to a suggestion of an alternative time frame
*   the likely cost of the exercise to the supplier
*   what they feel about the likelihood of winning the business
*   the extent that they will have to share confidential information.

Let's examine each of these bullet points.

All too often buyers assume that suppliers are always keen to win the business they are offering. Consider the situations described in the market management matrix, where a buyer has a strategic critical item and the supplier views that customer as a nuisance. How keen will the supplier be to undertake a costly appraisal with the buyer? In this case excuses about being too busy to participate may be the supplier's response. However, where a supplier sees a buyer as a development customer, the answer might be, 'How soon do you want to come?'

Where suppliers are given a full picture of the whole supplier selection process at the start of the process, and are kept updated as the process goes on, then they will normally be keen to participate.

Adequate information prepared, delivered and discussed with the people at the supplier, preferably face to face before an appraisal, will bring a keener response that a buyer who arrives without making the supplier aware of their needs. Remember that one of the buyer's key functions during the appraisal process is to motivate the people working for the supplier.

Do the people at the supplier know and trust the people working for the purchasing organisation or do they know and mistrust them? Are they neutral? Their response to the buyer will be coloured by these views.

Is the experience of the given supplier of previous supplier appraisals that they have:

- spent a lot of time in the process and got nothing out of it?
- won a significant amount of business through the process?
- been offered business following an appraisal, but at a barely profitable level by a very demanding purchasing organisation?

Two of these circumstances will make the supplier suspicious and cautious, one will make them keen. Remember that the appraisals that make the supplier suspicious may not have involved your purchasing organisation.

A reasonable time must be allowed by the purchasing organisation for suppliers to prepare for the supplier appraisal and ensure that the people they want to be present to best promote their offerings are available.

Timing an appraisal of a distributor to supermarkets in mid-December would not be well received as this could be expected to be a busy time for them. Buyers need to factor this into their planning schedule.

Where the buyer's reaction to a suggestion of an alternative time frame is 'take it or leave it', a supplier may choose to leave it or to only provide minimum support to the process. This is not in the buyer's interests.

Never underestimate the cost of the exercise to the supplier. Consider how many people will be involved in preparation and during the visit. For a supplier taking an appraisal seriously it may not be unreasonable for them to spend double the actual time taken during the visit in preparation and review. Suppliers will consider this as a factor in their decision to participate.

Where suppliers feel they have a strong likelihood of winning the business they will be keener to participate. A feeling that they are there to 'make the numbers up' (to three?) will deliver a self-fulfilling prophecy!

Sharing confidential information is a risk and suppliers need to feel sure that they can trust buyers with this information; otherwise they may be less keen to participate. Buyers must, when appropriate, be prepared to sign a confidentiality agreement.

Supplier feelings after an appraisal

Once you, the buyer, have left their premises, the people involved from the supplier will normally sit down and appraise the appraisal from their point of view. Their questions will include the following.

- How do we think we did?
- Did we get a fair chance to sell ourselves?
- What could we have done better?
- How did the people from the purchasing organisation treat us?
- Do we want the business?
- Do we want to/can we work with them?
- Do we have a clear picture of what they want?
- What did we learn for negotiation at the next stage of the process?
- Do we want to continue to the next stage of the process?
- What can we do to improve for another appraisal?

Note that many of these questions are the mirror image of questions which you as the buyer have been asking about them as suppliers!

After the appraisal and particularly once they have received the feedback from the buyer, a supplier feels that an appraisal has gone well and is pleased with the process or they may feel discontented with the appraisal and the process. Where they feel discontented they may feel that:

- they received feedback which is wholly negative and condemning
- they have been taken advantage of
- they were there to make the numbers up
- the purchasing organisation is using the process to exploit their power
- the buyer was only after information to drive prices down
- they did not get a fair chance to display their talents
- the buyer was not prepared to listen
- they were not prepared
- they let themselves down by not giving the best picture of their people and their organisation
- they had the wrong people there.

Where a supplier feels that an appraisal has gone well they may feel that they:

- got a chance to know the potential customers as people
- understand how they can best meet the needs of this customer
- received feedback which amounts to free consultancy
- received feedback which will allow them to reduce cost and apply the knowledge to all customers and their requirements without necessarily passing on the reduced cost to customers
- learned things that they can use in negotiation with the customer
- were listened to.

Self-assessment question 10.2

As a supplier to a prestigious corporate customer who is being required to undertake a supplier appraisal, prepare a table with one column of

(continued on next page)

10

potential costs and risks and another column with potential opportunities and benefits of the exercise from your point of view.

Feedback on page 191

10.3 The impact of supplier appraisal upon relationship development

The supplier appraisal process may be part of a tactical selection process for standard components, yet it may be part of a more significant selection process where the purchasing organisation seeks a partner. In this latter case the process will be much more intensive and far reaching.

Learning activity 10.3

Refer back to the supply positioning model. Imagine that you are seeking to initiate two supplier relationships, one for the purchase of 200 desktop computers, which you see as high within the tactical profit quadrant, and one for an organisation with whom to develop the next generation of your software, which will be a strategic critical relationship. What would differentiate the supplier appraisal process?

Feedback on page 191

All supplier appraisals will impact the development of the relationship between the buying and selling organisations. Without repeating them, many of the factors discussed in section 10.2 will impact the growth and development of the relationship.

Where the macho buyer approach is used, meaning that the table is banged and the emphasis of the appraisal is upon what the buyer can extract from the seller, the resulting relationship will not become a close and trusting relationship. Equally, the same will be true where the potential seller refuses to divulge information to the buyer. In these circumstances the relationship may not start or, if it does start under these conditions, it may last for only a short time, satisfying no one. Using the analogy of a firework, this relationship may be one that is lit, but smokes for 30 seconds and then goes out, leaving the person wondering whether to go back and try again risking an explosion or simply throw sand on the firework and walk away.

Where both parties view each other with interest and are prepared to share information and invest time in opportunities they recognise in each other, then a closer developmental relationship will evolve. Using the analogy of a firework, this relationship may be one that once lit soars to the heavens and provides a beautiful display.

Whilst recognising that the view that the parties have of each other within the market management matrix will drive their objectives, buyers and sellers must always be professional. This means that macho buyer behaviour is not acceptable even when price is a key driver. It is necessary for both parties to realise that supplier appraisal is part of a process of going from a situation where the parties are competing to get the best deal for themselves, towards a collaborative situation where they will be working together. Thus, even allowing for 'price' as a key driver, the supplier appraisal process must not be used by buyers as a means of unfairly exercising power and driving the hardest possible deal with the supplier.

The old adage that 'a man reaps what he sows' (Galatians 6:7) applies here, for a supplier appraisal used to drive a weapon to savage a supplier will harvest a relationship with a supplier who will do the minimum that is necessary to meet their customer's needs, whereas a supplier appraisal used as a means of exploring and developing for the benefit of both parties will deliver a relationship in which both buyer and supplier work together for their mutual benefit. This is the preferred situation. In this paragraph use of the word 'partner' has so far been avoided for fear of causing confusion. It must not be thought that the closer developmental relationship described as a result of the preferred relationship situation is limited to what has previously been defined as 'partnership'. For whilst the relationship described is appropriate for a partnership within the strategic critical quadrant of supply positioning, it could equally be appropriate when:

- seeking a supply solution to a strategic security monopoly
- assisting a supplier to organise and take away the work we find we have with tactical acquisition commodities
- developing a closer tactical relationship
- looking to develop a relationship which will provide some protection against price fluctuations.

10

Self-assessment question 10.3

Assume that as part of a supplier appraisal process a supplier is identified who could develop the capability to be an alternative source for a component for which there is currently only one source. The supplier currently has a full order book and the initial research is promising. Present arguments that you would use to convince the supplier to develop a capability that will meet your needs. You might need to be inventive with your arguments.

Feedback on page 191

Revision question

Now try the revision question for this session on page 322.

Summary

The deliverables of the supplier appraisal process to the purchasing organisation are:

- information in the form of facts and a more detailed understanding of the suppliers concerned, their people, their leadership, their processes

and their overall ability to meet the needs of our business for the duration for which we seek a business relationship
* an understanding of the likely total cost to the purchasing organisation of the supplier delivering the goods and services it seeks
* a stable ongoing relationship with the supplier based on a full understanding of the needs of both parties.

Buyers must consider the cost and risk that suppliers feel they are exposed to during the process and keep the suppliers fully informed on the process.

The relationship will not develop to maturity if one party seeks to exploit the other.

Suggested further reading

Review the material in the relationship management and supplier development section of CIPS knowledge works on the CIPS website.

Feedback on learning activities and self-assessment questions

Feedback on learning activity 10.1

You should have found that statistics are available on the financial health of the organisation, stock turnover, staff turnover, production of goods and even the delivery of some services, but less quantifiable measures are available on services and areas which are considered to be subjective.

Feedback on self-assessment question 10.1

Typically, this type of appraisal could include the following benefits:

* Internal stakeholders would be able to taste the food.
* Our catering people can assess the hygiene in the kitchens.
* It's a difficult contentious area and worth investing the time in.
* How will we know what they do unless we go and see them?
* We will be able to see what other diners feel about their service and their food.
* We will be able to understand what the service we can expect is likely to be.
* We will get an opportunity to talk to the person managing the contract for the other customer and learn from them how the supplier performs.
* We will be able to see the type of staff employed by the supplier.

Feedback on learning activity 10.2

You should indicate that you were pleased at the opportunity to get the business and want to make the most of the opportunity to sell to the organisation concerned.

You should indicate that four people for three days is a major undertaking and a very detailed analysis. You may be concerned about exactly what they want to see, whom they want to meet and what information they may want you to reveal. You may also be concerned that the supplier appraisal exercise is a disguise for an attempt to reduce your ability to make a profit in any given situation.

Feedback on self-assessment question 10.2

Your answer should resemble that shown in table 10.1.

Table 10.1 Opportunities, benefits, costs and risks of a supplier appraisal from a supplier's point of view

Potential opportunities and benefits	Potential costs and risks
Learning about the customer and their requirement	Cost of time in preparation, during and after the visit
Learning things we can use with other customers	Risk of loss of confidential information
Free consultancy	Rearrangement of other things to meet the time schedule of the customer
A chance to sell ourselves	Opening ourselves to be exploited by the customer
Opportunity of business to win	Risk of being there to make up the numbers
Opportunity of motivating your staff	Risk of demotivating our staff
Benefit of adding client name to your client list	Opportunity cost of the time spent
Benefit of business once won	

Feedback on learning activity 10.3

Desktop PCs

Standard appraisal, with financials, delivery performance, cost, warranty and support post-implementation as criteria. Very much a financially driven appraisal.

Software developers

Searching financial appraisal focusing on ownership, stability and long-term viability. Focus on methodology, previous customers, and the people who will be writing the software and their experience and knowledge. The ethos of the organisation, and our ability to work together and spark ideas. Very much a touchy-feely appraisal once the financial stability is determined.

Feedback on self-assessment question 10.3

Arguments could include:

* the size of the business possible
* assistance in the development processes
* financial assistance
* long-term contract available
* the capability can be used with other customers
* business diversification would be a good thing for the supplier
* the prestige of working for the purchasing organisation
* business from other group companies
* other business as well as this.

10

Process constraints applied to public sector purchasing

Introduction

In the UK the public sector has always taken its purchasing responsibilities seriously, that is to say, people purchasing within the public sector have always taken the view that they have a duty of care to spend public money in a way which both provides value for money and demonstrates that value for money is provided. To this end the competitive tender as a route to select suppliers has and is the basis of the preferred method of selection, although other countries have not always been as strong in their practices. Within the EuropeanUnion (EU), procurement procedures have had a major impact since 1992 and were updated in a major way in January 2006. This study session describes and differentiates the EU processes and assesses the impact upon relationships between public sector purchasing organisations and their suppliers. This study session deals with the public sector legislation effective from January 2006 and neither its predecessors nor its successors. The extent of the processes, procedures and nuances of this area of purchasing would fill a study guide on their own. This study session aims to provide an adequate level of understanding of the processes to assess their impact upon purchasing and supply relationships.

11

Session learning objectives

After completing this session you should be able to:

11.1 Contrast the process steps necessary in the public sector with the steps 'necessary' in the private sector.
11.2 Summarise the routes available to public sector organisations.
11.3 Argue the case for and against the current legislation.

Unit content coverage

This study session covers the following topics from the official CIPS unit content document.

Learning objective

2.4 Evaluate the constraints on supplier selection within the public sector.

Resources

The Office of Government Commerce website at Office of Government Commerce: http://www.ogc.gov.uk.

Timing

You should set aside about 8 hours to read and complete this session, including learning activities, self-assessment questions, the suggested further reading (if any) and the revision question.

11.1 Public sector processes contrasted with private sector processes

This section contrasts the purchasing processes which must be used within the public sector against those typically used by private sector organisations.

Learning activity 11.1

What additional legal issues must you be aware of when considering the process of purchasing in the public sector?

Feedback on page 207

Differentiating public and private sectors

First, what is meant by 'public sector'?

- The EU procurement rules apply to public authorities including government departments, local authorities and NHS authorities and trusts (for clarity these organisations will be termed 'public sector' in this study session).
- The utility functions of utility companies, where these utilities are not subject to competition, are also included within the rules (for the sake of clarity these organisations will be called 'utilities' in this study session).

You need to understand that the rules vary for the public sector and utilities. However, for your examination preparation *concentrate on what is termed 'the public sector' above*. The rules set out detailed procedures for the award of contracts whose value equals or exceeds specific financial thresholds as described in table 11.4.

'Private sector' refers to all other organisations, whether they are limited companies, partnerships or sole traders. Charities are also considered to be within the private sector.

In many circumstances it is appropriate for the private sector organisations to compare the goods and services offered by several suppliers. However, there are no legal requirements insisting that they do so. In what might be considered bad practice in any organisation, the owner of a private sector organisation may choose to buy from a friend, trusting that they are getting a good deal. The logic here is that the owner of the organisation and the people to whom he delegates authority have the freedom to spend his or her own money as they wish.

In the public sector the logic is different. Public sector purchasing organisations are spending the money of individual and corporate taxpayers,

11

whether it is levied at local or national level. Hence, the purchasing organisation and the people working in it have a duty of care to purchase in a way which both provides value for money and demonstrates that value for money is provided. The process of supplier selection must therefore be transparent and allow all suppliers an equal opportunity to win the work on offer. In addition, European public procurement policy seeks to open up European cross-border trade and to use public procurement as an enabling mechanism.

Basic concepts of EU legislation

Simply put, the concepts of EU procurement legislation are that:

* There is a free market within the EU and that all suppliers will have an equal opportunity to bid for work which is competitively tendered.
* A minimum duration in days is specified for notices of public sector requirements and supplier tenders.
* There are thresholds below which procedures need not be followed although the principles of openness, transparency and fair treatment, upon which the rules are based, must still be followed.
* Where a requirement is above the threshold, following the procedures is mandatory. Within the UK the processes are enshrined in our laws through statutory instruments.
* Not following the procedures can mean that contracts can be set aside or damages awarded.

Contrasting similar purchasing situations

Table 11.1 gives examples of the way which public sector organisations are impacted by the EU rules are provided. Please note:

* each example applies to every public sector organisation
* each case assumes that the purchase is above the appropriate financial threshold.

In the right-hand column a comment on private sector practice is provided as a contrast.

Table 11.1 Public and private sector practices contrasted

	Public sector practice	Private sector practice
1	A supplier who has never provided their service to a local authority will be considered equally with those suppliers who are veterans of working with local authorities.	A purchasing organisation could exclude a supplier it did not *feel* had appropriate experience to deliver the services if it wanted to, or submit them to a more searching examination than other suppliers it knew well.
2	A supplier who has made an outstanding contribution to cost reduction at a government department during the past five years will be considered equally with all other suppliers, known and unknown, during the reselection process at the end of the five years.	In this case a purchasing organisation would probably simply seek to work more closely with the supplier and given the benefits described, not even consider going to the market.

(continued on next page)

Table 11.1 *(continued)*

	Public sector practice	Private sector practice
3	Where a contract between a supplier and a blood transfusion service has a particular duration, the contract cannot normally be extended just because the parties agree that it should be extended. However, contracts can be extended by up to 50% to cope with the unforeseen or alternatively the option to repeat a contract can be included in the original advert e.g. a three-year contract with the option to extend for a further two years In practice it is best to seek expert advice in these circumstances to ensure that the right path is selected.	If the purchasing organisation and the supplier agreed, they could simply extend the contract.
4	Where a public authority sees an opportunity to purchase a large amount of a commodity at an especially low price, but the commodity will be bought by another customer if the purchase is not made today, the public authority cannot make that purchase without going though processes and allowing other suppliers an opportunity to bid.	The purchasing organisation would dive into the market and secure the supply before someone else did.
5	A local council which runs a fleet of 130 buses. In its locality is a supplier of new buses. The council cannot deal with the local supplier and exclude other suppliers, even if the supplier is going through difficult times.	If there were advantages in using the local supplier the purchasing organisation would use them and not consider other suppliers.
6	Workload pressures have prevented staff at a railway company getting round to placing an order for new uniforms. The unions are pressing for urgent action and the year end is approaching. If the budget is not spent this year the money may not be available next year. The railway company must still follow the EU processes. A positive aspect of the public sector is that planning has to be very good for procurement to be done effectively. Also if mistakes are made in the procurement process, it is more difficult to rectify in the public sector than it is in the private sector.	The private sector organisation could, if it was appropriate, negotiate a solution with a supplier in a matter of a week This may not reflect good practice. However, there are no restrictions on the private sector organisation.

Relationship impacts

Self-assessment question 11.1 below asks you to consider the relationship impacts of the situations outlined in table 11.1. As you do this exercise consider the relationship spectrum described in study sessions 3 and 4 and ask this question, 'Is is possible for public sector organisations to have the relationships described at the collaborative end of the spectrum when they

11

must re-bid the work at the end of the contract?' Some buyers will argue that it is possible to have partnership and co-destiny relationships within the public sector. However, others will point to the definitions of these relationships and indicate that the ongoing nature of the relationship, as defined, means that it is prohibited by the legislation reflecting the EU procedures, which insist that the contract must be put out to competition at its end. Although it is rare, some public sector contracts have a 25-year duration and in that situation it ought to be possible for close developmental working relationships akin to a partnership to develop.

Where there may be a meeting of minds is in the approach used by the parties to the business on offer. With a public sector purchasing opportunity, both parties realise that there is no choice but to use competitive processes and the competitive process is not therefore a signal as it would be in the private sector, that the purchasing organisation sees a given purchase as tactical, whilst it sees other purchases as strategic. The use of the competitive process acknowledges a fact of life – it has to happen. In a given circumstance, where the services or goods being provided are vital to the public sector purchasing organisation, both parties can approach the opportunity realising the importance of the requirement and the importance of the relationship. This can lead to a close developmental relationship throughout the contract and deliver benefits for both parties. However, it must be said that the formality of the processes used by public sector purchasing organisations can appear very cold to suppliers.

Self-assessment question 11.1

11

Take each of the six situations identified in table 11.1 and assess the impact upon the relationship between the public sector purchasing organisation and the supplier. Complete your answers within table 11.2.

Table 11.2 Relationship impacts of EU procurement processes

	Public sector practice	Relationship impact
1	A supplier who has never provided their service to a local authority before	
2	A supplier who has made an outstanding contribution to cost reduction	
3	Extending the contract	
4	The large purchase at a low price	
5	A local council with a bus manufacturer in its area	
6	The late railway order	

Feedback on self-assessment question 11a

Table 11.3 Feedback on relationship impacts of EU procurement processes

	Public sector practice	Relationship impact
1	A supplier who has never provided their service to a local authority before	The supplier will realise that they have an equal opportunity compared with other suppliers who have supplied many times to this organisation. The buyer must consider all suppliers equally.

(continued on next page)

197

Self-assessment question 11.1 *(continued)*

	Public sector practice	Relationship impact
2	A supplier who has made an outstanding contribution to cost reduction	No matter how brilliant the supplier performs, at the end of the contract they know they will be considered equally with all other organisations seeking to offer services. Although accepting the situation, this may discourage the people working for the supplier and possibly cause them to give priority to other clients or not offer further cost-reduction ideas towards the end of the contract. Internal customers within the public sector may feel frustrated that a service being delivered really well must be opened up for competition.
3	Extending the contract	Contracts can be extended by up to 50% to cope with the unforeseen, or alternatively the option to repeat a contract can be included in the *original* advert, for example a three-year contract with the option to extend for a further two years.
4	The large purchase at a low price	In this case there is no relationship impact because the contract cannot be made. Normal processes must prevail.
5	A local council with a bus manufacturer in its area	No help or preferential treatment can be given to the local manufacturer. There may be tension originating from the fact that the manufacturer and their staff, who are all local taxpayers, believe that they should receive help from the council.
6	The late railway order	Suppliers may offer to 'help', but no relationship can start until the EU processes are complete.

11

11.2 Purchasing routes available to public sector organisations

Before 2006 there were three procedures available to public sector purchasing organisations. However, four procedures and four tools are now recognised.

Figure 11.1

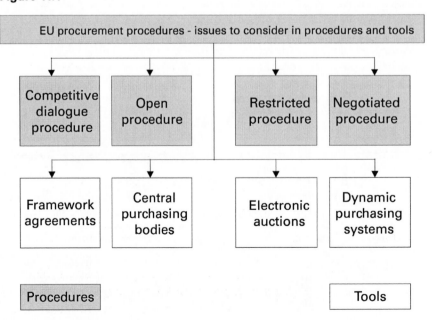

Please note: figure 11.1 portrays the issues which need to be considered graphically rather than using a bullet point format. It is not meant to demonstrate that there are eight procedures, there are only four procedures, three tools and the concept of central purchasing bodies.

Learning activity 11.2

Look at the OGC website (http://www.ogc.gov.uk) and download information to understand the processes and the support available to the public sector from the OGC.

Feedback on page 207

Basic concepts

Before each of the routes identified in figure 11.1 is considered, it is necessary to cover the following areas to understand the nature of the EU procurement directives and their impact upon purchasing and supply relationships:

- thresholds
- OJEU notices
- award criteria
- selection of tenderers.

Thresholds

Table 11.4 identifies the thresholds above which EU procurement procedures apply.

Table 11.4 Thresholds from 1 January 2006

	Supplies	Services	Works
Entities listed in schedule 1 of the Public Supply Contracts Regulations 1995 (Central Government)	£93,898	£93,898	£3,611,474
Other public sector contracting authorities (All other public bodies)	£144,459	£144,459	£3,611,474
Indicative notices	£513,166	£513,166	£3,611,474
Small lots	Not applicable	£54,738	£648,221

It will not be necessary to memorise these limits for the exam, simply to be aware of the implication of the limits on public sector organisations. Different thresholds exist for utilities. Organisations must follow these thresholds, which will be updated in the future. It is not permissible to avoid the threshold by creating two or more smaller requirements which fall under the thresholds when the total requirement is in fact above the threshold.

OJEU notices

One fundamental part of the process which ensures transparency is the requirement for public sector purchasing organisations to publish a notice of the goods, works and services they will purchase in a single location, the

Official Journal of the European Union (OJEU). In this way any supplier in any country within and beyond the EU is able to see the notice and bid for the work it contains. Practically, specialist organisations use the commodity codes included in the notice to alert subscribers to their service that the requirement is there to bid against. In this way an organisation in Greece may bid for the provision of street cleaning services in Antwerp. Notices must be placed within the journal for a minimum number of calendar days to allow potential suppliers to contact the purchasing organisation. For example:

- Where the open procedure is used, the 52 days is the minimum number, although this is reduced to 45 days if the process is fully electronic.
- Where the restricted procedure is used, the minimum time for requests to participate is 37 days, although this is reduced to 30 days if the process is fully electronic. This is followed by an additional 40 days for selected suppliers to complete tenders, although this may be reduced to 35 days if the process is fully electronic.
- Where a prior indicative notice (PIN) is used, timescales can be further reduced. A PIN indicates the contracts are being contemplated by a purchasing organisation during the course of the following financial year. It is not a notice of a requirement, but it serves to alert potential suppliers to forthcoming notices which may be of interest to them. Examples of how a PIN impacts the timescales are:
  - for the open procedure 52 days is reduced to 36 days, reduced further to 29 days if the process is fully electronic
  - for the restricted procedure the second stage of the process is normally reduced from 40 days to 36 days, although it can be as little as 22 days.

Award criteria

The directives state that contracts must continue to be awarded on the basis of lowest price or most economically advantageous tender, better known by the acronym MEAT. MEAT means that a supplier offering the service for a higher price is understood to have made a better overall offer in quality or total cost of ownership terms and may be selected on that basis. Where MEAT is used, the OJEU notice must provide both the selection criteria and the weight assigned to each criterion by the purchasing organisation and where this is not possible the award criteria must be stated in descending order of importance. MEAT may include environmental characteristics like energy saving or disposal costs. In this sense the purchase of electric light bulbs costing £1.50 each, but using less electricity per hour and having a longer projected life, could be considered *most economically advantageous* when compared with bulbs costing £0.50 using more electricity per hour and having a shorter life.

Disclosing this information is meant to provide suppliers with the best possible opportunity of meeting the purchasing organisation's needs.

Selection of tenderers

There are three relevant points here. First, a minimum of five bidders must be used for the restricted procedure and three for the negotiated and competitive dialogue procedures. Second, the minimum number of bidders must be stated and must be sufficient to promote genuine competition. And third, people found guilty of organised crime, corruption or fraud must be excluded from the bid list.

EU processes

The open procedure

The open procedure is a single-stage process where suppliers interested in supplying the public sector purchasing organisation must tender within the periods given within the legislation. This procedure can mean that a buyer might receive hundreds of tenders from suppliers. To avoid this outcome the restricted procedure is frequently used.

The restricted procedure

This procedure comprises a two-stage process whereby suppliers need to pre-qualify before being allowed to put their bid forward. The pre-qualification process allows buyers to set criteria for successful performance of the contract and evaluate potential suppliers' capabilities against these criteria without having to evaluate full tenders. In this case the buyer may request a large number of smaller pre-qualification documents from suppliers and then select a small number of suppliers to provide a larger tender document and present their offerings at a meeting.

The negotiated procedure

These notes only apply to the public sector; utilities have free access to the negotiated procedure. In most cases it is presumed that the open or restricted procedures will be adequate for the buyer's needs and that this procedure will only be used only in exceptional circumstances where:

- there is only one source of supply
- no suitable bids have been received in response to a previous notice using the open or restricted procedures
- an emergency occurs (this must not include situations where delays have been caused to normal processes and the requirement is now 'urgent')
- the purchasing organisation must replace goods on a partial basis, and they must integrate with goods which are already in use, for example an extension or upgrade to software where there is only one supplier of the software
- the detailed nature of the requirement is not known – here a notice is normally placed and suppliers pre-qualified before the negotiated procedure is used

The competitive dialogue procedure

The competitive dialogue procedure applies to what is termed as public sector only; utilities are normally free to negotiate. It was introduced in 2006 to complement the open, restricted and negotiated procedures. It is intended to be used for large, complex projects in circumstances where the procedure enables dialogue, meaning discussion and negotiation with

11

selected suppliers to define solutions to meet the business needs of the purchasing organisation. The steps in this process are:

1   A contract notice outlining broad requirements needs is published indicating that the competitive dialogue process is to be used. MEAT must be the evaluation criteria.
2   Several iterations of dialogue are conducted with suppliers and those unable to meet the need to provide value for money, as measured against the published aware criteria, can be dropped or can drop out.
3   When the dialogue is concluded the remaining suppliers are asked to provide tenders which are evaluated.
4   The contract is awarded.

Throughout the process all tenderers must be treated equally and in recognition of the efforts made by the suppliers, payment may be made to them during the competitive dialogue process.

This process would work well where software was required to perform a new requirement, but the detail of the requirement had not been developed. A local authority could therefore place a notice and develop a requirement with a small number of suppliers before asking them all to quote against the requirement developed. Note that the detail of each development with different suppliers could be different.

Tools used with EU procedures

Framework agreements

Framework agreements in the context of the EU directives are seen as agreements to agree. They set out terms applicable to contracts formed at a subsequent call-off stage and are used in the case of repetitive purchases to choose suppliers who, when the time comes, will be able to meet the purchaser's needs. The duration of framework agreements is limited to four years unless, exceptionally, a longer term can be justified. Framework agreements can be used in conjunction with any procedures, the contract notice must state the planned duration and the process can be summarised as follows.

1   A notice is placed using for example the restricted procedures indicating that a framework contract for the provision of specific goods and/or services is sought.
2   The restricted processes are followed and one or more suppliers are awarded a place within the framework contract, agreeing terms and conditions for supply *when supply is needed*. Note that the framework agreement does not 'order' any quantities of goods and services; it merely agrees the terms of their supply when required.
3   At a later date there is a need for specific requirements (a call-off) under the terms of the framework contract. The call-off may be:
1   awarded to the single supplier if there is only one supplier within the framework contract
2   awarded to the supplier who offers best value for money based upon the original framework selection criteria

11

3   the subject of a mini-competition related to the particular need at that time. All suppliers on the framework contract will be asked to participate.

Note that the call-off cannot substantially change the original framework agreement terms and that awards must be made on the basis of the criteria published for the framework award. Call-offs can extend beyond the life of the framework agreement, subject to a test of reasonableness.

Electronic auctions

Article 1(7) of the EU directive defines an electronic auction as:

> 'A repetitive process involving an electronic device for the presentation of new prices, revised downwards, and/or new values concerning certain elements of tenders, which occurs after an initial full evaluation of the tenders, enabling them to be ranked using automatic evaluation methods.'

Use of this electronic purchasing tool within the public sector is encouraged for goods, services and works subject to the following guidelines:

- Electronic auctions may only be used within the open or restricted procedures, framework agreements or dynamic purchasing systems.
- The contract notice must state that an electronic auction will be used.
- All aspects of the bid must be assessed at the initial evaluation stage.
- Only price and quality elements which can be expressed as a value suitable for incorporation within a formula can be used in the auction stage.
- Auctions are discouraged for the supply of intellectual services.

Process steps can be summarised as follows.

1   Tenders are invited in accordance with one of the procedures and a full initial evaluation is made.
2   Successful tenderers are invited simultaneously by electronic means to participate in the auction. Connection details and date and time of the auction must be stated, the auction cannot start sooner than two working days after transmission of the invitation and the invitation must state the number of phases and timetable.
3   If adopting most economically advantageous selection criteria, the invitation to participate must be accompanied by a full initial evaluation of the tender and the mathematical formula to be used in the auction to determine automatic re-rankings. Separate formulae must be provided for variants where these are permitted.
4   Invitations must state the information to be provided to suppliers during the auction and when this will be available (electronically); relevant information about the auction process; conditions of bidding and particularly, minimum differences required for a new bid.
5   During each phase of the auction, sufficient information to enable suppliers to understand their relative ranking within the auction must be communicated instantaneously. The number of participants in

11

a phase may be announced at any time but the identity of suppliers cannot be revealed at any time during the course of the auction.

Dynamic purchasing systems

Article 1(6) of the directive defines a dynamic purchasing system (DPS) as:

'A completely electronic process for making commonly used purchases, the characteristics of which, as generally available on the market, meet the requirements of the contracting authority, which is limited in duration and open throughout its validity to any economic operator which satisfies the selection criteria and has submitted an indicative tender that complies with the specification.'

In essence this option is an electronic framework agreement where indicative bids are made by suppliers to enter the agreement and subsequent call-offs are subject to a competitive tender in each case. Indicative bids can be made at any time, not just in response to the advert for the DPS. The process is as follows.

1   The open procedure *must* be used and an OJEU notice placed.
2   Suppliers may at any time register indicative bids for the product or service. The bids must be assessed within 15 days and the supplier informed as to whether they are admitted to the system. Note that at this stage there is no specific requirement for supply and the buyer may therefore have a multitude of indicative bids from suppliers latent, but filed in their system.
3   When a specific requirement arises a further simplified notice is published against which any supplier (not just suppliers already within the system) has 15 days to respond with an indicative bid.
4   Evaluate the new indicative bids from suppliers.
5   Invite final bids from all suppliers now within the system and award against the original criteria, which may be amended slightly by the call-off notice.

Central purchasing bodies

Central purchasing bodies (CPBs) already exist, they are organisations like Eastern Shires Purchasing Organisation and the Central Buying Consortium who are consortia, aggregating the spend of smaller public sector organisations and providing a purchasing service. Search the internet using http://www.espo.org. Since 2006 the provisions in the EU directives have reflected UK practice in this area, although there are no special or different processes for use by these organisations alone. There are, however, two important points to note:

1   Purchases may be managed through a CPB and organisations using the CPB are deemed to have complied with the directive in so far as the CPB has complied with them.
2   The CPB must be a contracting authority for this provision to apply. Public sector purchasing organisations are free to buy through private sector bodies acting as agents, however, in this case the public sector body is still responsible for ensuring compliance with legislation.

11

Self-assessment question 11.2

Attempt the following ten questions.

1 What is a PIN?
2 The restricted procedure means that buyers can avoid using suppliers they don't like. True or false?
3 I can organise an electronic auction for low-value low-risk goods within a week. True or false?
4 Describe a dynamic purchasing system.
5 The open procedure means I have to take the tenders of everyone and evaluate them, even if there are 255. True or false?
6 What does CPB stand for?
7 When might electronic auctions be used?
8 If the whole notice and tender process is carried out electronically, how many days may the timescale normally be reduced by?
9 Define MEAT. Provide an example of it.
10 If a local authority buys through a purchasing consortium can they pass the responsibility of complying with the EU procedures to the consortium?

Feedback on page 207

11.3 The case for and against the current legislation

To an extent the case for and against the current legislation is academic – if you work within in the public sector, you and your organisation must follow it. This brief subsection aims to consider present both the benefits and the costs of the legislation as it impacts public sector purchasing organisations.

Learning activity 11.3

Assume that you have moved from a job as a buyer in the NHS and you now work for an independent engineering company. Consider how not having to follow the EU legislation would impact your processes and relationships internally and externally.

Feedback on page 208

Benefits of the EU procurement legislation

The following are the benefits of the legislation:

1 Transparency means that it is possible to see where money is spent and to whom contracts are awarded. The principle of transparency is to make the process and the opportunities transparent to suppliers.
2 The time taken and the thorough processes ensure that supplier selection is made against predetermined and (hopefully) well thought out criteria.

11

3   The fact that the requirement is advertised means that the all suppliers who are interested have an opportunity to bid.

4   The current procedures mean that several different routes are available for buyers.

5   Suppliers who keep themselves informed will be able to understand when they will be called upon to bid and will be able to marshal their best resources to their offer. There are no surprises.

6   Public sector organisations who plan ahead and organise themselves can avoid last-minute panics

7   Suppliers are given every opportunity to understand the full nature of the requirement against which they are bidding.

8   The processes provide checks and balances which should eliminate personal, corporate or national preferences and ensure a free market within the European Union.

9   The processes are ethical and are starting to take account of environmental issues in setting evaluation criteria.

10   The processes promote ethical relationships.

The following are the costs of the legislation:

1   Without the procedures the time taken to place a requirement with a supplier in given circumstances could be shorter.

2   The fact that the requirement must be re-bid at the end of the contract may in some circumstances prevent buyers and sellers forming close developmental relationships that could benefit both parties.

3   Following the procedures could cost more in terms of human and systems resources than would otherwise be the case.

4   The inability to create a long-term relationship and the presence of relatively large amounts of business encourages some suppliers to view their sales to public sector organisations as *exploitable* within the supplier preferencing matrix.

5   The inability of the public sector buyer (this does not apply to utilities) to negotiate with just one or two sellers after having received tenders, or to be able to simply start by negotiating with a single preferred supplier means that in a number of cases public sector organisations pay more for a given requirement than they otherwise would do.

6   The cost and time required to make a bid to a public sector organisation may prevent some suppliers from bidding, particularly SMEs.

7   The ability of sellers to gain business from existing customers where a re-bid is not necessary may mean that those sellers apply their scarce resources to those customers and not public sector customers.

8   Limited flexibility for the public sector.

Self-assessment question 11.3

Assume that you do not work in the public sector. Consider how having to adhere to the EU legislation would impact your processes and relationships internally and externally.

Feedback on page 208

Revision question

Now try the revision question for this session on page 322.

Summary

EU procurement processes are a fact of life; they are enshrined in our laws and regulate purchasing activity and purchasing and supply relationships within the public sector across the whole of the European union. Key points include:

- the use of several different processes based upon competitive tendering
- there are thresholds above which the procedures apply
- notice provided to suppliers of forthcoming requirements
- transparency of the processes
- insistence that all suppliers must be considered
- time taken by the process
- ability of courts to set contract aside or award damages if they believe that the procedures have not been followed.

Suggested further reading

You could look at the following website:

- The Office of Government Commerce website http://www.ogc.gov.uk.

Feedback on learning activities and self-assessment questions

Feedback on learning activity 11.1

You should be aware that there is legislation governing public sector purchasing processes that, when triggered by financial thresholds, requires public bodies to:

- notify the supply market within the European Union that they have a requirement
- allow a specified number of days for suppliers to respond to the requirement
- treat all suppliers equally
- use only mandated processes.

Feedback on learning activity 11.2

You should have found a large set of overheads and PDF documents describing the procedures as they apply from January 2006.

Feedback on self-assessment question 11.2

1   A PIN is a prior indicative notice, it is used to reduce timescales by indicating the contracts are being contemplated by a purchasing organisation during the course of the following financial year. Unlike the Contract Notice, it is not mandatory.

11

2 False. The restricted procedure allows all suppliers to flag their interest in a buyer's requirement. However, it uses predetermined criteria to select the suppliers who appear to have the best opportunity of meeting the buyer's needs.

3 True if the requirement falls below the appropriate threshold, but false if it is above the threshold.

4 An electronic framework agreement where indicative bids are made by suppliers to enter the agreement and subsequent call offs are subject to a competitive tender in each case.

5 True.

6 Central purchasing body. A consortium purchasing on behalf of smaller public bodies.

7 Electronic auctions may be used within the open or restricted procedures, framework agreements or dynamic purchasing systems.

8 Seven working days for electronic notices and five days for electronic tenders.

9 Most economically advantageous tender. The purchase of electric light bulbs costing £1.50 each, but using less electricity per hour and having a longer projected life could be considered *most economically advantageous* when compared with bulbs costing £0.50 using more electricity per hour and having a shorter life.

10 Whilst the consortium or CPB may manage the purchasing processes, organisations using the CPB are deemed to have complied with the directive in so far as the CPB has complied with them. If the CPB has not complied with the procedures appropriately, the local authority will be liable with other authorities using the CPB.

Feedback on learning activity 11.3

Not having to follow the EU legislation would mean that:

- the time taken in any purchasing process could be reduced as notices would not have to be placed
- internal customers being able to initiate the purchasing element of their project later than would be the case within the NHS
- it would not be necessary to inform suppliers of the award criteria and their relative importance
- selection could be made from a small range of suppliers without needing to be seen to include everyone
- long-term ongoing relationships could be developed without re-bidding work.

Feedback on self-assessment question 11.3

Having to follow the EU legislation would mean that:

- much more time will be taken by a given purchase
- internal customers will be required to initiate the purchasing element of their projects much earlier than they would within the private sector
- it will be necessary to plan ahead much more to ensure that notices are placed in time to allow the selection process to take place, enabling the requirement to be available for use when internal customers need it

11

- it will be necessary to think through the evaluation criteria before the notice is issued (whilst this is best practice in all circumstances, it is suggested that buyers may be tempted to leave this 'chore' until tenders are received unless they must do it earlier)
- long-term relationships may be restricted.
- thinking ahead will be important if you want to place a PIN.

11

11

Reciprocal trading

Introduction

Reciprocal trading can be a great opportunity or can lead buyers to despair as it restricts their opportunities. This study session defines reciprocal trading, analyses its role within purchasing organisations and highlights possible alternative courses of action used by purchasing and supply practitioners.

We buy from them, they buy from us, but who benefits most?

Session learning objectives

After completing this session you should be able to:

12.1 Define what is meant by reciprocal trading.
12.2 State which purchasing processes are impacted by reciprocal trading.
12.3 Propose a policy for reciprocal trading.

Unit content coverage

This study session covers the following topics from the official CIPS unit content document.

Learning objective

2.5 Analyse the role of reciprocal trading in purchasing relationships.

Timing

You should set aside about 4 hours to read and complete this session, including learning activities, self-assessment questions, the suggested further reading (if any) and the revision question.

12.1 What is reciprocal trading?

Reciprocal trading is a business situation where two organisations both buy from and sell to each other.

An example of a reciprocal trading situation would be where a high street bank provides a banking service to a vehicle leasing company and in addition leases its fleet of company cars and delivery vehicles from the same company. (NB: This situation is considered to be largely a private sector phenomenon.)

12

The CIPS position on reciprocal trading is set out in the *CIPS Positions on Practice* document on ethical business practices, where the following statement appears:

'Reciprocal trading (countertrade) which makes a customer of an organisation a condition for being a supplier, is generally unacceptable business practice. In essence CIPS believes reciprocal trading to be only acceptable when:
- there is no coercion
- both parties are in agreement and
- there is mutual benefit and transparency.'

The CIPS position, put in a few words, is therefore that reciprocal trading is acceptable provided that there is no coercion and everyone benefits.

'Countertrade' mentioned above is where payment is made wholly or partially in goods and services rather than money. In terms of reciprocal trading it may arise when an organisation wants to sell electrical goods to a developing country which has no cash, but for example tonnes of coffee beans. The organisation wanting to *sell* is therefore persuaded that the sale is *only* possible if they take the coffee beans in exchange and the negotiation is therefore about how many tonnes of coffee beans equal a container of DVD players.

Learning activity 12.1

Consider situations like this within your own organisation. Talk to colleagues, ask them if they know of situations and how they work in practice.

Feedback on page 217

12.2 Purchasing processes impacted by reciprocal trading

Primarily it is the supplier selection processes that are impacted by reciprocal trading; processes like approaching the market, selection of terms and conditions, enquiry and quotation processes, negotiation and award of contract. However, other processes like expediting and payment may also be impacted. At this stage of the session it is deliberate that no comment is being made about the impact that reciprocal trading has on the purchasing organisation. Let us develop the situation described in section 12.1 as an early learning activity in the session.

Learning activity 12.2

Let's assume that the bank has a three-year contract for its vehicles with Megalease and that there are nine months remaining in the contract. With options to purchase as well as to lease, the bank's purchasing team consider

(continued on next page)

The following questions must be addressed by the organisation, not just the purchasing team:

- What benefits does the situation bring to the purchasing organisation?
- Should the purchasing organisation not be 'free' to select suppliers on merit?
- Is there any form of coercion being used internally or externally to attempt to insist that purchases are made in a given way, from a given organisation or at certain pricing levels?
- What is the greater good to the purchasing organisation?

Bringing benefits

Where the reciprocal trading relationship brings new technology, favourable delivery times or lower costs, then there is no question of the relationship itself being questioned. However, where these benefits are not present and, even worse, the relationship appears to be delivering only additional cost or risk of non-supply, it has to be questioned.

Free choice

The argument against reciprocal trading can be put like this: 'What is a purchasing team if it cannot select and negotiate the best deal for the organisation it represents?' The answer offered by those who promote this line of argument is, 'Nothing'. Some people feel that all other considerations are invalid if they interfere with a free selection process. This may miss the $64,000 question and be a little short-sighted. But as a principle, selection on total cost of ownership or most economically advantageous tender (MEAT) has much merit.

Coercion

Where a form of coercion is being used internally or externally to attempt to insist that purchases are made in a given way, from a given organisation or at certain pricing levels, it is most probable that a purchasing organisation

12

making this purchase from the given supplier under this type of pressure is not getting the best deal if the purchase is considered on its own. It may be that internal customers, possibly in a sales role, are attempting to clinch a major deal with the customer and the customer (supplier) indicates to the sales team that it would be helpful if the:

- forthcoming purchase which may be made from them by the seller's organisation could be 'assured', brought forward or 'netted off' the sales amount to them
- selling organisation could sell additional items to the purchasing organisation
- recent order pattern, which had shown a surprising decline, could find an upward trend.

Alternatively, discounts from the sales organisation to the purchasing organisation might mysteriously be 'under threat', lead times might extend or key service deliverers might be attracted to other customers. Reading this text the word 'blackmail' might just possibly occur to you and you would be right.

Pressure can come to the purchasing team via the other internal stakeholders within the purchasing organisation, for example technical specialists, or directly from the sales organisation in the form of a potential delivery problem or a new, higher, price proposal for items bought by the purchasing team. The circumstance will be presented as a totally separate issue or a coincidence, yet it will be linked.

The greater good

This is the $64,000 question. It is necessary for all parties within the purchasing organisation to calculate what is the greatest good for their organisation. Here are three situations:

1   Imagine the services being purchased by the purchasing organisation cost £10,000 per year and the goods being sold to the sales organisation by the purchasing organisation amount to £100,000 per year, on which £25,000 net margin is made. Here there is no contest and the purchasing team need to understand and accept the position, which may well be that a tactical acquisition item is, to suit the greater interest of their organisation, moving up into the strategic security quadrant with a supplier who will in effect become a monopoly supplier.

2   Imagine the situation if the services cost £40,000, which is £10,000 above other suppliers, the sales revenue is £100,000 and the margin £25,000. Here the purchasing organisation is bearing an additional £10,000 on its purchases to gain £25,000 and the net benefit is only £15,000. These figures ignore the prestige that the purchasing organisation may incur from selling to the sales organisation and other factors which the board of the purchasing organisation may consider worth the £10,000 reduction and again the purchasing team may have to accept the situation.

In this situation if the maths, once calculated, indicate that the additional sales margin is substantially less than the additional cost, a different view may be taken.

3   Finally, consider the situation where a sales organisation proposed to cease delivery of services to the purchasing organisation if a guarantee of a 'significant reduction' in a sales price of goods currently on offer to them is not made. Here it is probable that the most appropriate course of action is to call the supplier's bluff.

These examples bring to light the need to consider the situation at a higher level within the business, for neither sales nor purchasing will want to give way and wisdom may be required to accept a higher purchasing cost or lose sales revenue. The role of the purchasing professional in this case is to present a business case, assessing both cost and risk from both income and expenditure sides and allow a senior person within the organisation to make a decision based upon fact. In saying this, the customer might be so attractive that the decision is 'grin and bear it!'

Self-assessment question 12.1

Identify a checklist of points for consideration against a reciprocal trading proposal.

Feedback on page 217

12.3 A policy for reciprocal trading

In this section we consider the matter of a policy on reciprocal trading.

Learning activity 12.3

Review your own organisation's policy on reciprocal trading. If you work within the public sector and reciprocal trading is not an issue you have met before, then talk to trusted suppliers, explain that as part of your course of study you have to consider this issue. Ask what their experience of the subject is.

Finally, search the internet using 'reciprocal+trading'. There are a number of marketplaces and sites advocating reciprocal trading.

Feedback on page 218

Different organisations have different views on reciprocal trading. Some purchasing organisations will not entertain it at all, whilst others will attempt to make an assessment of their own best interests. The key issues are:

1   Retaining freedom of choice of supplier depending upon the technical and commercial evaluation of the offer being made by a supplier.
2   Assessing the greatest good of the organisation in any one situation.

12

As seen earlier, this may involve calculation and a high-level decision. A policy statement could look like this:

> 'This organisation will only participate in reciprocal trading where there is an absence of coercion and where reciprocal trading reflects the overall best interest of <insert organisation name> and its customers.'

This statement recognises the need to protect the purchasing organisation's interest and limits the use of reciprocal trading to those circumstances. Buyers also have an escape route if they feel they are being coerced.

Examples of policy statements

1 This is the policy statement of an organisation operating in Asia. It stresses that reciprocal trading is not policy, but then leaves the door open for it if all else is equal:
   'It is not corporate policy to indulge in reciprocal trading. The need for cost-effective procurement requires that best value for money is achieved, including the choice of best supplier in every case. All other things being equal, giving preference to suppliers who are customers can in some cases be beneficial to the corporation in protecting and developing relationships. Choice of supplier must always be made on a strictly commercial basis.'

2 The author is grateful to Steve Heywood, the Head of Purchasing AB Mauri, part of the Allied Bakeries group, for this example. It is interesting because, as a large manufacturer and provider of food and drink products, it actively promotes reciprocal trading. However, the caveat is that it also insists that there is a check on all such arrangements:
   'Reciprocal agreements
   Purchasing will encourage suppliers to use ABF's products exclusively. Where there is a potential benefit to the Company in a reciprocal agreement, any such agreement shall be first cleared by the Company's Legal Department to ensure there is no contravention of law as it relates to anti-competitive practices.'

Self-assessment question 12.2

Argue the case for and against reciprocal trading.

Feedback on page 218

Revision question

Now try the revision question for this session on page 322.

Summary

Where reciprocal trading is of benefit to a purchasing organisation and there is an absence of coercion, then it should be used as a legitimate purchasing technique.

Suggested further reading

Review the material in the relationship management and supplier development section of CIPS knowledge works on the CIPS website.

Feedback on learning activities and self-assessment questions

Feedback on learning activity 12.1

If you have situations like this you may find that purchasing colleagues feel uncomfortable about them, or feel pressured about them.

Feedback on learning activity 12.2

Options include:

- Mind your own business.
- Don't interfere.
- We make purchasing decisions on merit, not due to supplier pressure.
- We make purchasing decisions on merit, not due to bank manager pressure.
- Of course we'll do all we can to give Megalease the business.
- We'll do a full cost benefit analysis and if Megalease come out on top then they will get the job.
- Our purchasing policy means that we do not indulge in reciprocal trading.

Some of the above are too aggressive, others are too submissive.

Feedback on self-assessment question 12.1

The appropriate points are split into three groups, one focusing on sales, one focusing on purchasing and one on other considerations. Points should include the following.

Sales considerations:

- Sales volume and revenue from all areas of the supplier/customer to our business.
- Sales margin from all areas of the supplier/customer to our business; ability to replace the supplier/customer as a customer if the sales business is lost.
- Attractiveness of the supplier/customer as a customer to our business.

Purchasing considerations:

- Cost being borne by our business purchasing from the supplier/ customer because of the reciprocal trading arrangement.
- Alternative purchases.
- Alternative sources.
- Cost of the goods and services from alternative sources.
- Additional cost borne by our business purchasing from the supplier/ customer because of the reciprocal trading arrangement.

12

- Risks being borne by our business because of the purchase from the supplier/customer.

Other considerations:

- Our policy on reciprocal trading.
- Duration of the reciprocal trading situation.

Feedback on learning activity 12.3

Consider, from what you have heard and found, whether you believe that reciprocal trading is on balance a good or bad situation for your organisation.

Feedback on self-assessment question 12.2

The case for could include the following points:

- Builds a better relationship (if true).
- Reflects the greatest good of the organisation (if true).
- Delivers cost, quality or technical benefits (if true).

The case against could include the following points:

- May expose the purchasing organisation to extra cost.
- May expose the purchasing organisation to extra risk.
- May limit choice.
- May not reflect the greatest good of the organisation.
- May limit selection of alternative goods and services.

The risk and cost of changing supplier

Better the devil you know...

Introduction

Changing supplier involves cost and time. However, there is also the risk that the new supplier and the goods and services they provide will not meet our needs and even be worse than the previous supplier. To use another old adage, we could go from the frying pan into the fire. Frequently the term 'switching costs' is used to describe costs associated with these situations.

Session learning objectives

After completing this session you should be able to:

13.1 Identify the possible risks in a change of supplier.
13.2 Demonstrate what is meant by the cost of change.
13.3 Formulate strategies for reducing the exposure when changing supplier.

Unit content coverage

This study session covers the following topics from the official CIPS unit content document.

Learning objective

2.6 Analyse and explain how to mitigate against the potential risks of a change of supply source.

Timing

You should set aside about 4 hours to read and complete this session, including learning activities, self-assessment questions, the suggested further reading (if any) and the revision question.

13.1 Identify the possible risks in a change of supplier

The risks involved in a change of supplier focus primarily on the worry that the new supplier and the goods and services they provide will not meet our needs and may even be worse than the previous supplier. One of the most humbling tasks any buyer will face is returning to a supplier and renegotiating a contract three months after informing them that they were losing the business to a competitor.

13

Learning activity 13.1

Take two of your suppliers and contrast the risk of changing them. First, consider the risk of changing a tactical acquisition supplier, and second, consider the risk of changing a strategic critical supplier.

Feedback on page 225

An analysis of the risks of changing supplier could include:

- *The core activity of the organisation being brought to a halt because the new supplier cannot deliver:*
    - at all
    - to an appropriate level of quality
    - to the right place
    - in a way which meets our needs.

    These risks are perhaps the greatest risks associated with a change for their ability to 'stop the job' makes considering them vital.
- *A failure of systems or procedures for part of the interface between the organisations:* Imagine a new internet security supplier sending updates to the software they had installed and the purchasing organisation's electronic gateway not allowing the supplier access.
- *The learning curve:* The new supplier collecting and delivering the internal mail may not be able to find some locations or may leave mail for one Mrs Barlow at the desk of another Mrs Barlow. This may not matter, but if one of these ladies is responsible for running accounts receivable, cheques might not be processed on time and the organisation's cash flow impacted. The learning curve may work both ways, however, if the purchasing organisation faxes information to the wrong fax number at the supplier's premises.
- *Relationship issues:* The previous supplier's canteen team were considered part of the furniture; they were known and liked. The new team must build relationships with the customers of the canteen. Equally, a supplier of components may read a drawing in a certain way and make components 'incorrectly', because they are unaware of informal agreements made between the purchasing organisation's production team and the previous supplier.
- *Cost:* The new supplier may not, despite promises to the contrary, be able to meet the lower costs they had promised.
- *Total cost of ownership:* Here again the new arrangement may in some way not over time reflect the forecast situation.

Several of these examples are things which should not happen given adequate standards, processes and relationships. However, it is the element of change and the involvement of human beings which generate occurrences which would not previously have occurred, given the history of the relationship and the fact that custom and practice had ironed out the problems.

Finally here, whilst the impact of the risk upon the organisation is greater for a strategic critical contract than a tactical acquisition one, the likelihood of a problem occurring is not necessarily reduced and the embarrassment caused to those responsible can frequently be considerable when things go wrong.

Self-assessment question 13.1

Assume that you are responsible for the change of stationery supplier in your organisation. Like the old supplier, the new one will provide an electronic catalogue for staff to use to order goods and deliver the items to the desk of the people concerned. What risks might be associated with this change?

Feedback on page 225

13.2 Demonstrate what is meant by the cost of change

Getting down to specifics, what will the change cost us?

Learning activity 13.2

Take the change of a canteen service from one supplier to another. Identify areas of cost.

Feedback on page 225

13

Purchasing process costs

It can be argued that as a function and a team, purchasing is there to purchase. However, the cost of a full competitive exercise, whether tendering is used or not, will take much more purchasing and stakeholder time than a simple renewal of contract with an incumbent supplier. In saying this, it is recognised that this is not an option within the public sector, unless the extension was in the contract from the start. In a situation where resources are tight and there are a more purchasing projects than resources, a decision can be taken in conjunction with internal customers to renew a contract with one supplier rather than re-bid it and apply the resources of the purchasing team to other more critical situations. It can be argued that this may not represent best purchasing practice; however, the overriding issue may be the allocation of scarce resources within the organisation.

Phasing in/phasing out

These costs are primarily borne by the internal customers with the closest interface with the supplier and although purchasing are involved it is more in a supportive role. Nevertheless, a change of supplier will be one of the most important events of the year to some internal customers and specific costs can involve:

- inventories of stock, tools and equipment
- finishing batches ordered
- handling remaining and subsequent rejects
- detailed handover of ongoing projects
- changing systems and interfaces
- meeting and making new relationships, finishing old relationships professionally.

One HR manager, in the middle of a change of payroll service provider was heard to say, 'All this to do and my real job too!' These costs may not be obvious to everyone, yet they are real and busy internal customers with a full workload often incur them.

Transaction costs

At the lowest level there may be a new supplier record to create, but there may be new bank accounts to set up, there may be an access code and a desktop interface to create for hundreds of employees. If a supplier is servicing each of 50 locations from their local centres then there may be a large number of transaction addresses to set up and test during changeover and a similar number to remove.

Learning curve costs

A supplier replenishing vending machines at a large site may need to be shown around and may need to understand the detail of the different demand patterns. This again will probably fall to the internal customer to complete. Previous comments made about drawings and delivery locations also apply here.

13

Self-assessment question 13.2

Take the main headings given for cost in this subsection and identify specific areas of switching cost relating to a contract for the supply of computers and peripherals to be delivered via a web-based catalogue.

Feedback on page 225

13.3 Reducing the exposure when changing supplier

This subsection deals with formulating strategies for reducing exposure when changing supplier. The first action is to fully understand the circumstances of the existing contract and relationship.

Learning activity 13.3

Consider this situation, based upon real events. Monday was the first day of the new canteen contract and the purchasing manager was involved in a

(continued on next page)

Learning activity 13.3 *(continued)*

training programme. At 10 am he was summoned by the HR manager who had the manager from the new supplier with her. The new supplier wanted to know where the kitchen utensils were. Subsequently it was discovered that three years ago as part of a renegotiation the previous catering supplier had replaced all of the kitchen utensils at their cost. Obviously they had taken them with them on the previous Friday. The HR manager, the purchasing manager and the new supplier then drove together to a well-known high street shop and bought almost all of the utensils the shop had in stock.

How could this have been prevented?

Feedback on page 226

Prudent purchasing staff will set triggers within their systems to alert them to contract renewal well before the event. Understanding where the requirement sits within supply positioning is vital to the contract, the relationship and the processes for renewal. Discussions then need to take place with stakeholders about alternative courses of action and one of the considerations must be the switching cost and risk.

Some electronic reverse auction software will allow purchasing organisations to weight this element into the equation and where a change of supplier is a possibility a total cost of ownership matrix could include this as an option. Refer to study session 5 to review electronic reverse auctions.

The message here is similar to the risk identification and risk management methodology described in section 3.3, for it is necessary to identify the probable risks and costs of switching supplier before strategies can be put in place to reduce our exposure to them.

Ideally, a purchasing organisation should seek to deflect switching costs and risks to suppliers. However, this may not always be possible and sharing them may be the next best option, whereupon the purchasing organisation would budget for them, as it would if it had to bear them. Finally there is the option of setting aside a contingency and in all circumstances there is the issue of communication to consider.

Deflecting to suppliers

One basic contract clause that is often forgotten by buyers is one where the supplier agrees to help the purchasing organisation and the new supplier in circumstances of contract termination. Some buyers make these clauses specific, even including retention monies as part of the clause with the aim of reasonably committing the first supplier to assist in a transition from their role in serving us to that of the alternative supplier.

Where the new supplier is concerned, deflection of risk can focus on the key deliverables of the contract and be reflected in key performance indicators (KPIs). It is not unreasonable to construct, negotiate and agree a small set of KPIs to reflect the transition period as well as the main body of the contract.

In terms of cost, the purchasing organisation can invite the supplier to prepare separate costs for the transition or request that the terms of the

13

contract include the supplier bearing the switching costs. One note of caution here. A prudent supplier may include the switching costs in the ongoing contract rate and it may be that the imprudent buyer pays those costs several times over during the life of the contract!

Sharing and bearing costs

Sharing costs, if they can be identified, is an appropriate option in some cases. However, where the cost reflects assets or intellectual property there must be a clear contractual understanding as to future ownership. For example, is the supplier contributing to the cost of our kitchen tools or are we contributing to the cost of their tools used in our canteen? It is also worth bearing in mind that 'cost' does not necessarily mean that the purchasing organisation 'pays' in monetary terms. Valuable consideration can include services and therefore as part of the changeover our contribution could include the resources of our staff or our equipment to reduce the cost incurred by the supplier. Part of the negotiation can be to draw the supplier's attention to the areas and value of the costs which we are bearing as part of this transfer of supplier.

Contingency

Without wishing to overuse the word 'prudent', it is appropriate for purchasing organisations to set aside funds or plan the availability of human and other resources to be available during the changeover time. One example could be organising stocktaking at a weekend when suppliers were involved in a changeover. This would mean that if needed several pairs of hands were on-site, but if not needed they were usefully employed in the stores.

Communication

Often spoken of as an issue and yet often ignored, communication is a vital strategy here. It must involve stakeholders, both suppliers and the purchasing team. Ideally all parties to the existing contract should brief the new supplier on performance and in particular the nuances and peculiarities of the requirement, as it works out in practice. However, it may not always be possible to involve the incumbent supplier, but at least the team from the purchasing organisation should have such a discussion.

Self-assessment question 13.3

Who would you involve in briefing sessions for a supplier taking over a contract to refill vending machines at a hospital?

Feedback on page 226

Revision question

Now try the revision question for this session on page 322.

Summary

Switching costs and the risks that are associated with the activity of changing suppliers are a fundamental part of purchasing activity.

Risks arise from a number of different sources including purchasing process costs, phasing out costs, phasing in costs, transaction costs and learning-curve costs.

Buyers must identify costs and risks and seek to deflect them to the supplier, negotiate arrangements to share them and make appropriate contingencies.

Feedback on learning activities and self-assessment questions

Feedback on learning activity 13.1

The risks in changing the tactical acquisition supplier should be much smaller than the risks of changing the strategic critical supplier; in fact, the suggestion of such a change will send a shudder down the body of some internal customers.

Feedback on self-assessment question 13.1

Typical risks may include:

- non-arrival of goods
- delivery to the wrong location
- charging to the wrong cost centre
- access to the catalogue not available to all authorised users
- users still ordering from the catalogue of the old supplier which has not been removed from their desktop.

Feedback on learning activity 13.2

Costs could include purchasing process costs, phasing out costs, phasing in costs, transaction costs, learning curve costs.

Feedback on self-assessment question 13.2

Table 13.1

Cost	Examples
Purchasing process costs	Supplier selection, tendering, visits, testing sample equipment. Time attending presentations and meetings. Communication to user community.
Phasing out	Warranty on previous equipment, will the new supplier handle this? Removal of desktop links to supplier's site. Changeover or disposal of any stock specifically held for our organisation.
Phasing in	Creating links to new site, approvals and user IDs. Upskilling internal IT resource or contracted help desk supplier on the new equipment. Introducing key supplier representatives to their opposite numbers.
Transaction costs	Updating files and records at both sites. Cost centres linked to users, uploading elements of the catalogue to the purchasing organisation's website.

(continued on next page)

13

Table 13.1 *(continued)*

Cost	Examples
Learning curve costs	Supplier's staff understanding the preferences and standards put in place by IT, understanding site locations and any priority users within the organisation

Feedback on learning activity 13.3

This situation could have been prevented by updating the contract records and either including a requirement to provide the kitchen tools in the new requirement specification or buying them back from the incumbent supplier.

Feedback on self-assessment question 13.3

Your answer could include:

- the catering manager
- the contract manager
- representatives from staff using the machines
- representatives from staff using the machines frequently working night shifts
- members of the public who sit on the customer panel
- health and safety representatives
- trade union representatives
- the purchasing manager
- the quality manager.

The process of outsourcing

Introduction

Outsourcing is one reason why the importance of purchasing and its processes has grown over the last 20 years. A pie chart of an organisation's total spend would previously have shown much greater amounts of spend being allocated to people and capital within the organisation. Now a number of the areas have been outsourced, this spend has been moved to suppliers and should be controlled within purchasing processes.

Outsourcing is not a quick fix to a badly managed process or function. There is absolutely no reason to believe someone else will be able to sort out a problem that the organisation has failed to manage.

Session learning objectives

After completing this session you should be able to:

14.1 Distinguish between service contracts, outsourcing and subcontracting.
14.2 Determine why organisations are outsourcing and the benefits they seek.
14.3 Determine what organisations typically outsource.
14.4 Explain a process for outsourcing, taking into account the needs of the purchasing organisation's business.
14.5 Explain how recent UK legislation and case law impacts the process of outsourcing.
14.6 State reasons why some organisations are 'insourcing'.

Unit content coverage

This study session covers the following topics from the official CIPS unit content document.

Learning objective

3.1 Develop and apply procedures for undertaking an outsourcing exercise and maintaining effective outsourced relationships.

Timing

You should set aside about 6 hours to read and complete this session, including learning activities, self-assessment questions, the suggested further reading (if any) and the revision question.

14.1 Service contracts, subcontracting and outsourcing

The terms 'service contract', 'subcontracting' and 'outsourcing' are different. Let's define them.

14

A **service contract** is a legally binding contract for the supply of services by a seller to a buyer for a defined period of time.

An example might be the supply of office cleaning services to an organisation.

Subcontracting occurs when one organisation requests another organisation to undertake work which it may be capable of doing itself, on its behalf, within a short-term timescale.

One example might be when an engineering organisation is busy and offloads work to other similar organisations. When it is less busy it chooses not to offload the work. A second example is where an organisation uses the specialist skills of a second organisation to complete part of the larger task which they have undertaken to complete for their customer. For example, an event management organisation may subcontract the provision of staging and audio/visual requirements to a specialist organisation.

Outsourcing is the retention of responsibility for the delivery of services by an organisation, but the devolution of the day-to-day performance of those services to an external organisation, under a contract with agreed standards, costs and conditions. An example could be where a purchasing organisation devolves the responsibility of running its vehicle fleet or its information technology services to a specialist supplier.

Insourcing is the process of changing from an outsourced service to delivery of the service using the internal resources of the purchasing organisation. An example could be the decision to run and manage the vehicle fleet using internal resources at the end of an outsourcing contract.

Learning activity 14.1

Search the internet using the keyword 'outsource'. At this stage do this to gain an understanding of the range of services offered by providers of outsourcing services.

Feedback on page 239

What makes outsourcing different?

A number of factors distinguish outsourcing from service contracts and subcontracting. These include the:

- duration of the contract – outsourcing contracts are long-term, service and subcontracting contracts will vary from instant through short term and up to several years
- autonomy of the supplier to perform their tasks, which is high in the case of outsourcing and lower in other cases

- transfer of responsibilities from an internal department currently performing the service within the purchasing organisation to a supplier in outsourcing but not in other cases
- transfer of employees from the purchasing organisation to the supplier in outsourcing but not in other cases
- payment for services delivered is made to a supplier rather than employees in outsourcing – in-service contracts and subcontracting suppliers are still paid, but they are not paid instead of employees
- difficulty with which outsourced arrangements can be insourced at a later date – with subcontracting and service contracts the work may be changed with much less difficulty
- relationship with the supplier – with outsourcing the relationship will be closer than it would typically be with subcontractors or service providers.

Self-assessment question 14.1

Take the definition of outsourcing given above and unpack it into five key points.

Feedback on page 240

14.2 Why do organisations outsource?

Is it fashion, is it a trend or is it a hard-headed decision that attracts an organisation to outsource?

Learning activity 14.2

Carefully consider these points. Are they appropriate reasons to outsource a service?

- The managing director has heard that outsourcing is a good idea.
- It's a mess! Let someone else sort it out.
- No one really understands what goes on in IT.
- The competition have done it.
- It sounds like a good idea.
- It fits in with the new 'leaner' structure.
- The supplier can save us money – on current costs.

Feedback on page 240

Valid criteria for outsourcing

The following criteria are valid ones when making a decision to outsource. In saying this, they are valid when in a combination *appropriate to the business in question*, they form part of a rigorous business case which covers all of the costs and benefits of the proposition to outsource.

1   The supplier can save us money, over and above the best we can do. Organisations have outsourced because suppliers have offered cost savings and the area of improving cost within the existing business model has been forgotten. Improving the current situation should be the first task, followed by a challenge to the supplier to improve on that. Cost benefits accruing from suppliers here should include:
    (a) economies of scale from their greater purchasing power and preferred supplier arrangements in the area
    (b) more efficient and productive use of people and other resources from their greater experience and greater volume.

2   The area is not our core business. Determining the core business and focusing on that, whilst using the specialism of other organisations to perform non-core activities is key to business success. An organisation may therefore say, 'We run trains and not computers. Let's outsource the IT function to a specialist.' Once the non-core activities are outsourced, management time will be free to focus on core activities.

3   Improving return on net assets (RONA). RONA is a measure of how a business utilises its assets to make money by comparing sales with assets. If the assets are sold to an outsourcing supplier the organisation:
    (a) has less assets but the same sales turnover – as a percentage the turnover will therefore be higher
    (b) has to make less provision to replace the assets through depreciation
    (c) will have a single inflow of cash.

4   The high pace of technical change may mean that the purchasing organisation will prefer to use a specialist supplier to manage this as a service for them. It will mean that the specialists within the supplier will be able to better develop the resources to meet the changing needs of the business and in doing so, reduce the buyer's exposure.

5   We need a better service. Here the supplier may be more experienced at providing this service than the existing resources, may have the necessary accreditations and may be able to use their greater volume and diversity to cope better with peaks and troughs. The supplier may simply have the expertise when internally we are amateurs.

6   The supplier may be able to provide a 'one stop shop' consistently across all of the sites of the organisation.

7   It may not be possible for our organisation to obtain the skills necessary to run that area of our business effectively.

Self-assessment question 14.2

Consider why a bank outsourced the management of its fleet of company cars.

Feedback on page 240

14.3 What do organisations outsource?

Organisations outsource different parts of their business.

Learning activity 14.3

Consider your organisation. Talk to colleagues in purchasing and other functions to get their views on the activities that your organisation currently outsources, could outsource or would not outsource.

Feedback on page 240

The first consideration here is to identify the core activities of the organisation and then consider what else could be outsourced if it is felt that a business case can be made for such a decision. A core activity can be described in a number of ways. It may be regarded as the essence of the business, the critical activity, the reason for the business's existence or the source of competitive advantage. Activities which fall into these categories must not be outsourced. However, the dividing line may form a debate within the organisation. For example, an insurance company may see their software as a source of competitive advantage and retain development in house. However, the management of the data centre running the software could be outsourced.

Typical non-core activities outsourced by organisations are: catering, security, IT, site maintenance, internal post and mail services, travel, stationery, vehicles and freight. Other organisations have outsourced legal, HR, finance and purchasing.

Study session 18 considers the issue of tiering, where suppliers are grouped together and one supplier is asked to manage several other suppliers. Study session 3 considered the closer tactical relationship which is one means of achieving tiering. Many organisations have created an outsourced contract to cover the area of 'site services'. For example, for a government department with 200 buildings across the UK, this contract could aim to provide a consistently good service including office cleaning, catering, reception, vending machines, delivery and collection of internal and external mail, stationery, gardening, window cleaning and minor buildings maintenance. The outsourced supplier may be expected to employ the current staff in some cases and in others work with a number of local and national suppliers to deliver the services to the government department. In this case the government department will have one contract and one supplier, whereas the supplier may need to manage over 100 suppliers at the different locations and also interface with the government department's preferred suppliers in other cases.

Self-assessment question 14.3

Take the government department situation described above. Assume you were the buyer for the government department who has just appointed an outsourcing supplier with the core competency of buildings maintenance,

(continued on next page)

14

Self-assessment question 14.3 *(continued)*

but experience in managing the other areas. Consider where you would expect the outsourcing supplier to deliver the service for you using:

1   their own people
2   your national contracts
3   local suppliers
4   national suppliers.

To complete this task you will need to make assumptions about your contracts and the capabilities of the outsourcing supplier. There is therefore no wrong answer to this question; however, completing it will provide an understanding of the complexity of a major contract for outsourcing site services.

Feedback on page 241

14.4 A process for outsourcing

Many organisations have rushed into outsourcing and many of them have regretted it. Sometimes those who advocate processes which take time and cost money before making a decision are ridiculed as being over-cautious or trying to avoid taking a given route. In the case of outsourcing, the time invested in the early stages of the process will pay dividends during the life of the outsourcing contract.

Learning activity 14.4

Assume you were asked to consider the proposal to outsource one of the activities that your organisation currently performs in-house. Summarise the steps you would undertake to achieve this objective and review your proposed process with a colleague at work.

Feedback on page 241

A process for outsourcing must include the following steps:

1   strategic analysis
2   selection of target areas
3   specification of the requirement
4   supplier selection
5   implementation and review
6   ongoing relationship management.

1 Strategic analysis

This first step is the process identification of core activities and consequently non-core activities. This gets to the heart of the organisation and must involve key stakeholders and the board or management team, and even the owners of the organisation.

2 Selection of target areas

Once the core areas are identified and ring-fenced, areas of the business which form a target for outsourcing must be identified. Again, this must involve key stakeholders and the board or management team, and participants in this discussion need to understand the long-term nature of outsourcing and the consequences of decisions made. For each target area this process will involve:

- a supply positioning analysis, with particular emphasis on the risk
- an assessment of the extent to which problems in the target area can be corrected before outsourcing
- understanding whether a better return on investment can be obtained from retaining the area in-house or from outsourcers
- a clear understanding of the objectives of the outsourcing project, how they will be measured and who will be responsible for measuring them
- a clear plan of the project including stakeholder involvement and sign-off
- a clear statement of how and where this area interfaces with core processes
- considering other options like internal service level agreements, management buy-out or a joint venture
- considering the financial, tax and legal implications of all options against the status quo
- communication to members of the organisation impacted by the process.

An outline business case may be the vehicle which encompasses this information.

3 Specification of the requirement

The specification of the requirement must be based upon a full understanding of the current situation. Organisations have made mistakes by writing specifications which they *believe* reflect what happens in the area to be outsourced but not what actually does happen. This has led to them either paying for services not required or being invoiced for extras or contract variations by suppliers who have been asked to undertake tasks not in the original specification. The specification must:

- be clear and unambiguous
- include measurable performance criteria of the level of key performance indicators
- recognise any remaining problems and highlight them
- describe the relationship sought with the supplier
- reflect issues like confidentiality and security
- identify licensing issues and contract assignments necessary as part of the outsourcing contract where appropriate
- consider the terms and conditions of contract.

The specification must recognise that a supplier rather than a department will be performing the service and processes for change and development must be included.

14

Finally, there is the question of conflict of interest for the person drawing the specification. Where for example a vehicle fleet manager is to be transferred to the supplier with the team delivering the service, and the same person is asked to draw up the service specification, it would be possible to imagine circumstances when the specification may not be as demanding upon the supplier as it could reasonably be expected to be. Independent advice is needed here.

4 Supplier selection

Supplier selection must be rigorous and include a supplier appraisal, a tender process or alternatively a negotiation based upon the specification, due diligence concerning the supplier, and result in a business case which demonstrates clear benefit to the purchasing organisation before the outsourcing project goes ahead. Factors which need to be considered are:

- a supplier preferencing and market management matrix analysis
- whether the market will be interested in our requirement? (Normally the answer here is 'yes', but this cannot be taken for granted.)
- sharing any outstanding problem areas with potential suppliers
- assessing the cultural fit between the two organisations
- sharing sufficient information with the supplier to enable them to make their best offer to us – this may include the current costs of the area concerned and the variability of the requirement
- a site survey by the supplier and discussion with users and current deliverers of the service
- supplier relationships with their suppliers
- selection criteria not based simply on price – here the private sector could learn from the public sector's use of MEAT (most economically advantageous tender)
- discussion with the supplier over their normal performance measures
- appropriate terms and conditions, including the means of termination.

Remember that the outsourcing relationship will be a long-term one. In this context the searching and detailed examination is vital.

5 Implementation and review

Implementation of the contract may take a number of months and both parties must approach the process as one moving from the competitive process of selection to a cooperative process of working together. Communication internally is vital, particularly to people impacted by the change, and joint working parties need to be established with the supplier to discuss:

- contract management processes, including meetings, reporting and escalation processes.
- handover planning
- changes in working practices
- changes to procedures
- status of projects that will be live across the boundary of the outsourcing cut over
- linkages with other areas of the business and other suppliers

14

- processes for new employees of the supplier and also our employees who become employees of the supplier.

It is vital that communication channels remain open between the people managing the contract for the purchasing organisation and the supplier and employees on both sides who will be delivering the contact. At the end of the implementation phase it is appropriate for both parties to review the process they have been through and identify learning points for the future.

6 Ongoing relationship management

It is important to recognise we are now managing a supplier rather than a department. This is the subject of study session 15.

Self-assessment question 14.4

Identify five mistakes that you believe organisations may make by not following the process described in this study session when outsourcing, and their consequences.

Feedback on page 241

14.5 Recent UK legislation and case law impacts the process of outsourcing

The vital legislation here is the EU Acquired Rights Directives of 2001, which replaced the 1977 directive of the same name and is, within the UK, operated by the TUPE (Transfer of Undertakings (Protection of Employment) Regulations of 1981). At the time of writing, the 1981 TUPE regulations are being revised and it is understood that they will be issued in their revised form in 2006.

14

Learning activity 14.5

Download the document on TUPE within the knowledge insight part of CIPS knowledge works.

Feedback on page 241

Outsourcing agreements are often subject to this legislation, and it is therefore important that both parties to the agreement, that is, the purchasing organisation as the original employer and the supplier as the new employer, are clear as to exactly who is being transferred and who is not being transferred, and what their terms and conditions are.

Simply put, when outsourcing takes place and employees move between the two organisations, the regulations insist that they are transferred with at least the same terms and conditions of employment. It is as if their contracts of employment had been made with the supplier from the beginning and their length of service is counted as continuous from their original start date with the purchasing organisation. This means for example that:

- Cooks in a school cannot be offered a lower hourly rate by the outsourcing supplier than the local authority used to pay them.
- Engineers at a brewery who used to receive free samples of best bitter each week as a condition of employment must continue to receive them as employees of the site services employer. Here this benefit must be a 'contractual' entitlement, not just something given at the discretion of the management.
- An employee with six years' service with a purchasing organisation is considered to have seven years' continuous service after she has worked for one year as a programmer with the outsourced IT service provider.

This principle applies to all the terms and conditions of employment of public and private sector employees within the UK, except for occupational pensions, although the Pensions Act 2004 now provides some pension rights to employees affected by a TUPE transfer. It does not, however, apply to employees recruited after the outsourcing contract is in force and this is the cause of what has become known as the two tier workforce, where people sitting next to each other in an office may be paid different rates per hour or have different benefits packages. There is much more to the TUPE legislation than described in this section. However, the above is adequate to assess the impact upon purchasing and supply relationships.

The legislation also provides that where an employee objects to being transferred to the new owner, the transfer will have the effect of terminating the employee's contract of employment, but not in such a way that the employee can make a complaint of dismissal.

Case law

- *Lightways (Contractors) Ltd* v *W. Hood & Associated Holdings* [1998]: Street lighting maintenance had been contracted out by Strathclyde Council to Associated Holdings. Following local government reorganisation, the contract was put out to tender and a new contract awarded to Lightways. This involved no transfer of premises, stock or vehicles. Some, but not all, of the workforce previously employed on this work was transferred.
  It was held that TUPE applied because the previous contract had been run as an economic entity which was heavily dependent on the people it employed who were therefore an identifiable part of the losing contractor's business. When only a few key workers were transferred to the new supplier the appeal tribunal held that it was the essential nature of the roles of these people rather than their numeric significance that meant that TUPE applied to the whole workforce, who should also have been transferred.
- *Litster* v *Forth Dry Dock Engineering Co Ltd* [1989]: This case dating back to 1989 demonstrates that in the event of the dismissal of an employee by either the transferor (the purchasing organisation) or transferee (the supplier), either before or after a transfer, or where the dismissal arises out of said transfer, then the dismissal will automatically be regarded as unfair.

14

In this case employees were dismissed by a company going into receivership; very shortly (a matter of hours!) after this the business was sold to another company which then proceeded to recruit cheaper labour from elsewhere. The dismissals were held to be unfair with liability resting with the transferor (the logic of this argument was that technically the individuals concerned were not in employment immediately before the transfer). Obviously the transferor was in no financial position to offer compensation and it was decided by the court therefore that this liability should attach to the transferee.

The impact upon purchasing and supply relationships

Clearly a supplier considering and evaluating the cost of providing an outsourced service to a purchasing organisation must take account of the terms and conditions that the employees they are taking over are entitled to and factor that into their calculations, for they must reward the employees in exactly the same way and they cannot refuse to take the employees as part of the arrangement. Equally the purchasing organisation cannot make the employees redundant because their area of the business is being outsourced unless they wish to fully meet the costs of the likely settlement awarded by an employment tribunal to the employees concerned.

Circumstances could be envisaged where either the supplier withdraws from making a bid because the ongoing employee remuneration packages are too high or the purchasing organisation feels unable to accept the offer of supplier, because they reflect these costs back to the purchasing organisation in the contract offer. Circumstances could also be envisaged where service delivery is interrupted because of disputes arising from the two tier workforce situation.

Self-assessment question 14.5

Consider these questions.

1   An employee refuses to move to work with the supplier selected by his employer to provide security services. Can he claim unfair dismissal?
2   An employee of many years' service is on maternity leave when she is sent a letter dismissing her in the first week of the outsourced cleaning supplier's tenure of the contract. Can she claim unfair dismissal?
3   An IT outsourcing supplier informs their employees, recently transferred from the purchasing organisation, that they can no longer have their free meal in the canteen as they are not employees of the purchasing organisation. Is this within the TUPE legislation?

Feedback on page 241

14.6 Why are some organisations 'insourcing'?

Insourcing is the process of terminating an outsourcing contract and the delivery of the previously outsourced service to an organisation by employees rather than a supplier.

Writing in late 2005, the purchasing press, the IT press and even the national daily papers increasingly carried stories of large well-known corporate organisations who had decided to terminate outsourcing contracts with equally large well-known service providers, and re-establish groups of employees to provide the service to their business once again.

An article in *Computer Weekly* indicated that 'nearly two-thirds of firms have brought some form of outsourced service back in-house, according to consultants Deloitte'. The article goes on to indicate that whilst some analysts believe that the current insourcing trend is a fad, others believe that in the area of IT the volume of business being insourced makes the trend much more than a fad.

The basic reason why organisations choose to insource is that, for whatever reason, the given outsourcing agreement is not delivering the benefits it promised. Circumstances may include:

- poor specification of the requirement by the purchasing organisation
- poor terms and conditions of contract being negotiated by the purchasing organisation
- assumptions about cost reduction not being delivered by the supplier
- relationship breakdown
- inflexibility on the part of the supplier or the buyer
- disputes of what is and is not within the contract.

The *Computer Weekly* article also indicates that 80% of purchasing organisations attempt to renegotiate their outsourcing deal within its lifespan and 15% are renegotiated within the first 12 months.

Too much emphasis must not be placed on one article or one outsourcing area. In the same time period there are also articles concerning outsourcing successes. However, imagine a situation where for whatever reason your business finds itself in a situation where the promised savings from outsourcing are not being delivered, service appears to have deteriorated, there are constant arguments with the supplier and costs are rising. What would you do? The following steps are appropriate.

1   Review the circumstances against the contract.
2   Review the current situation openly with the supplier and attempt to understand the supplier's position.
3   Agree steps to improve matters with the supplier, even if this means renegotiating key elements of the contract. Review progress and changes.

14

4   If an acceptable resolution cannot be achieved then the purchasing organisation will need to invoke the termination clause in the contract.

Self-assessment question 14.6

In your first week as a purchasing manager within XYZ Plc, a private sector organisation, your managing director indicates that she is not satisfied with the current service provided by the logistics organisation to whom you outsource the running of your warehouse and customer delivery operation. Indicate the steps you would take to resolve the situation.

Feedback on page 242

Revision question

Now try the revision question for this session on page 322.

Summary

Outsourcing is a vital part of business life and the role of purchasing in the process of outsourcing is vital. Purchasing's role includes undertaking these tasks or ensuring others do them:

* ensuring a business case is made
* ensuring that the requirement is specified completely
* assessing all of the risks involved in the opportunity are understood within the purchasing organisation
* ensuring that all alternatives are considered
* understanding the real costs of the current operations
* calculating the payback realistically
* conducting the commercial process of the project
* setting up workable ongoing contract management arrangements
* ensuring that the organisation retains a way out.

Suggested further reading

Review the material in the relationship management and supplier development section and other sections of CIPS knowledge works on the CIPS website.

Feedback on learning activities and self-assessment questions

Feedback on learning activity 14.1

You should find many sites attracting you to venture into them and consider outsourcing services as wide ranging as transcription, recruitment, web design and telemarketing.

Feedback on self-assessment question 14.1

The definition can be unpacked to the following five key points:

1   The purchasing organisation is still responsible for the provision of the service undertaken on their behalf by the outsourcer, as it impacts their customers.
2   Outsourcing hands over the day-to-day running of the service and the people performing the service to the supplier.
3   A supplier is paid rather than employees.
4   A legally binding contract is vital.
5   The focus of the contract with the supplier is around improvements in cost, performance and delivery.

Feedback on learning activity 14.2

None of the reasons listed above are appropriate reasons to outsource, yet organisations have used them as part of a decision-making process to outsource. Consider the comments again.

- *The managing director has heard that outsourcing is a good idea.* We must make a decision on a business case using cold figures not impulses.
- *It's a mess! Let someone else sort it out.* Are we not managers? Should we not sort out our own mess?
- *No one really understands what goes on in IT.* Then we are negligent and if we outsource we do not know what we will be outsourcing.
- *The competition have done it.* Does that mean it is right for our business too?
- *It sounds like a good idea.* Lots of things sound like good ideas, but you cannot make a business case for them.
- *It fits in with the new 'leaner' structure.* Lean we may be or want to be, but that does not mean that we should outsource.
- *The supplier can save us money – on current costs.* Here we need to take the view that we will outsource if the supplier can do better than the best we can do.

Feedback on self-assessment question 14.2

A bank may outsource its fleet of company cars to:

- save money by using the supplier's purchasing volumes
- gain access to specialist fleet managers
- concentrate on its core business of providing a banking service to customers
- obtain a better service from specialists
- provide a professional service to its employees
- better interface with the supply market
- have a 'one stop shop' for all company car issues.

Feedback on learning activity 14.3

Typically, areas like catering, logistics, IT, security, site services, cleaning and maintenance may be outsourced. However, depending upon the nature of

14

your organisation, you might outsource other areas. There is no hard and fast list of functions to be outsourced.

Feedback on self-assessment question 14.3

Your answer might be:

- catering – national supplier
- delivery and collection of internal and external mail – own people
- gardening – local suppliers
- minor buildings maintenance – own people
- office cleaning – own people or national supplier
- reception – own people, local suppliers
- stationery – national supplier or government contract
- vending machines – national supplier
- window cleaning – local suppliers.

Feedback on learning activity 14.4

You should have included activities like a strategic analysis, the selection of areas as targets for outsourcing, specification of the requirement, supplier selection, implementation and review, ongoing relationship management.

Feedback on self-assessment question 14.4

1 Not planning, with the consequence that the process does not include all of the necessary steps.
2 Not taking the full extent of the existing operation into account, with the consequence that the supplier also does not have the full picture and is asked to perform extra duties which become contract variations.
3 Allowing the person moving to the supplier to draw up the specification without an independent assessment of the specification, with the consequence that the supplier is asked to perform to a lower standard than would normally be the case.
4 Not fully evaluating the supplier, with the consequence that they may not be fully able to meet our needs or that they, for example, use sources of supply that do not meet our CSR standards,
5 Not communicating to people impacted within the change, with the consequence that they worry, suffer stress and even start to perform less well than they are able.

Feedback on learning activity 14.5

The topic reference file will provide background to the legislation and more detailed information.

Feedback on self-assessment question 14.5

1 The employee cannot seek compensation for dismissal.
2 Yes, the employee can seek redress for unfair dismissal.
3 The employees are entitled to their meal now if they were entitled to it before.

14

Feedback on learning activity 14.6

The answer is that the organisations concerned are not getting the benefits that they expected and probably did not use a carefully structured approach taking all factors into account! In other cases the business model or the market may have changed.

Feedback on self-assessment question 14.6

Steps would include:

1 Ask the MD and other stakeholders for specific examples of what 'not satisfied' means in practice.
2 Review the performance statistics from the supplier.
3 Review the contract.
4 From these fact-finding exercises, attempt to understand whether XYZ has a genuine reason for feeling that performance is not what it should be. If this is not the case, discuss the situation with the MD and other stakeholders. If this is the case, prepare factual examples for the supplier and get the backing of the MD and other stakeholders.
5 Discuss the situation with the supplier and attempt a resolution, seeking performance as per contract and perhaps a little redress or a change to the contract.
6 Assuming this is successful, monitor the situation.
7 If action 5 or subsequent performance was not successful, commence a project internally to review the options which may include a change of supplier or insourcing.

Study session 15
Managing and maintaining an outsourced relationship

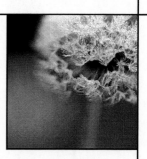

Introduction

As with any contract, buyers can breathe a sigh of relief when the contract is signed. However, those who think that the matter is now closed are mistaken. Ian Taylor, a former president of CIPS, is quoted as saying, 'Negotiation really starts when the contract is signed'. Whilst this may have been said tongue in cheek, there is some truth in it, for often it is only in implementation of the arrangements that we have negotiated with suppliers that both parties start to understand what they each actually meant and what the reality of working together will be like.

> 'Outsourcing is not an end result in itself. It is simply a tool that you are using to achieve organisational objectives.'
> **Michael Corbett, The Outsourcing Institute**

Session learning objectives

After completing this session you should be able to:

15.1 Evaluate the differences in relationship between an internal customer department and a service department to that internal customer before and after the service department is outsourced.
15.2 Contrast the objectives of the purchasing organisation and the outsourced service provider over the life of the contract.
15.3 Calculate the typical areas of cost and benefit of outsourcing.
15.4 Formulate performance measures to ensure delivery of promised benefits.
15.5 Compare 'outsourcing' relationships with other relationships within the relationship spectrum.
15.6 Evaluate the change in relationships between the people delivering and receiving a service when that service is outsourced.

Unit content coverage

This study session covers the following topics from the official CIPS unit content document.

Learning objective

3.2 Explain how performance should be managed in outsourcing exercises.
3.3 Evaluate the impact of outsourcing on relationships between customers and providers.

Timing

You should set aside about 6 hours to read and complete this session, including learning activities, self-assessment questions, the suggested further reading (if any) and the revision question.

15.1 Differences in relationship with outsourced departments

This section evaluates the differences in relationship between an internal customer department and a service department to that internal customer before and after the service department is outsourced.

Learning activity 15.1

Imagine that you are a senior manager within your organisation, you have been in the company for many years and you know and are known to everyone. You need a new report on the budgets and so you walk down to IT, where they offer you a coffee and you chat through your requirement with Sandra. Sandra agrees your requirements can be met given her current workload, says she will add it to her job list and it should be ready by the month end once the programs are tested. What are the benefits of this situation?

Feedback on page 253

Assume that the situation described in learning activity 15.1 above is a little more formal than the words used, assume that 'Sandra' manages her time professionally and the situation described may well reflect a private sector organisation where an internal team provide a service to internal customers and use their common sense to evaluate priorities.

Now assume that the department run by Sandra has been outsourced. Will it be possible to 'walk down to IT' and discuss the needs as informally? The answer is almost certainly no. The department will now be a supplier and their time will be monitored in a more searching way. The process set up in the outsourcing agreement might be like this.

1   The originator of the requirement drafts a requirement specification outline and emails it to the purchasing organisation's contract manager.
2   The contract manager reviews the outline, works out which of the variations or project types it fits within and forwards it to their main point of contact within the supplier's team. This may be Sandra.
3   Sandra evaluates the request, estimates a start date and agrees or disagrees which of the project types it fits within, as per the agreement.
4   When the outline is agreed and the costs estimated, a request to approve the change will be forwarded to the budget holder for approval. Here there may be a debate with the originator about the necessity and the cost.
5   Assuming the request is approved, the contract manager will then ask Sandra to make an appointment with the originator to assess the requirement in detail.
6   When the detailed assessment is complete a fully budgeted fixed cost may be provided and signed off.
7   Work will commence and the development will be successfully delivered.

To make the contrast come alive it has been an objective to paint a picture of two extremes and it is accepted that many professional in-house IT

15

teams have more formal procedures than the ones alluded to in the learning activity. The point is that when the people running a function within your organisation are your employees, you, as the owner or manager, can directly instruct them within the changing priorities of the business. When the people running a function within your business are not your employees, you, as the owner or manager of the business, must go through the agreed processes to ask them to meet your changing needs and pay at the agreed rate.

Finally, consider the supplier's view. Work undertaken informally may in the final analysis be considered 'unwanted' by the purchasing organisation's contract manager and will not be paid for. Work undertaken in one area of the business may impact delivery in another area of the business and may mean that a performance indicator is not met in that area, therefore reducing the payment to the supplier. It is therefore appropriate to respect the professionalism of suppliers delivering an outsourced service and agree reasonable and *workable* business processes with them.

Self-assessment question 15.1

Imagine that you are the site manager of an organisation and you have now outsourced the canteen. Consider how your communication to the people working in the canteen will be impacted if an employee survey reveals the need for a significant change in the menus, and contrast that with the situation before the canteen was outsourced.

Feedback on page 253

15.2 The objectives of the organisations over the life of the contract

This section contrasts the objectives of the purchasing organisation and the outsourced service provider over the life of the contract. It is assumed that the supplier is keen to win the business, though as supplier preferencing teaches us, this is not always the case.

Learning activity 15.2

Contrast the objectives of the supplier keen to get the business with those of the supplier who has just been informed that the purchasing organisation is terminating the agreement and bringing the function back in-house.

Feedback on page 254

If the life cycle of the contract is separated into five stages, it is possible to see how the buyer's and seller's objectives will differ in some cases and be in harmony in others. Each stage is analysed in table 15.1 and a private sector environment is assumed in this case.

1   Bidding and negotiation, through to reaching an agreement.
2   Transition and initial service performance.

15

3   Ongoing performance.
4   Approaching renewal.
5   Termination and handover.

Table 15.1 Buyer's and seller's objectives by contract stage

	Buyer's objectives	**Seller's objectives**
Bidding, negotiation, agreement	One clear objective here will be to minimise risk through a secure contract. Others will focus on meeting the business needs as expressed in the specification and will include service and value for money objectives as well as the basic need to reach agreement.	Two objectives are the same, minimising risk and reaching an agreement. Risk to the supplier might be around the shape of the agreement and the terms which may have to be accepted, but the basic risk of working with the organisation will be considered. Reaching an agreement means that business is secured, but this will not be accepted at any cost, for the consideration of revenue and likely margin to be made will also arise here.
Transition, initial performance	Here time, uninterrupted supply of service and people issues will be the focus for the buyer. Time in both the sense of urgency and achieving the agreed plan, uninterrupted supply in the sense that ideally no one should notice the changeover and people issues relating to the workers transferred to the supplier's employment will concern the buyer, who will feel responsible for them at this stage. Buyers will also be keen to see early benefits being delivered to confirm the wisdom of the approach selected.	Implementing the transition on time will also be an objective for the supplier and one where to some extent the supplier may 'throw money' at issues to meet the schedule and not start off by being late. Sellers will share the need for early success to prove their worth to the organisation and to do this they may select 'low hanging fruit' as a clear demonstration of their value. Factors like maximising economies of scale as soon as possible will also be clear objectives and potential areas of conflict. Identifying future economies of scale is also a key driver at this stage for suppliers.
Ongoing performance	Maximising the promised benefits in line with the stated objectives, delivered as hard and soft savings and/or improvements to services, will be key to the buyer at this, the longest of the stages. Review meetings, reportage and incentivisation mechanisms are ways of achieving this objective. Continuous improvement and benefits flowing from further improvements will also be an objective for the buyer.	Making and increasing target margin whilst keeping the internal customer stakeholders happy are key combined objectives for the supplier throughout this stage of the contract. The previously identified economies of scale can be driven through and shared with the customer insofar as the agreement calls for them to be shared. These objectives may therefore cause conflict with the customer, particularly where the benefits arising from the economies of scale are perceived as going in the supplier's direction or reducing service quality.
Approaching renewal	Here the buyer wants to learn from the experience of the selection process of last time and the	Suspicious buyers will say here that the incumbent supplier 'suddenly' proposes ideas for cost-saving solutions or

(continued on next page)

15

Table 15.1 *(continued)*

	Buyer's objectives	Seller's objectives
	experience of working with the supplier throughout the years of the agreement. In a perfect world, both sides should have been sharing ideas and improving together as time went on, but this may not be the case. A clear objective for the buyer upon renewal, which might include a market test, will be to raise the bar on the performance standards and the measures that they reflect. At this stage some buyers may grow a little colder to the supplier, which may not be entirely productive.	improvements and that buyer wonders why the ideas were not proposed before! In reality suppliers may realise that they need to provide a little extra to secure renewal. However, the relationship fostered by the buyer may have had something to do with why the ideas were not generated. Keen suppliers will point to future trends and improvements that their expertise will allow them to make, working with the buyer. Finally, whilst the objective will be renewal, there may be circumstances where the supplier feels that they have not been able to recover costs and these will need to be addressed.
Termination and handover	Once contractual issues are resolved with one or both suppliers, the buyer's objectives here return to those of the transition and initial performance phases, where uninterrupted supply, time and people issues are again important.	Once termination is formally confirmed, the seller's objective will be to exit professionally, at minimum cost and with minimum bad feelings or bad publicity. Imagine how the suppliers feel when the trade press print articles describing that a high street store has terminated their logistics contract.

It must be commented that the objective of the supplier to maximise the benefits to them from the identified economies of scale is entirely legitimate and that they cannot be expected to share those benefits with the customer further than the agreement calls for them to be shared. Suppliers are in business to make a profit and buyers who latterly realise that they have negotiated a deal which, with the benefit of hindsight, does not share enough of the benefits to them must learn from the lesson and renegotiate at an appropriate time. This is one reason why an outsourced relationship is considered to be less open than a partnership. A partner in similar circumstances would share benefits, even if they were unforeseen by both parties at the start of the agreement.

15

Self-assessment question 15.2

Consider the transition and initial performance stage of the contract and identify practical steps that you would take to achieve the objectives of on time implementation, uninterrupted supply of service and happy people.

Feedback on page 254

15.3 Typical areas of cost and benefit from outsourcing

Section 14.2 considered the reasons why organisations outsource. These reasons translate into benefits which should accrue to organisations from their decision to outsource, and this section will not therefore repeat the discussion of them.

Learning activity 15.3

Review the reasons why organisations outsource in section 14.2 and make a short list of them as benefits.

Feedback on page 254

The costs of outsourcing can take a number of forms and include:

- cost – literally the outsourced operation could cost more than the previous operation or more than its budget or target
- failure to supply – the service fundamental to the contract is not delivered
- transition or mobilisation costs – costs here can include changes to buildings or facilities to accommodate the new arrangements. Similar costs will be incurred if the function is insourced or there is a change of supplier
- changes to processes – these may be part of transition costs, but it has been known for suppliers to insist on changes to processes during the life of a contract
- loss of control – this must include control of the day-to-day operations, but it may include a loss of the control of the future direction of that function. However, this may not matter and the direction and foresight of the supplier in this area may in fact be one reason why we selected them
- contract management costs – the cost of people managing the contract. In many organisations this may simply be part and parcel of the work of one of the people in the purchasing team. However, one UK government department has a team of four people managing outsourced contracts in one area of its business
- loss of skills – the purchasing organisation may lose the skills to perform the functions outsourced. However, this again may part of the plan
- a lessened capacity to innovate – here the innovation may pass to the supplier's and the purchasing organisation become too dependent on them. If this is the case the question has to be asked, 'should this area have been outsourced?'
- hidden costs – costs that will not be apparent at the start of the contract and may even not be apparent during the contract unless there is an extensive audit. These costs can include the following *long* list:
  - ambiguous requirements, which cost money to clarify or put right
  - buyer's staff duplicating supplier duties
  - buyer's staff bypassing the agreed processes
  - buyer's staff undertaking supplier duties 'to help out'
  - changes to business operations necessary to suit supplier ways of working
  - differentiation of requirements previously standard to become specials

15

- loose definition of the contract requirement
- failure to identify full extent of existing service
- settling on fixed costs in a descending cost area
- locking into ageing technology with supplier
- over-specified requirements
- payment in advance when this is not absolutely necessary
- production of unused output, again probably because of an inaccurate specification
- paying again for items already bought, for example software licences.

It is worth noting how many of the hidden costs arise from a poor specification of the requirement.

Self-assessment question 15.3

Take five of the hidden costs identified in this section and, recognising them as potential risks, indicate how you would seek to avoid them during the life of the outsourcing contract.

Feedback on page 255

15.4 Performance measures in outsourcing

Performance measures are a vital aspect in outsourcing contracts, but they need to be considered carefully. In section 15.3, an example of a UK government department was given, where four people manage outsourced contracts. These four people manage 200 IT systems, each with its own performance measure!

Learning activity 15.4

Consider how you would measure a cleaning supplier to whom you had outsourced the cleaning of offices.

Feedback on page 255

15

The example within the learning activity 15.4 above has both hard and soft measures. Hard measures are measures which can be easily quantified by reference to metrics like time, cost and other factual evidence. Hence the time taken to complete the cleaning, the fact that bins are empty and the indexation of cost can be measured accurately. Soft measures are those that are more a matter of opinion and interpretation, and these aspects are frequently measured using questionnaires. Soft measures can in some cases be linked to cost as well. In the above example measures relating to politeness and appearance may be considered soft measures. Removal of stains would require the use of common sense between the parties and include consideration of how the stain was caused and the attempts made to remove it.

It is not appropriate to detail individual measures for different outsourcing contracts here, but it is important to consider how the purchasing organisation should determine the measures it uses. The following principles are key in this process:

1   relating the measure to key business needs
2   keeping the measure as simple as possible
3   getting agreement from the stakeholders that the measure is appropriate and relevant to their needs
4   getting ownership from the supplier that the measure is appropriate and can be met
5   making suppliers aware of the measures we are interested in at the earliest possible stage in the process
6   listening to suppliers about the measures used and performance against them in other similar situations
7   having a few vital measures
8   selecting measures that are robust.

Self-assessment question 15.4

Debate the pros and cons of listening to suppliers about the measures used and performance against them in other similar situations.

Feedback on page 255

15.5 Outsourcing relationships within the relationship spectrum

This short section aims to remind us of where the outsourcing relationship sits in the relationship spectrum.

Learning activity 15.5

Go back and read parts of study session 4 concerning the outsourcing relationship and also review figure 4..

Feedback on page 256

Outsourcing relationships are strategic to purchasing organisations, for they deliver a range of services without which the organisation could not function normally. However, purchasing organisations must not expect too much from them when compared with a partnership, a strategic alliance or a co-destiny relationship. Study session 14 emphasises that one of the reasons for selecting areas to outsource is the fact that the areas were non-core and logic therefore leads us to recognise that the purchasing and supply relationships that we rely on here are relatively less important to the success of our organisation than relationships delivering requirements that closely and directly impact core processes.

Outsourcing relationships are, however, significant and relatively more important to us than other more tactical and adversarial relationships and our investment in the development, planning and management of these relationships must reflect that.

15.6 Changes in relationships when services are outsourced

This section evaluates the changes in relationships between the people delivering and receiving a service when that service is outsourced. People are at the heart of this subsection.

Learning activity 15.6

Re-read learning activity 15.1 above. Consider the senior manager – let's call him David – and his relationship with Sandra. How does David perceive Sandra? How does Sandra perceive David? You only have limited information on which to work so make some assumptions.

Feedback on page 256

Take the relationship outlined and developed in learning activity 15.6 above and imagine that the two people work in a group of companies where head office has decided to outsource IT. Everything is fully explained to Sandra who moves to work with the outsourcer and is now the site manager reporting to the supplier's account manager responsible for the 24 sites of the group of companies. Consider how the relationship may change in these circumstances.

1   Less flexible processes are introduced and Sandra now has to account for every hour of her team during the week. The report of the activities of the team is circulated and people within the organisation start to question the value of the output received from the department which is now a supplier. Sandra points out that nothing has changed, the service is still the same, but a cost-cutting initiative is started with the outcome that one of Sandra's team is considered surplus to requirements. The impact of this situation on Sandra and the team delivering the service is that they feel less valued, will now work to rule, do absolutely nothing additional and deliver things on time but never early. They will not look for further cost savings, in fact they will seek to justify additional cost wherever possible. The relationship has deteriorated to a point where there is very little trust between the parties.
2   David now asks for another change to the budget report, citing the case two years ago, which Sandra's team did for her within the week. Sandra now puts the requirement through the development process agreed

15

in the contract and provides a cost of £4,500 to David. David shakes his head and indicates that he feels that Sandra is trying to 'rip off' the purchasing organisation.

The impact of this situation is also a loss of trust. Actually, the change may have cost nearly £4,500 two years ago, but as it was not individually costed, the amount was absorbed within department and company budgets.

Relationships inevitably become more formal when a department like IT or catering move to become a supplier. Typically relationships between the people involved can be impacted in the following ways.

1   They become more formal and both sides draw back to their side of the table.
2   People receiving the service can look at costs and processes much more than they did before.
3   Some people who know each other very well and have a personal friendship which transcends the work relationship will carry on as normal and even use their relationship to get 'favours' done. The cost of the favour will be hidden and/or charged elsewhere.
4   Information may not be shared as readily as it was on previous occasions. For example in the case involving Sandra, would she still be invited to the monthly management meeting?
5   Chains of communication may be lengthened. Again, in the case of Sandra, would all requests be routed via the company wide account manager, then to Sandra?
6   People may use the new situation to settle old scores.
7   People delivering the service may use the processes to create unnecessary steps, or restrictions on activity.
8   People delivering the service may look for additional areas of revenue for their organisation, particularly if they are on a revenue-based bonus.

To overcome issues like this, everyone involved needs to recognise the changed circumstances but be reasonable, flexible and participate in an information exchange. Where difficulties arise it is important to be open and honest and seek a resolution.

15

Self-assessment question 15.5

You still run the fleet of 30 vehicles for the bakery even though you now work for an international logistics organisation rather than the bakery. At a one-to-one meeting, the bakery's contract manager, who is someone you trained when he first joined the organisation 15 years ago, has just 'thrown out' your proposal for a new routing plan which you believe will save one vehicle. Previously, you would have just implemented the change. What are your options now?

1   Do nothing – throw the plan away and let the bakery bear the additional cost.
2   Go above the contract manager's head and talk to the bakery manager, someone you have a weekly 'pie and a pint' with.

(continued on next page)

3 Refer the issue to the account manager above you in the chain and sit back.
4 Table the proposal for the next contract review meeting.

Feedback on page 256

Revision question

Now try the revision question for this session on page 323.

Summary

Finishing where we started in this study session, outsourcing is not an end in itself, it is a tool to achieve objectives and:

- The purchasing organisation will have different objectives to the supplier at some stages of the process.
- People in both organisations will have changing roles and aspirations as the process of outsourcing progresses.
- Simple, relevant and robust measures are required, acceptable to buyer, supplier and stakeholders.
- Costs must be identified and eliminated.

It must be recognised that suppliers of the outsourcing service have a legitimate objective of exploiting economies of scale on their own behalf insofar as they are allowed to do this within the agreement.

Suggested further reading

Review the material in the relationship management and supplier development section and other sections of CIPS knowledge works on the CIPS website.

Feedback on learning activities and self-assessment questions

Feedback on learning activity 15.1

The benefits of this situation are flexibility, a good timely response, a good team spirit, a good-quality job, assuming that Sandra works to the agreed standards, and the high probability of on time delivery.

Feedback on self-assessment question 15.1

Changes in menus may impact the cost of the food and the time necessary to prepare it. With an outsourced contract the supplier would want to evaluate the cost of the changes and their impact on the services provided, the supply chain and the staff delivering the service. Where changes could not be made within what the supplier considered to be the existing contractual arrangements, the supplier would reasonably seek an increase

15

in their charges to reflect this additional cost. Communication of the change would need to go through the people and processes laid down in the contract, probably HR and the contract manager on both sides.

Before the contract was outsourced the change could be implemented though an internal meeting involving HR, the canteen manager and the site manager.

Feedback on learning activity 15.2

In the first circumstance the sellers will (and these feelings are expressed from the buyer's viewpoint and experience) promise almost anything to get the business, and in the latter case the seller's objective may appear to be to do the absolute minimum in every way from now on. These comments are a little biased, as we shall see.

Feedback on self-assessment question 15.2

For on-time implementation, joint project planning and monitoring with the supplier, the previous supplier (if appropriate) and the internal and external stakeholders would be needed.

For uninterrupted supply of service, again project planning would be vital. However, contingencies with both suppliers should be discussed, involving core parts of the organisation impacted by service.

Happy people may in some cases be unachievable. However, staff from human resources and unions should be fully involved with the employees and counselling might be provided if necessary. Employees impacted by the change must be briefed at all stages of the process. It may even be appropriate to work with the supplier on team-building events and on presentations of how relationships can change once the new service starts.

Feedback on learning activity 15.3

You should have noted:

- cost saving – the supplier can save us money, over and above the best we can do, including:
    - economies of scale from their greater purchasing power and preferred supplier arrangements in the area
    - more efficient and productive use of people from their greater experience and greater volume
    - more efficient and productive use of resources from their greater experience and greater volume
- concentration on core business
- improving return on net assets (RONA)
- access to expertise
- management of changing technology situations
- a better service
- a 'one stop shop'
- a consistent approach.

15

Feedback on self-assessment question 15.3

Full analysis of the existing operation, including talking in detail to the current service deliverers and internal customers, would help avoid:

- ambiguous requirements
- differentiation of requirements previously standard to become specials
- over-specified requirements
- production of unused output
- failure to identify full extent of existing service
- loose definition of the contract requirement.

Monitoring of the new service with the internal customers immediately after implementation would help avoid the buyer's staff:

- duplicating supplier duties
- bypassing the agreed processes
- undertaking supplier duties 'to help out'.

Knowing the market and the supplier would help avoid:

- settling on fixed costs in a descending cost area
- locking into ageing technology with supplier
- payment in advance when this is not absolutely necessary.

A full understanding and discussion of terms and conditions would help avoid paying again for items already bought, for example software licences.

The development of a good working relationship at all levels of the relationship will help avoid changes to business operations necessary to suit supplier ways of working.

Feedback on learning activity 15.4

Measures might include:

- cleanliness of offices
- empty wastepaper bins
- absence of fingerprints on glass doors
- stains removed from carpets, walls and other surfaces
- compliance with recycling policy
- appearance of staff
- politeness of staff
- time taken to compete the tasks
- cost of equipment purchased indexed to inflation.

Feedback on self-assessment question 15.4

Points for listening to suppliers:

- They have done it before and should know what works.
- We can talk to their customers and get their views.
- Getting the supplier's buy-in is important to the relationship.

15

- The supplier cannot complain about the measure if they suggested it in the first place.

Points against:

- Suppliers will not suggest measures they find difficult to achieve.
- The measures suggested may not meet our needs.

Feedback on learning activity 15.5

The review will remind you of the definition and description of the relationship and where it sits within the relationship spectrum.

Feedback on learning activity 15.6

It would be reasonable to assume that both David and Sandra have great respect for each other, they have probably known each other for many years and to David, computers are probably a mystery, but he sees Sandra as the person who can solve his problems, or at least explain in plain English to him why his problem can't be solved. David is someone Sandra can trust, she knows he won't make unreasonable demands; she respects his judgement and his position in the organisation and she knows he wouldn't ask for a change if he didn't need it. There is a long-term trusting relationship here.

Feedback on self-assessment question 15.5

Option four is the preferred option, as your proposal is then formally recorded and the bakery can then make a conscious decision about the change. Whichever decision it makes, it will bear the consequences.

The impact of organisational culture upon relationships

Introduction

This study session concentrates on the culture existing within an organisation and how it impacts purchasing and supply relationships within supply chains. Culture is a mixture of a number of things. It includes beliefs, customs, ideas and values and in understanding and working within the culture of an organisation, human beings will need to understand the past experiences of others to understand the current situation and look forward to how the culture will act and react in the future.

The culture of the organisation will affect the behaviour of the people who work within it and the behaviour of the people within an organisation will impact its culture.

Session learning objectives

After completing this session you should be able to:

16.1 Identify different cultures and their impact upon relationships within the supply chain.
16.2 Appraise the different cultures and pick out circumstances where cultures may compliment and conflict with each other.

Unit content coverage

This study session covers the following topics from the official CIPS unit content document.

Learning objective

1.8 Evaluate the role of culture and relationship values within supply networks.

Timing

You should set aside about 5 hours to read and complete this session, including learning activities, self-assessment questions, the suggested further reading (if any) and the revision question.

16

16.1 The impact of culture on supply chain relationships

The objective of this subsection is to identify different cultures and examine their impact upon relationships within the supply chain. It is important to understand the culture of an organisation when studying purchasing and supply relationships, because the culture of some organisations makes it almost impossible to use some of the relationship types identified within the relationship spectrum.

Learning activity 16.1

How would you define the culture of your organisation?

Feedback on page 266

Aspects of culture

Let's look at some aspects of culture and then some types of culture.

Beliefs

What we as human being believe impacts the way we act, but beliefs are not facts. The owner of a business may believe that some of her employees could work faster and produce more, a purchasing manager may believe that one of his buyers is too close to a supplier and the management team of a business may believe that they are under threat from another organisation and have to make changes to survive. Beliefs also lead us to do or not do some things. Our belief in an ethical approach to purchasing will, for example, not allow us to take a bribe.

Customs

Over the years customs develop and become good or bad practices. This study guide is evidence that the custom of training purchasing professionals has developed into a practice which demands standards and levels of achievement. Within organisations customs will develop – in law they talk of custom and practice – in areas like the time tea breaks are taken, or monthly meetings with key suppliers. It may also be the custom for engineers to discuss their technical specifications with suppliers they trust and this may lead to conflict as discussed earlier.

Ideas

Some organisational cultures welcome ideas from employees who they see as 'team members' rather than 'employees'; other organisations will question the 'soundness' of people wanting to change. How ideas are received in an organisation can determine its future. Organisations do not operate in a vacuum and both internal and external influences will bring about change, require a response in the form of ideas. But are ideas from *everyone* welcome? Or is the experience of some people that their ideas are never welcome and so they have given up making suggestions?

Values

What are the values of the people working in the team? Is it acceptable to go to a football match with a supplier? Is it acceptable to re-use suppliers who we know are not performing because it takes more effort to change them? Does the purchasing team share their experiences of what worked well in negotiation? The values of the people working within an organisation will directly impact purchasing and supply relationships. For example, when suppliers talk to each other about buyers, purchasing teams and organisations, they will reflect upon the extent to which they trust us. Here there is also a link to the discussion of CSR in study session 7.

Types of culture

Each organisational culture is different, because it involves people. However, the following broad types of culture can be identified amongst others:

- bureaucratic
- paternalistic
- aggressive
- laid back
- dominating
- progressive.

Each of the six broad types will be defined and their characteristics considered against the impact upon the organisation, the impact upon internal relationships and the impact upon supply chain relationships.

A bureaucratic culture

When we think of a bureaucratic organisation we think of one which is characterised by its hierarchy, its adherence to fixed rules, its red tape and its inability to see the need to change.

In this culture the organisation will seek to be what it always has been, it will seek to perpetuate a status quo and it may resist those who want to develop and change. The civil service may be one example of such an organisation, but those working within some civil service departments will advise you that there is quite a climate of change at this time (early 2006). This environment may mean that people value and rely on long-term relationships and question new people, new ideas or new suppliers. Internally, people may be satisfied with the current situation and whilst realising that there are other alternatives they feel that they want to retain the known and trusted situation. The process of decision making may also be long and tedious, with sellers having to meet several people at different locations to get a decision.

One European private sector organisation known to the author has five levels of approval before any purchase is made, even for tactical acquisition items.

A paternalistic culture

A paternalistic organisation may be a small family firm, where a father/mother figure who set up the organisation is the dominant person, but the authority they clearly have as the owner is fairly exercised as if the employees are their children.

Here the organisation is firmly, if tolerantly, steered by the father/mother figure, major decisions are all made by that person and in many cases the organisation is restricted because nothing major can be decided without their involvement. There is a stage within the development of an organisation when the father/mother figure has to step back and let others make that decision, and where that step has not been taken the organisation can suffer.

Imagine the situation where the owner was negotiating a deal to buy 100,000 mobile phones for his organisation to sell and delaying the deal

16

to squeeze the last ten pence from the supplier. At the same time the shops selling the phones had no stock and were losing sales, yet the only person who could make the decision was the owner. When eventually the cost of lost sales over several days was pointed out, the deal was done very quickly, without the last ten pence, but the point was that people in the business were deferring to the owner and not questioning his negotiation tactics.

All internal relationships in this situation defer to the views of the father or mother figure and phrases like 'he won't have that' are heard around the organisation. Frequently this can mean that ideas are not brought forward and the organisation is poorer as a result. External organisations very quickly work out that the decision maker is the father/mother figure and target him/her, rather than the purchasing manager. The supplier and the father/ mother figure reach an agreement and the purchasing manager is instructed to 'do the paperwork'. Whilst the owner clearly has the authority, they may not have the negotiation skill or market understanding and the deal may not be as good for the purchasing organisation as it might have been.

An aggressive culture

An aggressive organisation is one marked by its readiness to challenge or fight, which may be a characteristic of the market it exists in. Here there is blatant energy and a driving force and the working environment of the organisation may be ruthless and intensive.

External relationships with aggressive organisations are characterised with a lack of trust and classically they are found towards the adversarial end of the relationship spectrum. Here, purchasing organisations will be demanding more and more from suppliers and wanting to give nothing in exchange. It may be that the purchasing organisation is operating in a cut-throat market which sets the conditions in which all of its participants must operate. However, it may also be the essence of what is perceived as success or a strategy to get the organisation to where its leaders want it to be. Internal relationships may or may not follow the external model, for aggression in the supply market may be one strategy, yet paternalism to the 'team' may be the internal model. However, aggression within the organisation may also be the model and people may be placed in situations where they have to fight amongst each other to survive.

One situation known to the author involved the leader of the organisation informing one manager that three other colleagues were poor performers and he wanted them to be given a hard time. The other three colleagues were separately given the same message and conflict ensued until one of the managers asked the others what had been said. When they all realised they had been given the same message, they cooperated, to the frustration of the 'leader'.

Aggressive organisations can be stressful to work in and frequently have difficulty in trusting and being trusted by suppliers and customers alike.

A laid back culture

A laid back organisation is one where there is a tolerance of individualism and an apparent lack of drive. However, appearances can be deceiving.

16

Technical experts who are absolutely assured of their eminence in their profession may give the impression that they are unconcerned about commercial and relationship aspects. In a research and development centre these experts may be unconcerned about cost or giving information to suppliers. A small family firm, secure in its position in a local community, may also not see the need to extract the last penny out of a deal with a supplier, and may therefore reject the purchasing and negotiation strategies proposed by a new purchasing specialist. This may in some circumstances be appropriate if the small family firm is able to provide its services to other organisations on the basis that they will not be squeezed for every last penny.

One senior person in such an organisation known to the author said that a given tactic could not be followed because, 'our suppliers would not like that!' Another comment was, 'I'm not comfortable in asking them to quote with others, they've always done a good job for us, haven't they?'

These organisations will question the very need for a specialist purchasing team and rely on relationships that they can build with suppliers, it might be called 'the old boy network'. Purchasing professionals will find these organisations frustrating places to work, as their skills will not be valued and they can see, but are not allowed to take, opportunities.

Dominating culture

Within a dominated organisation some people are able to exert a supreme determining or guiding influence because of their position within the organisation.

There are characteristics of the paternalistic and the aggressive organisational culture here, the former when the father/mother figure is intolerant and the latter when the aggression is focused on the people within the organisation. A ruthless father/mother figure may own these organisations or they may be corporate organisations, but their common denominator will be the pressure to perform and achieve.

One organisation known to the author sent a text message to a delegate on a week-long offsite training programme indicating that their email inbox was full and that they were required to travel back to work that evening after the training programme and clear their emails. The culture in this organisation also seems to demand that buyers keep in touch by email on their holidays.

In another organisation the owner asked a buyer to get a price for a new component. Two weeks later the buyer returned with the information, let's assume the figure was £24.98. The owner said, 'I know; I went to the suppliers myself. I was just checking up on you.'

The dominance can be turned into a demand for conformance to what is perceived as the norm by the top people within organisation, those who do not conform are not valued by those who try to conform and conflict can result from the demands of those at the top. Failure to conform can result in those people being ostracised, or even dismissed. The organisation goes in the direction set by those at the top, who frequently do not listen to ideas offered by others. Internal relationships can be characterised by fear and externally this type of organisation probably treats suppliers towards the adversarial end of the relationship spectrum.

16

In one example known to the author a senior person ran a purchasing team in this way and then become aware of partnerships and supplier development as a possible way forward. The approach to suppliers, who had little trust in the team as a whole, was received by suppliers as an *instruction* to follow this new relationship style. The suppliers were suspicious and slow to adopt the new view painted for them, whereupon the senior person said he had his adversarial view confirmed, and abandoned the project for the old aggressive style.

Dominating cultures find it difficult to make alliances and partnerships, although they can be found as a dominant partner in a co-destiny relationship, where they extract their needs from the other members of the supply chain by applying power. Study session 18 considers this aspect further.

A progressive culture

A progressive culture is one characterised by new ideas and development, working towards an objective and seeking to exploit business opportunities. This culture will change and evolve if it sees a need or an opportunity to be seized. The speed of change will vary from organisation to organisation and sector to sector, but the common denominator is the search to do better. Processes and relationships are not fixed in stone within this type of environment and are adapted towards customers' needs and in these circumstances there is something of the agile relationship defined in study session 7 as 'using market knowledge and a responsive supply network to exploit profitable opportunities in the marketplace'. This is therefore probably a private sector environment.

Internally people accept the need to change and develop new solutions, they generate ideas and options and are stimulated by them. It may be that a development implemented only three months ago is recognised as redundant now because a member of staff has conceived another, better solution. Relationships with customers and suppliers react to the needs of one and develop solutions with the other and these relationships are towards the collaborative end of the relationship spectrum.

Progressive cultures reward idea generators and tend to regard people who do not generate ideas less highly, but a good manager will realise that a mix of people is required within a successful team.

Summary

Organisations may change cultures with the introduction of new people or they may bend and force the new people into their mould, and different parts of an organisation may have different cultures.

16

Self-assessment question 16.1

What issues might exist between a paternalistic family firm employing a firm of city-based management consultants with a dominating culture to carry out a review of the family firm's business processes?

Feedback on page 266

16.2 Conflict and benefit emanating from culture

The objective of this subsection is to appraise the different cultures and pick out circumstances where cultures may compliment and conflict with each other.

Learning activity 16.2

Consider the culture types described in section 16.1 and reflected in figure 16.1. Assume that the organisations in the left-hand column have the cultures indicated in the boxes, indicate by drawing lines to the boxes on the right-hand side of figure 16.1 where you feel there may be particular conflict between organisations which need to work together in a purchasing and supply relationship. You may finish the exercise with many lines between the boxes.

Figure 16.1: Potential conflicts between cultures

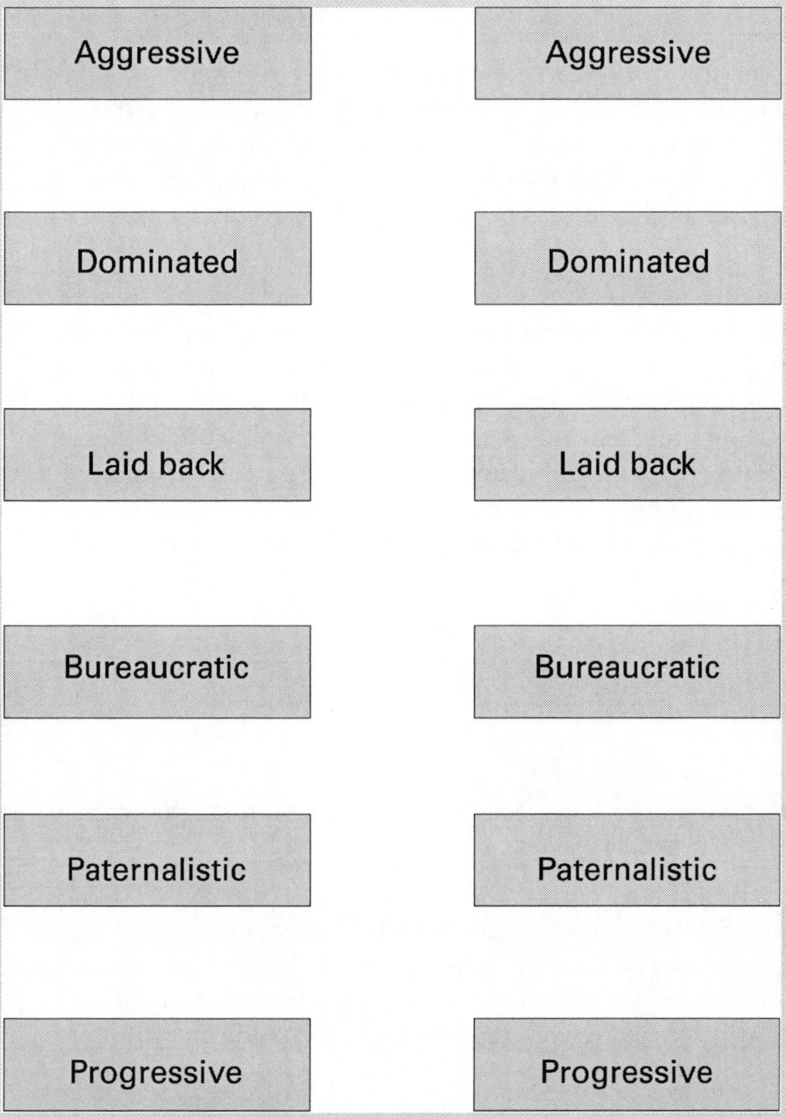

Aggressive	Aggressive
Dominated	Dominated
Laid back	Laid back
Bureaucratic	Bureaucratic
Paternalistic	Paternalistic
Progressive	Progressive

Feedback on page 267

16

Aggressive cultures will probably conflict with most other cultures and be at their most explosive when trying to reach agreement with an organisation similar to their own, or an organisation with a dominated culture. Within the Market Management Matrix these situations will be viewed as tactical profit to exploitable and may be visualised as a boxing ring with two opponents fighting it out. Dominated cultures may conflict in the same way as aggressive cultures.

The bureaucratic culture will not tolerate the aggressive or dominated one and may feel threatened. The aggressive culture will be quietly sidelined and if demonstrated by a supplier, the supplier may not be awarded the contract. The problem for the bureaucratic culture occurs when it has appointed a supplier who has not appeared aggressive or dominating until after the appointment is made. Anecdotal evidence based upon conversations with employees from some UK government departments seems to indicate that suppliers have exerted or attempted to exert aggression and dominance when they are performing against contracts. This may result from the conflicting cultures and business objectives of the organisations concerned.

Paternalistic cultures work well with cultures of their own kind and may also be tolerant and accepting of laid back cultures. However, as self-assessment question 16.1 above demonstrates, these cultures will not happily tolerate other aggressive cultures. Paternalistic cultures may accept progressive cultures if they see a value in the change being advocated by them.

Progressive cultures may be immensely frustrated with laid back cultures and reject both them and bureaucratic cultures as their kind of supplier, seeking in preference a similar culture with whom they can enjoy the changing and challenging relationship. The progressive culture will probably seek to bend the aggressive or dominated culture towards its way of thinking, but may in the end seek other parties if this is not possible. The paternalistic culture will be recognised and probably accepted by the progressive culture, but at the same time they will want to stretch and develop that culture towards their vision of life.

Self-assessment question 16.2

Consider the culture types described in this study session and reflected in figure 16.3.

Assuming that the organisations in the left-hand column have the cultures indicated in the boxes, indicate by drawing lines to the boxes on the right-hand side where you feel there may be particular synergy between organisations which need to work together in a purchasing and supply relationship.

(continued on next page)

16

Self-assessment question 16.2 *(continued)*

Figure 16.3: Relationship synergies

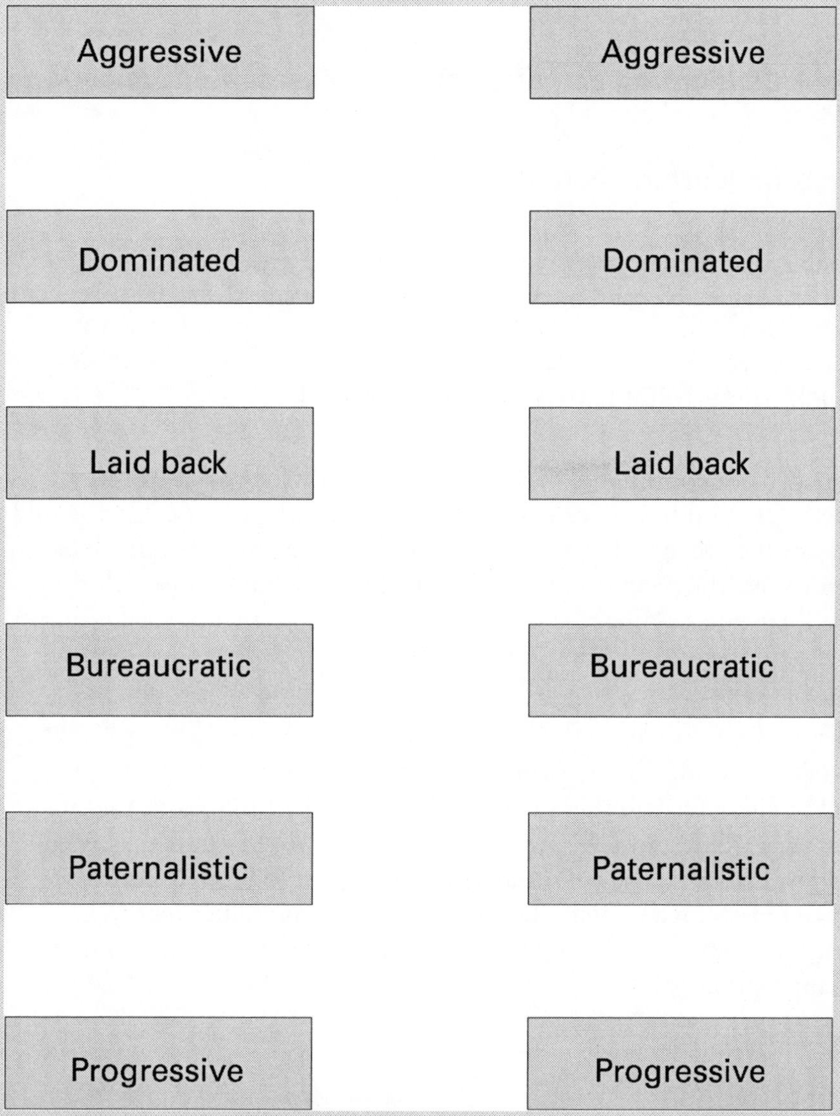

Aggressive	Aggressive

Dominated	Dominated

Laid back	Laid back

Bureaucratic	Bureaucratic

Paternalistic	Paternalistic

Progressive	Progressive

Feedback on page 268

Revision question

Now try the revision question for this session on page 323.

16

Summary

The culture of the organisation will affect the behaviour of the people who work within it and the behaviour of the people within an organisation will impact its culture. There are noticeable traits of cultures which can mean that they are seen as bureaucratic, paternalistic, aggressive, laid back, dominated or progressive.

The culture of one organisation can cause conflict with other organisations.

The culture of one organisation can mean that organisations and their people complement each other.

Feedback on learning activities and self-assessment questions

Feedback on learning activity 16.1

It is possible that you may have used words such as bureaucratic, paternalistic, aggressive, laid back, dominating or progressive.

Feedback on self-assessment question 16.1

The management consultants would view the family firm as sleepy, lazy, slow, inefficient and having values from the nineteenth century. They would want to tear the organisation apart and introduce efficient processes. They would not value the people and the history of the organisation which they might well regard as a dinosaur fit for the scrapheap or a takeover. During the project they would cast doubt on the existing processes and the people carrying them out.

The people within the family firm would feel that the consultants were prepared to give advice to them without knowing anything about the business, they would not feel understood and they would not feel listened to. They would regard the consultants' people as over-educated under-experienced Flash Harrys, who did not understand the values that their organisation aspired to and were trying to apply experience from elsewhere in an inappropriate way.

16

Feedback on learning activity 16.2

Your answer should look like figure 16.2.

Figure 16.2: Potential conflicts between cultures: answer

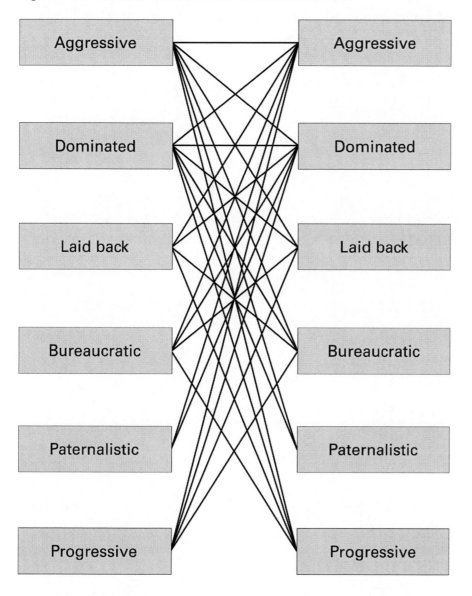

Feedback on self-assessment question 16.2

Your answer should look like figure 16.4.

Figure 16.4: Relationship synergies: answer

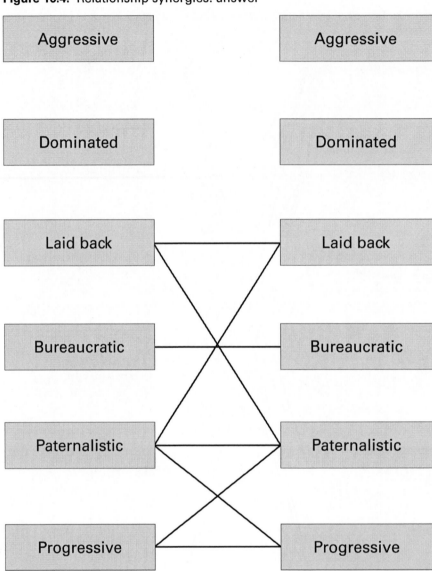

Study session 17
Relationships in an international setting

When in Rome, do as the Romans do.

Introduction

Wherever you are based, dealing with people in different parts of the world brings additional challenges. They may not speak your language, their customs may be different and it may be difficult to contact them.

Session learning objectives

After completing this session you should be able to:

17.1 Evaluate the differences of maintaining relationships with suppliers in different parts of the world.

17.2 Assess the steps that may be taken to protect the position of an organisation buying or selling on an international basis.

17.3 Evaluate how multinational organisations use their power.

17.4 Evaluate the benefits that multinational suppliers bring to multinational customers.

Unit content coverage

This study session covers the following topics from the official CIPS unit content document.

Learning objective

4.5 Appraise the relationship aspects of international supply contracts.

4.10 Analyse the relationship challenges of multi-national suppliers in the context of a global supply chain.

Timing

You should set aside about 5 hours to read and complete this session, including learning activities, self-assessment questions, the suggested further reading (if any) and the revision question.

17

17.1 Maintaining relationships with worldwide suppliers

The objective of this subsection is to evaluate the differences of maintaining relationships with suppliers in different parts of the world.

Learning activity 17.1

Assume that you are a purchasing manager in Nigeria. Indicate the additional challenges that you feel you would face in obtaining supplies from the United Kingdom and Japan, compared with obtaining supplies from your own country.

Feedback on page 279

There are many reasons why maintaining purchasing and supply relationships with suppliers in different parts of the world is more difficult. They include:

- communication: there are different time zones and it may only be possible to talk to and get a response from a supplier for a short period of your working day
- language: not everyone speaks the same language, there are even significant differences between the English spoken in the USA and the UK
- geographical distances: this impacts four factors:
  - transport costs can be significantly more when obtaining delivery from another continent
  - delivery time can be significantly more when obtaining delivery from another continent
  - packaging requirements may need to be more robust to take account of the type of journey
  - length of time that communication takes to reach the other person. Today this consideration has almost been eliminated when organisations have access to high-speed internet connections
- the political and economic stability of the nations and organisations which may form our sources of supply
- the differing legal systems the nations have evolved and which law will be the one under which the contract will operate
- organising payment when one party does not want to release the goods until they get paid and the other party does not want to pay until they receive and examine the goods
- differing cultures and ethical standards: one culture may expect to give and receive a gift and the other culture may feel that this is inappropriate in a business situation
- duties and taxes may be imposed and need to be accounted for by someone
- the issue of using different currencies, which may fluctuate, leaving the buyer or the seller with different costs to bear over the lifetime of the arrangement
- inflation rates, which may need to be factored in to the cost model
- holidays: different countries have public holidays at different times and this will impact communication and delivery
- supplier management costs: the cost of a visit to a supplier on another continent will be much greater than a journey 50 miles down the road.

17

Not all of these factors will affect every situation, but maintaining a relationship and conducting business with people in a different language, time zone and culture adds an additional dimension to the purchasing and supply relationship.

Self-assessment question 17.1

Imagine that you work for a French company which is part of a US parent organisation making office equipment. You are working on a team to develop a new photocopier with colleagues in the US. One of your potential suppliers is in China. Everyone has high-speed internet access and you intend to organise a videoconference next week with all three parties. What additional considerations would you need to make in these circumstances?

Feedback on page 279

17.2 Protecting your position when dealing internationally

The objective of this section is to assess the steps that may be taken to protect the position of an organisation buying or selling on an international basis.

Learning activity 17.2

Search the internet using the terms 'freight forwarder' and 'incoterms', particularly http://www.iccbo.org. Assess the services offered and the diversity of the terms. The objective of this search is to make you aware of the services provided by freight forwarders and also the types of INCO terms which can be used to help increase security when purchasing from other countries.

Feedback on page 279

The conundrum here is that the seller of goods in, for example, China, will not want to release the goods to the customer in France until they are assured of payment, yet the customer in France will not want to pay until they receive and examine the goods. How is this resolved? There are a number of options open to the parties and these include:

- the use of agents
- letters of credit
- INCO terms
- local people working for your organisation
- setting up in different countries.
- CSR and other issues.

The use of agents

Both buyers and suppliers can appoint agents to act on their behalf in different countries.

17

271

In this case the French buyer could appoint an agent to inspect and even test the goods on their behalf in China. Once the agent was satisfied, the shipment and payment processes could commence.

Likewise the Chinese supplier could appoint a French or European agent or distributor to receive the goods and then allow inspection or deliver the goods to the French customer.

Both of these options incur cost, assume that the agent is trustworthy and minimise the risk for the organisations concerned. It is common for vehicle manufacturers in Japan to have local dealerships and then the purchase takes place totally within France in this example.

Letters of credit

The letter of credit is the solution evolved by traders and the international banking community to solve the conundrum posed at the start of this section. For the sake of clarity the conundrum is repeated: the seller of goods in, for example, China, will not want to release the goods to the customer in France until they are assured of payment, yet the customer in France will not want to pay until they receive and examine the goods. A letter of credit is defined as a financial instrument under which the issuing bank (buyer's bank) gives its irrevocable undertaking that payment will be made to the seller's bank if all the terms of the letter of credit are met and the specified documents provided.

The importance of the letter of credit is that it solves the conundrum, because both parties are able to find a local organisation that they can trust to help them assure their position. Trust is expanded across the world using the probity of international banking system, where bankers deal with other bankers they can trust. A summary of the letter of credit process follows.

1   The French buyer would therefore go to their bank and indicate that they wished to purchase goods from China, naming the supplier and the supplier's bank.
2   The French bank would ensure that the Chinese bank was a bona fide bank and report back to the buyer.
3   The buyer and seller would agree details of the deal (price, delivery, INCO terms and the terms of the letter of credit).
4   The French bank would create the letter of credit, possibly insisting that the French buyer placed the amount of money concerned in an account to be available when needed.
5   A copy of the letter of credit would be sent to the Chinese supplier and at this stage the Chinese supplier has a guarantee that if the terms of the letter of credit are met, they will be paid. The guarantee exists because if the Chinese bank presents the French bank with the letter of credit and the necessary documents, the French bank is *obliged* to pay.
6   The goods would be made and shipped and the terms of the letter of credit met.
7   The supplier then presents the letter of credit to his bank, his bank presents it to the French bank and the French bank takes the money from the account of the French buyer.

17

One vital consideration is that it is the *terms of the letter of credit which must be met* and not the fitness of purpose of the goods. Hence, if the terms of the letter of credit were triggered on delivery to the buyer without inspection, then the supplier could supply goods which turned out to be defective and get paid for them. Care must therefore be taken in constructing a letter of credit. Where buyers and sellers are new to each other, misunderstandings and doubts of this nature can be cleared by appointing a third party inspector and triggering the letter of credit based upon such a report. Another point to remember is that the letter of credit is often referred to as an irrevocable letter of credit, for the buyer cannot change the letter once the bank issues it.

INCO terms

INCO stands for International Chamber of Commerce and the terms are used to describe where and when the risk associated with the transport and carriage cost passes from one party to another. Examples of INCO terms are:

- FOB: Free on board
- CIF: Cost, insurance, freight
- DDP: Delivered, duty paid
- EXW: Ex works

Each of these terms is linked to a place. In the example of the French buyer and the Chinese supplier FOB, CIF and DDP may be linked to the port of Shanghai or the port of Le Havre. Where FOB is used risk and cost pass from one party to another when the goods go over the ship's rail at the port, CIF will be paid by one party to the given location and DDP will include all of the costs and the duties needed to be paid to get the goods to the location. Location of course may be a more specific address than simply 'the port of Le Havre'. Ex works means that cost and risk associated with the transport is the responsibility of the customer from the supplier's factory gates.

In this case protecting the position of the parties to the deal is simply knowing who will pay what and where the risk lies for which parts of the journey. Obviously, in our case the French supplier would prefer the risk and cost to be with the Chinese supplier as far as Le Havre, rather than only as far as Shanghai, and this will become a point of negotiation.

Setting up in different countries

Rather than appoint agents, both the buyer and the seller could set up an organisation within a foreign country and as the buyer, some large corporate organisations also have purchasing teams comprising expatriates and local people working in locations like Shanghai and New York. This gives them a presence on the ground to purchase the goods and even take the delivery and inspection locally if needed before shipping the goods within their control. As the seller the reverse is true. An article in *Supply Management* on 15 December 2005 indicates that Sainsbury's have opened offices in Poland and Hong Kong to purchase goods locally. The article identifies cost savings and greater control of the supply chain to provide greater flexibility and more responsiveness as drivers for this move.

17

CSR and other considerations

Protecting the image of the purchasing organisation when dealing with suppliers based in low-wage economies is also a consideration. This is not to say that the purchasing organisation would only care about its image and being caught out rather than the fundamental CSR issues, it is to recognise that the distance and many other differences between the buyer and the seller in this situation make the situation worthy of examination. Purchasing organisations must therefore attempt to ensure that their suppliers in far-flung parts of the world do adopt their CSR standards, so far as that is possible. This could particularly include environmental issues where, for example, at the time of writing (early 2006) there are several stories in the press of the impact of industry on the rivers in China. You may want to return to study session 7 and look again at the issues highlighted under the umbrella of CSR in the context of this session.

It is vital that buyers fully cost the foreign purchase, for whilst the purchase price of a component made in a low-wage economy can be much lower than a local economy, the cost of duties and shipment may be higher and there can be cost of quality issues.

Freight forwarders are specialist organisations which undertake the shipment and organise customs clearance of behalf of buyers and sellers. This means that organisations not having high volumes of international importing and exporting can gain access to specialists who are used to the processes and procedures and have a network of local contacts. These organisations obviously charge a fee, but they can remove some of the risk and provide a door-to-door service, allowing others to concentrate on their core activities.

Self-assessment question 17.2

You work in South Africa. Your sales manager has just won a large contract in Ireland. Advise her on steps you would take to protect your organisation's interests.

Feedback on page 279

17.3 Multinational organisations and their use of power

The objective of this subsection is to evaluate how multinational organisations use their power. Firstly let's define a multinational organisation.

Learning activity 17.3

How would you define a multinational organisation and a global organisation?

Feedback on page 280

Multinationals seek to use their power in a number of ways, which include:

- leveraging supply markets
- standardisation
- determining which products and services will be sold where
- determining pricing policies for its sales
- attempting to determine cost models for its supply bases
- determining road maps
- quality
- CSR.

Leveraging supply markets

The vast spend of a multinational organisation, frequently more than the economic output of small nations, enables it to attract and possibly dominate suppliers anywhere in the world. A supplier may be prepared to tolerate harsher terms and conditions for the vast volume on offer. Simply put, the logic that we pay a lower unit price for a purchase of 100 than a purchase of ten is extended further to a purchase of 1,000,000 items. Multinationals will view many items as tactical acquisition and tactical profit and seek to reduce their operating costs and ensure minimum levels of service. To meet the needs of the multinational organisations, for example oil companies, supplier organisations have themselves become multinational by acquisition or they have formed strategic alliances with regional and local suppliers to meet the needs of the multinational organisation.

Standardisation

With crude leverage comes a requirement for the goods or services provided to a multinational in Brazil to be the same as the goods or services provided to the same multinational in Finland. This may be in terms of the configuration of hardware, software and communications, in hotel rooms and travel, in the provision of a logistics service and in the provision of brand. Catering is one area where standardisation would be difficult.

Determining which products and services will be sold where

Strategic selling may mean that multinationals will seek to exploit the different markets with different products. For example, the market in the US may be where there is an expectation that new and or more technically advanced versions of products will first make an appearance, whilst during the same calendar year the European market will not be offered that model and the third world markets may still be offered an even older model. The situation where IT suppliers offered models 12 months later to the European market led some UK organisations which rely on technology to set up purchasing teams in the US and although multinationals have attempted to resist these moves, purchasing organisations have been successful. Organisations in markets where the latest technology is held back are restricted and may not be able to be as competitive as other organisations with access to such technology.

Determining pricing policies for its sales

The pricing policy adopted by multinational organisations will in one sense be the same as any other seller; they will charge what the market will bear,

17

yet the question still exists: why should an organisation in, for example, the UK pay more for a given item made by a multinational in Argentina than an organisation if France? Are the shipping costs significantly more? If the price is greater in the UK, why can the UK organisation not make the purchase in France? The answer here lies in the fact that many of the customers will be smaller organisations, or may only purchase small quantities of the items and may not therefore see benefit in such activity. However, where the purchase is strategic then purchasing organisations will act to purchase on more favourable conditions.

Attempting to determine cost models for its supply bases

Given the power to award or not award large-scale business to suppliers, and the competitive nature of some of the sales markets faced by multinationals, one reaction used is to 'work with' suppliers, examine their cost model and reduce the costs. Study session 16 discusses this aspect in terms of culture and study session 18 discusses it in terms of power and dependency. Suffice it to say that multinationals can exert a high level of power on their suppliers for a long duration.

Determining road maps

All products and services develop, but the development direction, particularly for a complex product is referred to as a 'road map'. Assume that a piece of equipment has a worldwide market and there are several demands on the manufacturer to develop the already good performance of the equipment. Which direction should the development take? What influences the decision? Internally within the multinational organisation the debate between technical specialists and sales teams will take place, but to what extent are customers listened to, and which customers are listened to? Supplier preferencing would indicate that development and core customers' needs might be addressed first and other factors include the position of the product in its life cycle, the business and sales strategies of the organisation and the impact of the competition on the multinational. An alternative view of this situation is that the multinational has a right to set its strategies and sell its products, within legal and ethical boundaries, as it sees fit.

Quality

Multinationals can and do demand quality from local suppliers. However, this can be a significant benefit to the suppliers, the business community and the nation as a whole. One multinational known to the author moved a factory to a low-cost country and as part of the development process assisted the country to create a Standards Institute. That institute, with the support of the multinational, introduced the business community to the ISO standards. Power that demanded quality therefore became power that influenced the national concept of quality for the good and enabled other suppliers in that country to compete in world markets.

Corporate social responsibility

Multinationals can influence CSR issues in developing countries by providing basic rights for workers, or they can take advantage of poor practices by using, for example, child labour.

Self-assessment question 17.3

What alternative courses of action are open to a buyer faced with a
multinational organisation dominant in its own local supply market?

Feedback on page 280

17.4 Benefits multinational organisations bring to each other

The objective of this section is to evaluate the benefits that multinational
suppliers bring to multinational customers. The essence of the proposition
of the multinational supplier here is: 'We are where you are'. This section
uses an airline as the example of a multinational customer, but the customer
could be a car assembler, an IT software provider or a financial institution.

Learning activity 17.4

Imagine that you were an international airline. How would the
multinational supplier be of benefit to you?

Feedback on page 280

Multinational organisations become both customers and suppliers of other
multinationals. Imagine the airline used as an example in the learning
activity 17.1 above. From Boston to Bogotá, when an aeroplane lands, the
plane itself, the passengers and the crew will have common requirements
and the airline might choose to ally itself with multinational providers for
services such as:

- in-flight catering
- refuelling
- maintenance
- customer services
- baggage handling
- cleaning
- IT.

In some cases the organisation delivering the service may arrive in an
airline uniform or a vehicle painted in airline colours, but they may work
for a supplier. What benefits do such arrangements bring the purchasing
organisation?

- A consistent service level: The airline customer can expect the same
  level of service at Bogotá as they can at Heathrow or Boston, the cutlery
  loaded on to the plane which has the airline's logo and the meals offered
  would be identical to meals served for the airline anywhere in the world.

17

- Absence of need to deal directly with local suppliers: The multinational serving the airline becomes the tier one supplier, dealing with local refuellers, caterers and hoteliers on behalf of the airline.
- Assured quality: The multinational discusses the quality required with the airline and imposes it on other tier providers.
- Guaranteed availability: In theory, the size of the multinational should guarantee availability, as if one tier two supplier is unavailable, another can be recruited.
- Cost is known: The airline can agree cost centrally and, for example, standard costs could be set by types of aircraft or numbers of passengers etc.
- Reciprocal trading: If beneficial, this could be a feature of the multinational-to-multinational contract.
- The ability to buy where cost is lowest: Multinationals could identify the purchase price of given items as being lowest in, for example, Mexico, purchase them there through a local office and ship them to other countries. Shipment costs, warranty, duties and INCO terms need to be evaluated fully in this case.

Benefits to multinational service providers include:

- The prestige of working with other multinationals: The kudos of being able to say to any potential customer 'we have the worldwide contract for XYZ', where XYZ is a well-known global brand, is immense.
- The opportunity to expand their business: Business expansion is frequently an objective for all organisations. A contract from an airline which required a presence in Bolivia might provide the base load for a multinational to expand there. Previously a cost/benefit analysis would have prevented that organisation opening up in Bolivia.
- The opportunity to drive economies of scale: Assume now that the multinational already has a presence in Bolivia; there can be economies of scale and rationalisation to be gained from the larger volume available with the new contract. These savings will not necessarily be passed on to the customers concerned.
- Achievement of business objectives: The multinational-to-multinational business may allow the supplying party to meet key business objectives.
- Reciprocal trading: If beneficial this could be a feature of the multinational-to-multinational contract.

Self-assessment question 17.4

The power of multinational suppliers should be curbed – discuss and reach a conclusion on the basis of your reading.

Feedback on page 280

Revision question

Now try the revision question for this session on page 323.

Summary

Purchasing items from other countries introduces additional dimensions, which include:

- cost, risk and commonality of specification
- communication difficulties
- language difficulties
- customs and duties.

Multinational organisations use power on both suppliers and customers. In some cases this power brings benefits to local organisations, but in other cases it imposes requirements and restricts the goods and services on offer in given markets.

Feedback on learning activities and self-assessment questions

Feedback on learning activity 17.1

You might have mentioned language, time difference, currency, the ability to trust someone so far away, lead time, shipping cost and transit time.

Feedback on self-assessment question 17.1

1 Time of day: China may be eight hours ahead of France and the US seven hours behind us.
2 Language: Will everyone speak the same language? Will you need a translator?
3 Are there any public holidays I need to be aware of?
4 Will we be able to view drawings and samples?
5 Are we aware of the cultural differences that our US colleagues and our Chinese supplier may exhibit? Will they be aware of our French culture?
6 Connection protocols, and connection issues.
7 Basic communication issues including who has the floor, over-talking and the satellite gap.
8 Basic meeting issues: Who is taking and circulating notes? Confirmation of buy-in to decisions.

Feedback on learning activity 17.2

You should have found many entries relating to INCO terms and other entries describing the services of organisations transporting goods across the world. You can even get an INCO terms wall chart!

Feedback on self-assessment question 17.2

Advice would include:

- ensuring that an irrevocable letter of credit was in place before the contract was finalised
- understanding the INCO terms to be applied and the costs associated with those terms

17

- ensuring that the legal system being used in the contract was fully understood
- checking the solvency of the customer
- shipping through an agent or group company if appropriate.

Feedback on learning activity 17.3

A multinational organisation is one which operates across national boundaries, typically having a presence in several countries. A global organisation is one which buys from a worldwide supply base and sells to a worldwide customer base.

Feedback on self-assessment question 17.3

Alternatives include:

- working with the multinational to get a better deal, increasing attractiveness
- purchasing in another country
- working with other buyers to leverage the multinational
- making, not buying
- starting a supplier development initiative with local suppliers
- accepting the multinational's offering as the one for them and seeking to leverage elsewhere
- being persistent to express their needs.

Feedback on learning activity 17.4

You could have said that the multinational can provide a presence, a consistent known service and a common level of service wherever the airline lands.

Feedback on self-assessment question 17.4

Points for multinationals

- They do provide goods and services to everyone in the world.
- They provide goods and services not available from indigenous suppliers.
- They can provide innovation, higher quality and thought leadership.
- They can influence society in developing countries through the introduction of quality and CSR.

Points against multinationals

Multinationals seek to use their power to:

- restrict what is sold where
- control road maps
- control too great a proportion of markets
- control prices
- control cost models of suppliers.

17

Your conclusion could indicate that you feel that multinationals are too powerful and mechanisms are needed to allow more control to be vested with local organisations, or your conclusion could indicate that on balance the benefits outweigh the costs.

17

Power, dependency and multi-tiered relationships

'Responsibility walks hand in hand with capacity and power.'
Josiah Gilbert Holland (1819–1881)

Introduction

Tiering is a concept that many purchasing organisations use. This study session explains the concept, gives practical examples and discusses how power can be used and abused in tiered and other relationships. The study session also discusses the issue of dependency and how purchasing and selling organisations can become over-dependent upon each other.

The examples used throughout the text in this section frequently refer to a car assembler, as the motorcar industry is a *prime* user of supplier tiering.

Session learning objectives

After completing this session you should be able to:

18.1 Show diagrammatically how a supply base may be tiered to provide advantage to the buyer.
18.2 Assess the benefits of supplier tiering.
18.3 Consider control mechanisms of delivering benefit from a tiered supply base.
18.4 Analyse the circumstances when dependency is a critical issue in supply relationships.

Unit content coverage

This study session covers the following topics from the official CIPS unit content document.

Learning objective

4.2 Evaluate the impact of both power and dependency on the management supplier relationships.
4.7 Explain a range of techniques for managing multi-tiered supply relationships.

Timing

You should set aside about 5 hours to read and complete this session, including learning activities, self-assessment questions, the suggested further reading (if any) and the revision question.

18

18.1 The concept of tiering

The objective of this subsection is to use diagrams to demonstrate how a supply base may be tiered to provide advantage to the buyer. This principle is most common in the manufacturing environment, but it is also applied through outsourcing in a number of other sectors.

Figure 18.1 tries to demonstrate the situation where a car assembler – perhaps Ford, Renault or Vauxhall – will have to deal with many suppliers where the supply base is not tiered. The reason this diagram only *tries* to demonstrate the situation is that there are probably 1,001 or more suppliers who contribute to the supply of items for a typical car and the dimensions of this document restrict the diagram!

Figure 18.1: A non-tiered supplier base

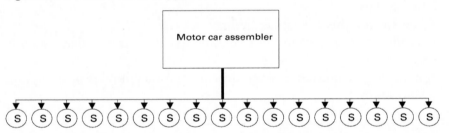

Tiering separates the supplier base into several levels. Figure 18.2 demonstrates the same number of suppliers as figure 18.1, yet in this example the car assembler manages five major suppliers and not 22 suppliers as shown in figure 18.2. The figure of five suppliers in tier one has been selected for diagrammatic convenience; however, it is understood that some car assemblers have as few as seven or eight tier one suppliers.

Figure 18.2: The same supplier base tiered

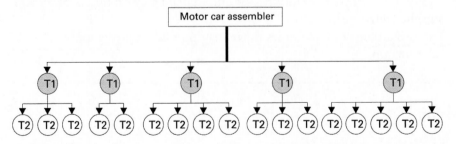

In figure 18.2 the 'T2' suppliers will receive orders and day-to-day instructions from the 'T1' supplier and deliver and invoice that supplier. There will be little or no routine contact with the car assembler.

Figure 18.3 extends the diagram further and adds levels three and four to one of the tier two suppliers. Typically most of the tier two suppliers will have their own suppliers and so it may be expected that the diagram will explode to perhaps 15 levels with the 1,001 suppliers all mapped into position.

Figure 18.3: Adding further tiers

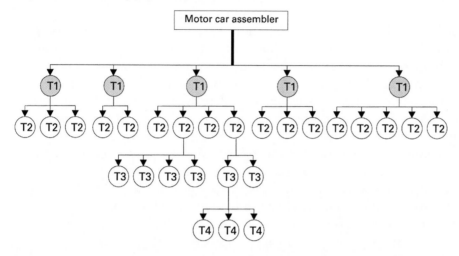

How would you define the concept of supplier tiering described in this subsection?

Feedback on page 293

18.2 The benefits of supplier tiering

Supplier tiering is a fundamental part of organising and managing purchasing and supply relationships. In one of the early study sessions supply positioning was used to identify more important suppliers through the dimensions of risk and cost and we return to that issue here.

Learning activity 18.2

Consider how many suppliers you deal with on a regular basis. What would the impact be if your boss asked you to deal with three times the number of suppliers?

Feedback on page 293

18

Supplier tiering offers a number of benefits to the purchasing organisation. Consider two of the many suppliers supplying a car assembler. One supplier supplies the screws that fix the handles that wind the windows up and down to the car door, whilst the other supplier supplies the gearbox. Ask yourself three questions about these suppliers.

1   Are these suppliers of equal importance?
2   Do they have the same propensity to stop the assembly line?
3   Should an assembler of cars invest time in a relationship with a supplier of the screws that fix the handles that wind the windows up and down?

In sequence, the answers to the questions are no, no and no. The gearbox itself will have many parts and whilst you could conceivably let a car leave the production facility and fit the handles to wind the windows at a later date, even at the dealer before the car was delivered to the customer, without a gearbox it would be impossible to complete the assembly of the car. The gearbox supplier would thus become a tier one supplier and the screw supplier a tier four or five supplier. In developing the relationship with the tier one supplier the value of the spend with that supplier increases, as does the risk, because the supplier becomes responsible for a greater proportion of our requirement, yet the single relationship delivers many benefits when compared with the multiple relationships. This movement and delegation is the fundamental rationale behind tiering, from the buyer's point of view. Given this rationale, what advantages does tiering bring to buyers and suppliers?

To the purchasing organisation the advantages of tiering a supplier base are:

1   There is less administration. At the mundane level of space required to store records of suppliers, less records will be required.
2   There will be fewer transactions with the purchasing organisation. Take the example of figure 18.3, where one of the central 'T1' suppliers has four levels extending to 13 suppliers including themselves. If the purchasing organisation were to deal with all of the suppliers then there would be 13 times the transactions that there are with the tier one supplier alone (13 times the orders, deliveries, receipts and invoices to coordinate).
3   Coordination is easier. Imagine the additional coordination required to get individual parts from several suppliers to the main subcontractor.
4   Suppliers have their own trusted specialist subcontractors. T1 suppliers may have a close relationship with several key suppliers to them. In asking the T1 supplier to organise the delivery and even the design of components, the purchasing organisation is able to harness this expertise.
5   Closer, better relationships with fewer key suppliers. The T1 supplier becomes a key supplier, if not an ally or partner. This relationship can develop into a co-destiny relationship such that the parties work together on the design of the next generation of products and services and would never consider an alternative customer or supplier.
6   The closeness and duration of the relationship makes the investment in technology to design, produce and transact the relationship worthwhile. These investments bring the benefits of lower cost and faster time to market. In this environment the collaborative development fora discussed in study session 5 are used to shorten design cycles and within industries like vehicle assembly and aerospace, EDI is used to cascade requirements, therefore eliminating waste. For example the

18

car assembler can issue 17,000 requirements for next week by EDI between 17.00 and 18.00 on a Thursday. These transactions in a standard format are read by the tier one suppliers and processed through their own **MRPII** (manufacturing resources planning) systems on Thursday evening. EDI instructions concerning the tier one supplier's requirements for next week can then be sent to the tier two suppliers during Friday. Optimisation will also allow several tiers to be processed in a 24-hour period.

7   With effective supplier tiering less stock will be required within the supply chain.

In the last two decades purchasing organisations have increased their use of concept of tiering such that they have termed themselves 'assemblers' rather than 'manufacturers' and they rely on tier one suppliers to deliver main modules, rather than components. This has further reduced the number of tier one suppliers and also allowed the assembly time to be reduced further.

In a sense, when the tiered supplier base works together effectively, it is the supplier base as a whole which is competing against the tiered supplier base of other organisations.

Self-assessment question 18.2

Consider the benefits that suppliers might expect to gain from being part of a tiered supply chain.

Feedback on page 293

18.3 Controlling a tiered supply base

The objective of this section is to consider control mechanisms of delivering benefit from a tiered supply base and its impact upon relationships. Previous subsections have alluded to the tiered supply base being an environment where day-to-day control is moved from the purchasing organisation to the tiered suppliers. Whilst this is true there will, however, be a strategic influence set by the original purchasing organisation who may seek achievements from the supply base and on occasion other members of the supply chain may receive this 'influence' as interference. For example, key objectives for fuel consumption on the new car may translate into cost reduction or supplier selection during the development process.

Learning activity 18.3

Consider the extent to which the EDI systems described in section 18.2 lead to the car assembler being in control.

Feedback on page 293

18

Within the supply chain supplying cars, there is no doubt that the dominant player is the car assembler and within the UK food industry many people currently feel that the supermarkets are increasingly dominating the supply chain. With the dominance comes power, power for example to decide:

- what is made, through the design and specification (aimed at meeting dominant player's customer's needs)
- when the manufacture takes place, through the schedules required by the dominant organisation (aimed at eliminating waste (muda))
- the suppliers used as tier two suppliers because they are 'preferred' by the dominant organisation (aimed at ensuring quality and other performance from sources known to the dominant player)
- what a standard product looks like; as the dominant organisation feels, for example, that a banana should be straight (here the aim is to meet the perceived needs of the dominant organisation's customer)
- when other supply chain members will use the contracts of the dominant player, thus reducing cost – this may be for raw materials or transport and may involve benefit flowing to the dominant player and no one else (the aim here is cost control and benefit for the dominant player)
- the acceptable cost of the item (aimed at reducing or holding cost)
- the annual cost down target (aimed at reducing or holding cost)
- the profit margin made by the suppliers (aimed at reducing or holding cost)
- the use of given computer systems, formats and protocols (aimed at reducing cost and waste though more effective systems).

Let's consider each of the above issues in turn. Many of the following factors can bring benefit to the dominant player within the supply chain and all other suppliers working with them; however, there are situations where theory and practice do not meet, as the text highlights.

What is made

The design may well be the responsibility of the car assembler, but their view may dictate given options within the specification and organisations at lower tiers may well feel that they will not be listened to if they propose alternatives.

Schedules

Schedules are again the responsibility of the assembler or supermarket, both of whom are using technology and lean and agile approaches to reduce waste.

Selection of suppliers

Where the dominance extends to the selection of suppliers from lower tiers, the higher tier supplier may be less comfortable, as they may have a long-term relationship with an alternative supplier. If the assembler insists, then the tier one supplier's relationship with their partner may be damaged and the tier one supplier's relationship with the supplier who has been forced on them will not be the most cordial ever known. If this enforced supplier fails in any way, then the tier one supplier will turn to the assembler and say, 'I told you so'! A managing director of a tier one supplier is paraphrased as follows, 'If you want me to manage the tiers below me then allow us to choose the resources to deliver what you need'. In some supply chains there is an 'overlapping responsibility', where the assembler has released control in theory, yet in practice they are still too closely involved with the lower tier suppliers and tier one suppliers feel they have *responsibility* not *authority*.

Standard products

Farmers and growers of vegetables are frustrated when they have to plough crops back into the land which, whilst being nutritious and tasty, do not conform to a supermarket's vision of, for example, what a carrot should look like. They argue that the supermarket's view is too strict, but the supermarket clearly has the power to put the items on their shelves or not!

Use of 'our' contracts

The assembler may dictate the choice of raw material supplier to all others in their supply chain and even the terms that the other suppliers buy at from the raw material supplier. This makes sense to the assembler who has the volumes to leverage a worldwide deal. There is anecdotal evidence here of two situations which could cause alarm to other suppliers in the supply chain. First, the dominant player in the supply chain may receive a retrospective rebate on the purchases from a worldwide deal. Second, imagine how the suppliers felt when the dominant player agreed an 11% increase with the worldwide supplier, yet insisted that the other suppliers in the chain kept their prices unchanged.

Acceptable cost, cost down targets

Dominant organisations may well feel that they can determine what the acceptable cost of an item is and therefore what is not acceptable. Supply chains may face demands for a percentage reduction with the words 'or else' ending the sentence and the negotiation! In the retail sector supermarkets deduct amounts from suppliers' invoices for placing items on the end of an aisle where it is felt more likely that customers will buy the products. In February 2005 one UK national newspaper reported that a national retail chain had written to its suppliers requiring them to supply goods for a number of new stores free of charge and to contribute to the refurbishment at others. Suppliers were also expected to contribute to special discount days run by the store.

In one case known to the author the dominant player insisted on an 'x%' decrease in January and the purchasing manager successfully negotiated that amount. Rather than receiving a pat on the back the purchasing manager was instructed to ask the supplier for a cheque to cover the same percentage reduction for the last year's business. After the purchasing manager protested that this was unethical he was told to 'do it or leave'. The person concerned relayed the message, ensuring that the supplier understood that 'others' were driving this request. The supplier complied; the purchasing manager found a new job within four months and the supplier gave the dominant player notice that they were terminating supply

18

just as the peak season started, having taken the time to find alternative customers.

Profit margin erosion

Where dominant players use open book costing to understand their supplier's material, labour and overhead costs as well as their profit margin, supply chain power can be used to reduce the profit of suppliers. In the guise of a cost reduction project, teams from the dominant organisation will visit suppliers and examine their processes, insisting that all reductions are returned to them in the form of lower prices. Where suppliers are heavily dependent upon these dominant players, relationships suffer when suppliers see their profit margins squeezed by organisations who are not interested in sharing benefits. This has led to anecdotal stories of suppliers having different sets of financial data ready to show the cost reduction teams from different dominant organisations.

The use of systems

EDI and bar-coding systems have become the norm in some sectors and suppliers in all tiers are expected to use the common system or protocol. If a supplier works in several sectors their systems will, however, have to bear the overhead or be able to determine the appropriate formats for individual requirements.

Self-assessment question 18.3

Imagine that your business is a tier one supplier for an aircraft manufacturer. The aircraft manufacturer insists that your organisation now uses company AA as a major tier two supplier as they feel that AA will bring considerable savings. Whilst you know of company AA you have a long-term relationship with company FF. How do you feel? How will this impact your relationship with all three organisations?

Feedback on page 293

18.4 Dependency in supply relationships

The objective of this subsection is to analyse the circumstances when dependency is a critical issue in supply relationships. Dependency means that one thing depends or relies upon another.

Learning activity 18.4

Evaluate your own business. Who is your biggest customer and what percentage of your business relies on them? Ask questions like the extent to which you are exposed. Reverse the process and consider your supply base. Ask the same question again, but this time, consider both parties. Finally, do you have any customers who are very dependent on you?

(continued on next page)

18

Learning activity 18.4 *(continued)*

If you work within a public sector organisation you may feel that you can only complete half of this activity, but think again. Who else do you depend upon?

Feedback on page 294

Many purchasing organisations place a limit on the proportion of a supplier's sales turnover that they will purchase; typically this may be 30%, with the logic that the supplier should not be over-exposed to one customer. This example has the supplier's interests at heart, though an arbitrary figure may frustrate both parties.

Other purchasing organisations will see security in a supplier being totally dependent on them and there are anecdotal stories from the retail sector where clothes manufacturers have been in this position when fashions or policies have changed and the high street store has chosen a different supplier causing the original one to cease trading. This example can be seen as an abuse of power, particularly if the purchasing organisation, in previous years, has persuaded the supplier to work 100% for them.

Clearly, where a supplier works within a supply chain that has dominant organisations prepared to exercise their power selfishly, the supplier will be dependent on one or several of these organisations for their livelihood and, considering CSR, responsible purchasing organisations must recognise this. However, in the final analysis survival for a purchasing organisation may depend upon a change of supplier and sentiment may play a small part in the decision. For suppliers the solution may lie in diversification, for it may be possible to sell themselves in different sectors, and by doing this they may become less dependent on any one sector.

Partners, allies and organisations in co-destiny relationships are by definition highly dependent upon each other. They should have risk management processes to provide early warning of problems.

Purchasing organisations can also become over-dependent upon niche service and product suppliers. Supply positioning, supplier preferencing and the market management matrix can be tools for understanding these situations, which in a number of cases are deliberately developed by sellers who seek to capture customers such that they become their advocates once 'lock in' is achieved.

Dependency becomes a critical issue for one party when their:

- Ability to make strategic business decisions is restricted by another organisation within their supply chain. Examples here include:
  - a dominant member in a supply chain insisting that a supplier must use given processes and standards which curtail their ability to win other business
  - a relationship agreement which, although not legally enforceable, restricts the activities of one of the parties. For example, it may be that a customer sees no benefit in a given product, but 'prefers' that their partner does not offer it to other customers. The supplier

18

may feel that their best interest is in not upsetting the customer who may be, for example, 47% of their turnover. In the short term this may be appropriate; however, in the long term an appropriate strategy may be to decrease the dependency on that customer.

- Survival is threatened by the activity or lack of activity of another organisation within their supply chain. Examples here include:
  - a dominant customer changing supplier
  - a dominant supplier ceasing supply, increasing costs or changing specification
  - an innovation making the need for this product or service redundant
  - a dominant customer not going ahead with a given project.

Buyers must know the extent to which suppliers are dependent upon them and openly discuss the issues that knowledge brings with people from the supplier organisation. It may be appropriate, for example, to recommend a supplier to another purchasing organisation in an attempt to bring about a lower dependency. Equally, a vital purchasing strategy is one which lowers risk and dependency on suppliers, where a close mutually advantageous situation is not sought or is not delivering the benefits expected. These issues were discussed in the context of the market management matrix in study sessions 3 and 4.

Self-assessment question 18.4

Assume that your site within a national organisation buys printed forms from a small local family firm on behalf of the whole group of companies. The printer has two employees and provides a good service at a low cost. The wife of the proprietor tells you one day that of their £60,000 turnover your organisation currently accounts for £20,000. Complete a SWOT analysis of this situation for both your organisation and the supplier.

Feedback on page 294

Revision question

Now try the revision question for this session on page 323.

Summary

Tiering is an appropriate way of managing the scarce resources of a purchasing organisation, it:

- removes the need for buyers to manage so many suppliers
- benefits buyers and suppliers alike
- can lead to an abuse of power by dominant organisations within a supply chain
- can lead to dependency and over-dependency of lower tier suppliers on the dominant player.

18

Dependency works both ways. Buyers can be dependent and over-dependent on suppliers and conversely suppliers can be dependent and over-dependent on buyers.

Feedback on learning activities and self-assessment questions

Feedback on learning activity 18.1

You should have realised that there are thousands of parts in a car (a recent article said 2,500) and if the car assembler dealt individually with each supplier there would be thousands of relationships to maintain.

Feedback on self-assessment question 18.1

Supplier tiering is a process of dividing the total number of suppliers into logical groupings and sub-groupings and establishing control and coordination processes to enable the purchasing organisation and the suppliers to operate efficiently and effectively.

Feedback on learning activity 18.2

Assuming that you have a reasonable number of suppliers already, then you are going to be very stretched if you have to deal with three times that number. You may feel that you would not be able to get to know everyone in an appropriate way.

Feedback on self-assessment question 18.2

1   A closer relationship, particularly for tier one suppliers.
2   Certainty of supply: an agreement may be reached for the lifetime of an aircraft or car.
3   Efficient and effective transactions: the advantages described for the purchasing organisation above also accrue to the suppliers.
4   Customers searching on your behalf for business. A tier two supplier can work closely with the tier one supplier who will be searching for business for both them and the tier two suppliers.
5   Demand forecasting and integration of systems can reduce the need to carry stock.

Feedback on learning activity 18.3

There can be no discussion or flexibility of when items are required, the 'tight' system of relaying information gives the car assembler total control of this aspect of the requirement.

Feedback on self-assessment question 18.3

You feel unfairly pressured by the aircraft manufacturer and not trusted because you know your job. Also, there is more to a relationship than cost. However, if supplier AA fails you will feel less responsible for them as they were not your choice.

18

You wonder whether the supplier FF will want to continue to deal with you if they feel let down by your organisation.

Company AA may feel that the power balance has swung towards them as they have been selected by the aircraft manufacturer and your relationship with them may get off to a difficult start.

Feedback on learning activity 18.4

You may find that your biggest customer accounts for 11% of your sales turnover and the exposure is significant but would not threaten the survival of your organisation. However, if your largest customer accounts for 76% of your business then your business will be heavily dependent upon them. Equally, your suppliers will be in the same position with your business.

Public sector organisations will have the same supplier issues; however, they may also depend upon local or central government for funding and changes of policy may impact them substantially. Grant-maintained organisations and charities might also be highly dependent in this way.

Feedback on self-assessment question 18.4

Table 18.1

SWOT	For the purchasing organisation	For the supplier
Strengths	You can dictate terms to the supplier. You will be at the front of the queue in times of urgent need or shortage. A good service at a low cost.	Good relationship. Ongoing stream of business.
Weaknesses	What backup is there if the supplier has a fire? What if the people are ill?	Whilst the firm is busy meeting your needs they may not be selling to other customers. If your organisation has a cash flow problem or a systems failure they will have a cash flow problem if you do not pay.
Opportunities	If the supplier offers a good service, can we help them get other customers to lower their dependency? Possibility of good low-cost long-term deal.	More business from you. Referrals to other customers to lessen the dependency.
Threats	Family relationship problems may cause you a problem.	A change in your corporate policy could move the purchasing of these items to another part of the country. Other customers may feel that they are too focused on you. Another supplier could beat their costs and they could lose a third of their business.

Study session 19
Supplier and relationship development

Introduction

Working in a relationship with people from a supplier does not mean working in a constant or static state of existence. Circumstances change, either in a way that we cannot control or because we want them to, our supplier wants them to or we and our supplier, working together, want them to change. This study session is about developing changes with our suppliers.

If you always do what you've always done, you'll always get what you always got!

Session learning objectives

After completing this session you should be able to:

19.1 Define supplier and relationship development.
19.2 Give examples of supplier development.
19.3 Give examples of relationship development opportunities.
19.4 Evaluate costs and benefits of development opportunities to both buyers and suppliers.

Unit content coverage

This study session covers the following topics from the official CIPS unit content document.

Learning objective

4.6 Evaluate a range of techniques to develop stronger relationships between purchasers and suppliers.

Timing

You should set aside about 6 hours to read and complete this session, including learning activities, self-assessment questions, the suggested further reading (if any) and the revision question.

19.1 Supplier and relationship development defined

Refresh your memory of the relationship life cycle model described in study session 6 and the concept of the relationship life cycle. Consider the

19

295

analogy of human relationships and the process of courtship as a preliminary relationship to marriage. Both personal and business relationships take time to evolve and mature. This subsection defines the terms used for the maturing process.

Learning activity 19.1

Define the terms 'supplier development', 'supplier relationship management' and 'relationship development'.

Feedback on page 305

Unpacking the definitions

Supplier development

Supplier development is about giving, yes, giving! The definition from Compton and Jessop (2001) indicates that we as the purchasing organisation provide assistance to suppliers in a number of forms, with the aim of enabling them to provide something which we need. The 1982 quote from Peter Drucker tells us that over 20 years ago management theorists saw the opportunity offered in supplier development and yet many organisations still seem reluctant to take it seriously. One final quotation from the now defunct magazine *Purchasing* in 1991 comes from Dave Nelson of Honda: 'Suppliers are given huge support in meeting their productivity, quality and cost goals. Working with suppliers is a full-time job for Honda engineers assigned to Purchasing.' So in 1991 Honda had engineers working full time with suppliers on development. Honda must see supplier development as important.

Supplier relationship management

Here the two-way travel principle is identified. This means that purchasing organisations have to acknowledge that they don't 'know it all' and that listening to suppliers may well be necessary. Listening also has to be turned into action in both cases, as improvements may be needed within the purchasing organisation.

Relationship development

Put your mind back to the courtship analogy. Getting closer only occurs when trust increases, and trust increases with the activities of the people in the organisation working together.

19.2 Examples of supplier development

Supplier development can take a number of forms.

Learning activity 19.2

If supplier development is about giving assistance or working with suppliers to help them to improve to help us, think of ways in which you and your organisation could work with suppliers on development projects.

Feedback on page 306

Why undertake supplier development?

Buyers should undertake supplier development to improve the current position to meet their business objectives. Specific reasons include the:

- recognition that goods and services are a greater proportion of total business cost now that outsourcing is common
- need to develop our supply base to deliver better in terms of goods and services or in terms of the way suppliers interface with us
- fact that technology has increased and become more specialised; we can't, shouldn't, won't make everything – we should encourage our suppliers to be specialists
- fact that we don't have a monopoly of ideas and cannot 'know it all'.

Supplier development is proactive and seeks new ideas and opportunities before they become problems or situations that have to be reacted to. Examples include:

- agreeing to contingent (ongoing) liability: when making an arrangement with a supplier we agree to share the cost if, for example, the predicted sales volumes do not materialise
- conducting training programmes with suppliers in best practice approaches
- enhancing working relationships by communication and team building events
- increasing performance goals with suppliers, for example to cut waste and improve delivery
- providing capital to assist in the development of a new project, perhaps in the form of a loan at a low rate or an investment in a project
- providing equipment, either loaning equipment at a peppercorn rate or selling it, for example for £1
- providing progress payments during the development of a project
- providing support personnel to assist in meeting quality, cost or delivery targets
- requiring supplier capability improvements to the ways in which we interface or the goods and services themselves.

You may note that the above list is alphabetical. It is taken from research in 1995 by Monckza and Trent quoted in the book *Purchasing and Supply Chain Management* (Monckza, Trent and Handfield, 1998). Their research considered how many organisations practised the form of supplier development in the list. Table 19.1 shows the above list sorted into the

19

percentage of organisations within the survey who practised each form of supplier development.

Table 19.1 Organisations practising forms of supplier development

Form of supplier development	Percentage of organisations practising this form
Enhancing working relationships	72.1%
Increasing performance goals	68.1%
Requiring supplier capability improvements	51.5%
Providing support personnel	27.9%
Conducting training programmes	25.3%
Agreeing to contingent liability	17.6%
Providing capital	10.3%
Providing equipment	11.8%
Providing progress payments	8.8%

Source: Monckza, Trent and Handfield (1998)

Table 19.1 shows that supplier development options which did cost purchasing organisations little were the most commonly ones practised, whereas the ones costing more and demanding more involvement from the purchasing organisation were least practised. It is, for example, relatively easy to offer to enhance working relationships, whatever that means in practice. Providing capital, equipment and progress payments are serious commitments to suppliers and the relationships with them.

One clear message from the survey is that purchasing organisations were not active in supplier development where it was necessary to input resources to assist their suppliers, yet many were keen to get the suppliers to do more, presumably for the same cost.

Practical examples

Five practical examples of supplier development are provided here.

1   The purchasing organisation sees great benefit in moving 250 tactical acquisition suppliers to purchasing cards. Research indicates that 75 suppliers do not have this capability at present. Calculations are done and it is established that purchasing and giving the terminals necessary to enact the transactions to these suppliers would cost less than the annual cost currently borne by the purchasing organisation in placing normal computer-generated orders with the suppliers and receiving paper-based invoices. The machines are purchased and distributed, but the suppliers pay the connection charge and line rental. The purchasing organisation receives the savings.

2   A supplier is viewed as proactive and go-ahead by the purchasing team and the engineer assigned to the purchasing team. A supplier appraisal reveals major savings to be made if the supplier's manufacturing processes are updated. A deal is struck whereby the supplier supplies:

    (a)   this purchasing organisation at audited cost, which after 18 months of the project is a reduction of 60% on the previous cost

    (b)   the competitors of this purchasing organisation using normal pricing but using the cost reduction techniques and keeping the difference.

3   A purchasing organisation needs additional space in its factory. It decides to outsource the production of modules forming a major part of its own production to a supplier and with the deal a unique machine has to be transferred to the supplier. The machine is rented for £1 per month and a deal is done to share the revenue from use of the spare capacity of the machine at the supplier.

4   One of three good suppliers of printed stationery is asked by a purchasing organisation to manage the delivery process of all four of the stationery suppliers to all of the 30 UK sites of the purchasing organisation. The selected supplier does not know the price charged by the other suppliers, they simply receive the delivery, store some items and despatch when requested. The purchasing organisation uses the space previously used for storage for other purposes and the people previously involved for other core activities.

5   One of the purchasing organisation's tier one suppliers is experiencing a significant cost in travelling to and managing suppliers on behalf of the purchasing organisation. The purchasing organisation has a volume purchasing travel agreement with an international travel services provider and suggests that the supplier uses that agreement to lower cost. The supplier is provided access to the appropriate website.

Self-assessment question 19.1

Identify five barriers to the use of the supplier development examples in the research of Monckza and Trent.

Feedback on page 306

19.3 Examples of relationship development opportunities

Relationship development is different to supplier development, although it must be said that one of the aims of supplier development and the deliverable if the process is successful will be a better relationship between buyer and seller. Where relationship development differs is that it involves giving and getting (it is two-way); it assumes that the development is about the relationship rather than the goods and services; and it frequently starts from an existing good position between the parties. By contrast, some supplier development projects are reactive and focus on solving problems.

Learning activity 19.3

If the analogy of courtship in human relationships, discussed earlier in this study session, is followed, consider how you would develop a relationship with an existing supplier who you considered best of breed.

Feedback on page 307

19

The process of relationship development

Assuming that we have a need to develop a relationship, the process of development could have four stages.

1   We have an ongoing relationship with what we might regard as a normal or acceptable supplier. Here the focus is short term on the delivery of goods and services and we may be in tactical acquisition.
2   Our need and the needs of our customers increase, so we prefer to use the given supplier and might consider them to have reached a 'preferred' status. Assuming volumes have increased, we may be moving along the 'X' axis in supply positioning. However, if we are getting closer to the supplier who we may not want to test in a competitive market, we are also moving upwards and approaching the centre of the supply positioning model. The focus moves towards service and product development with a supplier (supplier development?). Perhaps our relationship is described as single sourced or closer tactical.
3   Our need and the needs of our customers continue to increase and working together closely becomes essential to meet the needs of our customers. From the good basis we have in stage two, we approach the early stages of the strategic alliance or partnership.
4   Evolution has taken us to the stage where we realise that we must sit down and optimise the relationship if we are to allow it to reach its full potential, for we cannot imagine doing what we do without the other party. Here we are already in a strategic alliance or partnership and developing towards co-destiny.

Examining the issues in relationship development

To examine the first bullet in the list of the feedback to the learning activity, review the purchaser–supplier satisfaction model and the text with it in section 20.4. This model presumes both parties want to do better and will allow issues affecting the relationship to be discussed and solutions developed. It offers a practical way forward to developing solutions and eliminating issues that could cause problems in a relationship.

Asking a person from a supplier 'what is your organisation looking for from our relationship?' will surprise them, it's not often that sellers are faced with this question from buyers! When we understand those needs and aspirations we may be able, at little cost to ourselves, to move towards them.

The people within the supplier's organisation are frequently what make the organisation succeed or fail on our behalf. Again, understanding where the people in the selling organisation want to take the organisation, or what their personal or team aspirations are, can assist in developing the relationship.

Assuming that we have ideas ourselves, discussions with suppliers concerning joint product and service developments and joint approaches to markets and customers can pay dividends. Again we are assuming that we, as the buyer, are in the lead position here. Have we invited the people from the supplier to propose ideas and opportunities? It may be that we can set the scene at an initial meeting and invite people to return in a month and have a development session.

Taking the relationship development forward

Many of the above issues are 'touchy-feely' and as written may offer little hard evidence of benefit. However, acknowledging and working with 'touchy-feely' aspects is one of the essential elements of being in a relationship of any kind with another human being. There is a sense that we are starting out on a journey to which we do not know the destination, rather like Christopher Columbus! But consider your closest purchasing and supply relationship. Did it start as a partnership on the first day? Almost certainly not, it evolved. Let's consider how a good relationship, perhaps a strategic alliance or partnership, could evolve further, making the assumption that we are well into stage three or at early stage four of the process identified above. Note that many of the comments below link back to comments made in previous study sessions.

Terms and conditions

There is a time when trust is great enough to become the prime backstop in preference to terms and conditions. A strategic alliance agreement and one partnership agreement seen by the author have one thing in common. Both documents were no longer than two sides of A4 paper. Some buyers will feel uncomfortable with this and many large organisations will not feel secure with such short agreements. Another partnership agreement seen by the author was 109 pages long. The essence in this kind of relationship is *trust*. Can we not construct a short agreement that defines the parties, states the objectives, the titles of the main players, the basis of the financial rewards and the escalation procedure when problems occur? Within this agreement we may negotiate separate terms and conditions for specific projects and then get on working together.

People

Primarily we are concerned with the buyer/seller relationships. However, in relationship development we, as members of the purchasing team, may step backwards and, having set the parameters in the terms and conditions, leave the actual development to technical specialists, people from marketing and even top management. These people know the business and where they want to develop it, and within a secure trusting relationship we can let them develop opportunities with people from our ally or partner. Perhaps they will use the collaborative development forum described in section 5.2.

Processes

Processes are vital to successful organisations and the relationship may develop to a situation where there is enough trust to stop sending 'purchase orders' and send formatted transactions. Review the text in section 4.3 as the destination here.

Opportunities

People are imaginative, and in a situation where the day-to-day problems have already been worked through, and, given an environment where together with others they can search for, conceive and develop opportunities

19

with the resources of two organisations rather than one organisation, they can deliver surprising results.

Students may be able to identify and discuss other issues that those described above, for example 'time', where immediate results may not be shown.

Self-assessment question 19.2

Take the supply positioning model. Draw the four quadrants and then use the process described under the heading of 'the process of relationship development' to position the four stages on the supply positioning model by drawing small circles for the four stages. Then join the four circles with a line.

Feedback on page 307

19.4 Costs and benefits: of development opportunities

This subsection evaluates costs and benefits of both supplier and relationship development opportunities to both buyers and suppliers. Everyone involved in development will have costs and benefits. Review the information below and consider how these factors would impact your organisation.

Buyer's costs and benefits

Typical costs to be borne by a purchasing organisation in supplier and relationship development include:

- time identifying, researching and developing suppliers, even convincing them of the opportunity
- travel to and from meetings and suppliers' sites
- extra people to work on projects
- direct cost of machines, systems and materials applied to the project
- loss of interest (pounds, dollars, euros etc.) when funds are used on these projects; opportunity cost
- risk of sharing new technology/new ideas which may be taken and abused by others
- risk to our reputation if the project fails.

Typical benefits delivered to a purchasing organisation in supplier and relationship development include:

- greater profit from reduced supply chain costs
- improvements in quality, punctuality, time to market, reliability, service
- reduced unit cost in absolute terms
- reduced unit cost against market trend
- reduced process cost from optimised transactions
- additional sales volume through new opportunities or lower costs

- additional purchasing volumes within our volume purchasing agreements where suppliers use our agreements
- lower costs from using supplier volume purchasing agreements
- new ideas.

Typical costs to be borne by a supplier as part of supplier and relationship development include:

- time taken identifying and developing customers, developing the opportunity
- time taken assessing customers' proposals
- travel to and from meetings and customers sites
- extra people to work on projects
- direct cost of machines, systems and materials applied to the project
- loss of interest (pounds, dollars, euros etc.) when funds are used on this project; opportunity cost
- risk of sharing new technology/new ideas which may be taken and abused by others
- risk to the supplier's reputation if the project fails
- being tied to the customer and not able to work with others.

Typical benefits delivered to a supplier as part of supplier and relationship development include:

- greater profit from reduced supply chain costs
- improvements in information on customer and customer's customer requirements
- reduced unit cost against market
- reduced process cost from optimised transactions
- additional sales volume through new opportunities or lower costs
- referrals from customers to other customers
- additional purchasing volumes within our volume purchasing agreements where customers use our agreements
- lower costs from using customer volume purchasing agreements
- new ideas
- longer-term security of business and the planning advantages that affords
- ability to improve:
    - quality, punctuality
    - time to market
    - sales volume, profit
- security to invest in equipment, processes and people
- new customers
- use of knowledge from the development project with other customers.

The concept of the cost of quality

This concept can allow specific measurement of development projects undertaken with suppliers, although it starts by identifying the cost of lapses in quality and cost which can be called the 'cost of no quality'. The concept focuses on four areas, the cost of:

- prevention
- appraisal

- internal failure
- external failure.

This concept is most easily applied to a manufacturing environment where there is a natural need to control quality. However, the concept can also be applied to services.

The cost of prevention

Here the focus is on steps taken by both organisations to prevent failure. It involves an examination of where failures occur now, consideration of how they may be prevented and an examination of any other potential failure. 'Failure' may be a non-arrival of the notes for a training programme, the CD player that stops working after six weeks or the hand rail that falls off a new building. Designers, existing customers, purchasers and many others will investigate how a potential quality problem could be avoided within the goods and services being delivered.

The cost of appraisal

Here the focus is on the costs of ensuring that everything is done to appraise potential situations, before during and after the delivery of the goods or services. Included here is the cost of supplier appraisal and the costs of the quality control or quality assurance processes used by both buyers and sellers. The cost of these actions can be understood if the cost of inspection departments and their equipment are assessed, and the cost of supplier appraisal and vendor rating systems is evaluated.

The cost of internal failure

The focus in this area is the costs associated with goods and services that do not perform as required within the purchasing organisation. Examples include the machined component which broke during the internal test of the equipment to which it was fitted or the external outsourced IT maintainer which failed to fix a network problem in a call centre, halting sales calls for six hours. In these circumstances the cost of the failure can be ascertained in time taken to resolve, scrapped components and the cost of replacement components. Additionally the cost of overtime may be incurred to complete work within deadlines.

The cost of external failure

In this case, two of the prime costs may be reputation and repeat business for, although the cost of warranty claims and the people needed to work with customers to resolve the issues created may be easier to assess, unhappy customers are less likely to reorder or reuse the service and also they will be keen to tell others of their experience. Consider the publicity received by a car manufacturer who feels it necessary to place an advert within a national newspaper recalling all vehicles with a serial number between 'x' and 'y' for safety.

As part of supplier and relationship development exercises it is possible to make examinations of these areas of cost and make meaningful reductions in the costs by revising business processes. For example, a purchasing organisation works closely with the supplier of components and understands the extent of the supplier's inspection processes. It may be that both organisations are carrying out similar tests of the products, one as part of post-production processes and the other as part of goods received processes. Clearly there is an opportunity to reduce cost. Could the purchasing organisation trust the supplier sufficiently to eliminate their inspection completely? If this decision is taken then a clear saving in cost and time can be accrued by the purchasing organisation.

Self-assessment question 19.3

Take the headings under 'cost of quality' (cost of prevention, appraisal, internal failure or external failure) and provide three sub-points as examples of costs that might be incurred by the purchasing organisation against each main point.

Feedback on page 307

Revision question

Now try the revision question for this session on page 323.

Summary

Supplier development is not easy. Relationship development is harder to practise than supplier development. Buyers intending to develop in either or both directions must commit to:

- giving time and resources
- seeking to understand the objectives and requirements of others
- listening to the others
- taking opportunities which may also be risks
- taking an existing good situation and wanting to do better
- identifying areas within the concept of cost of quality.

Suggested further reading

Review the material in the relationship management and supplier development section and other sections of CIPS knowledge works on the CIPS website.

Feedback on learning activities and self-assessment questions

Feedback on learning activity 19.1

Supplier development

'The provision of finance, technology or other forms of assistance by the buyer to the supplier to enable the supplier to offer a product or

19

service which meets the buyer's needs, or to interface with the buying organisation in a mutually appropriate way.'

Compton and Jessop (2001)

'Nowhere in business is there greater potential for benefiting from interdependency between customer firms and their suppliers. This is the largest remaining frontier for gaining competitive advantage – and nowhere has such a frontier been more neglected.'

Drucker (1982)

Supplier relationship management (SRM)

'The process of managing the interaction between two entities – one of which is supplying goods, works or services to the other entity. SRM is a two way process in that it should improve the performance of the buying organisation as well as the supplying organisation and hence be mutually beneficial.'

CIPS (2006)

Relationship development

A two-way process between buyers and sellers where activities jointly undertaken bring the organisations and the people working within them progressively closer towards a more trusting and mutually beneficial state.

Feedback on learning activity 19.2

You could have said:

- cost reduction projects
- communications projects
- technology road-map planning
- designing new goods and services
- planning to attack a new market.

Feedback on self-assessment question 19.1

Examples include:

- absence of adequate communication
- day to day and long term
- absence of two-way feedback
- concentration of supplier performance
- no interest in buyer's performance
- executive management support in theory, but deny resources in practice
- lack of buyer credibility: the buyer demands from others what they themselves cannot deliver
- supplier unwillingness to participate due to:
  - not being able to trust the buyer
  - the requirement being too small
  - the perception that they have no need to improve

19

   – the supplier having a monopoly
   – the supplier already having a close relationship with competitor.

Feedback on learning activity 19.3

You could have focused on:

- identifying and eliminating the problem areas
- understanding the needs of the other organisation better
- getting to know the people in the other organisation better
- considering opportunities for development of joint approaches to given markets and customers
- considering a joint product or service development.

Feedback on self-assessment question 19.2

Figure 19.1 forms the feedback to this question.

Figure 19.1: Relationship development

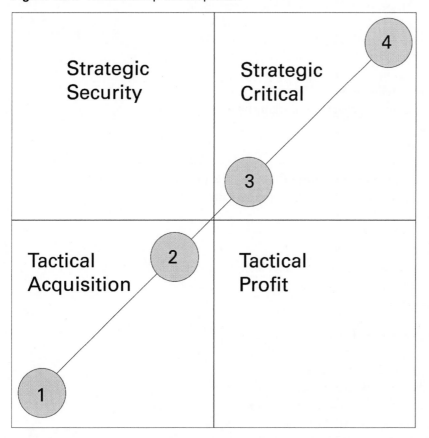

Feedback on self-assessment question 19.3

The cost of prevention:

- goods receipt
- inspection:
    - incoming
    - outgoing

    – at our supplier
    – at our customer
- FMEA (failure mode and effects analysis)
- statistical process control
- equipment and systems
- value analysis and value engineering.

The cost of appraisal:

- the sourcing process
- searching
- enquiry
- evaluation of goods and services
- supplier appraisal/ongoing audit
- quality audits
- commercial audits
- environmental audits
- capability audits
- supplier development initiatives
- negotiation of performance measures.

The cost of internal failure:

- verification of fault and cause
- express delivery of replacements
- sorting and segregation of material
- scrap
- rework
- communication of:
  - acceptance/rejection of failure to supplier
  - putting the relationship right again
- machine downtime
- service unavailability
- overtime for employees
- internal panics/galloping backlogs
- invoice mismatches
- concessions.

The cost of external failure:

- returns from customers
- verification of fault and cause
- express delivery of new 'right' goods
- repeated service to ensure customer satisfaction
- higher-level technical support to put things right
- sorting and segregation of material
- scrap
- rework
- refund of costs to customer
- invoice mismatches
- credit notes
- penalties.

19

Study session 20
Measuring relationships and their development

Introduction

Measurement of both the arrangements we make for the delivery of goods and services and the relationships entered into is important, but whilst we can create many measures, they won't on their own deliver the service or the relationship sought.

'A hundred objective measurements didn't sum the worth of a garden; only the delight of its users did that. Only the use made it mean something.'
Lois McMaster Bujold, *A Civil Campaign* (1999)

Session learning objectives

After completing this session you should be able to:

20.1 Evaluate why and when buyers would benefit from measuring supplier performance and the strength of relationships.
20.2 Assess how sellers see the relationships with buyers.
20.3 Give examples of measures used in supplier performance measurement for both goods and services.
20.4 Give examples of relationship measures.

Unit content coverage

This study session covers the following topics from the official CIPS unit content document.

Learning objective

4.8 Evaluate a range of measurement tools to assess the performance of suppliers and the strength of relationships between purchasers and suppliers.

Timing

You should set aside about 5 hours to read and complete this session, including learning activities, self-assessment questions, the suggested further reading (if any) and the revision question.

20.1 Measuring supplier performance

In this subsection we will evaluate why and when buyers would benefit from measuring supplier performance and the strength of relationships. The drive to measure frequently comes from the security motive and, underlying that, the risk that we run in entering into purchasing and supply relationships.

Learning activity 20.1

Take a supplier currently working for you in the tactical acquisition quadrant of supply positioning and indicate how you currently measure their performance.

Feedback on page 319

Why purchasing organisations measure

The objective of supplier performance measurement is 'to obtain and distribute relevant and timely data on the performance of both suppliers and buyers, using the minimum resources'. Reasons why a purchasing organisation undertakes measurement include:

- Ensuring contract performance. We have made an agreement and it is important to us that the supplier meets the agreement. Whilst this objective is the prime objective it must not be the dominant one in all relationships.
- Identifying process improvement opportunities. Improvement is a vital aspect of many business situations and in measuring it we may, together with the people from our suppliers, identify opportunities for improvement and the removal of muda.
- Identifying cost savings. Cost and the removal of unnecessary cost is a vital factor.
- Demonstrating shortcomings. Note that this does not have the word 'supplier' attached to it, it covers both parties.
- Learning for the future.
- Creating a benchmark against which to compare future performance.

Principles of measurement

The principles that follow are vital considerations before specific measures are determined.

1   We must measure what is vital to us. This means that we need to concentrate on strategic goods and services.
2   We must use measures that are relevant to the needs of our stakeholders and our business. For example, it may be easy to measure and compliment a supplier on delivery performance and miss quality and cost reduction issues which are key business issues and may be more difficult to measure.
3   The acronym 'KISS' meaning 'Keep It Simple Stupid' is another factor. Simple measures tend to work and absorb fewer resources.
4   The measures must be robust. They must work again and again.

5   Effective measures are 'owned' by suppliers' key people. Where people believe in the measures proposed, they support them and ensure they are delivered.
6   Listen to suppliers' ideas. It is probable that the supplier will have their own ideas and know measures that will work successfully.

Where to measure

The principles above touch on this when they emphasise measuring what is vital. We must understand the risks we face and in strategic areas work with suppliers' people to ensure that we measure, report and act upon what is likely to cause pain to our organisation, our customers and our suppliers.

Whilst it is relatively easy to measure the delivery and cost of stationery, many organisations would not consider this vital. For a retailer the availability of the stationery used in credit card machines and tills will, however, be vital.

For a motor-car assembly line the non-arrival of components can halt production very quickly. Measurement here might include knowing or being able to find out if necessary, where the components are on the road network, being alerted if components were in a traffic jam on the M25 and working with suppliers to minimise this in the future.

For a high street bank a key measure is the availability of cash machines for customers and working with and incentivising maintenance suppliers to improve availability.

Benefits

In the three situations highlighted above, consider the benefits of measurement to the organisations concerned. What is common between them all is that if the goods and services are performed as needed, they are able to carry out their primary business processes. The retailer is able to sell to customers, the car assembler is able to produce and the bank's customers are able to get their cash on demand. Measurement is not, however, the end of the process, for the measures identified could lead to process improvements for all three organisations.

The retailer may decide that secure delivery could mean a reduction in stock of the stationery, although the criticality of the stationery and its relatively low cost may mean that stock is a solution.

The car assembler would seek to use technology and accurate forecast data to further reduction of stocks in the supply chain.

The bank could work with suppliers and maintainers to identify the failure rate of components and technology to review the distribution of maintenance engineers against their footprint of cash machines.

In summary, measurement should play a role in delivering what internal and external customers really want, prioritise the benefits sought and generate strategies positively impacting upon cost drivers and cost itself.

20

Self-assessment question 20.1

Contrast what you would seek to measure in a partnership and in an adversarial relationship.

Feedback on page 319

20.2 Assess how sellers see their relationships with buyers

The supplier preferencing model, discussed in study session 3, is a prime tool for assessing how suppliers see buyers. In terms of performance measurement suppliers will measure and compare their customers.

Learning activity 20.2

Indicate five ways in which you believe a supplier may measure a purchasing organisation's performance during a contract.

Feedback on page 319

Being human beings, just like buyers, suppliers will measure from a risk motive. From the first they will consider the risk of not getting paid and where they perceive that as a high risk, they will look for other customers. However, during the delivery of the contract they will measure the extent to which:

- payment is received on time: where this is a problem the seller may seek to recover the cost of the late payment in other ways
- terms and conditions agreed to are fulfilled: this may be lead time afforded by the buyer against lead time agreed, timelines of reportage provided on performance, early payment discount taken, or volumes proposed and received
- changes are made to schedules, deliveries, basic requirements, specifications, people dealing with the supplier
- errors are tolerated: is every little error made a major issue when it originates from the supplier, but swept under the carpet when it originates from the buyer?
- communication is good, or on a need-to-know basis or simply absent: supply positioning may impact this from the buyer's point of view though
- the supplier feels they are given an opportunity to perform well
- costs and risk are shared, if that is what has been agreed – or does the buyer seek to pass cost on to the seller even though there is an agreement to share cost and risk?

Buyers need to be able to see how their suppliers measure them. Consider two of your suppliers, sitting in a hotel coffee shop and talking about you and your organisation. What would you want them to be saying about the way they were treated? Will it be:

- 'Yes, Rosemary gives us a fair chance to do a good job, we get the information and we mostly get paid on time, they are driving for cost reduction but they have involved us in the process and we have delivered what they asked.'

or:

- 'Ah Rosemary, wouldn't trust her as far as I could throw her. Pays late, always on the phone changing things and then changing them back again. I can see from the fact that you're nodding that she's like it with you. How much are you putting on next year to cover all the problems?'

We would prefer the first of these two conversations to be about us. However, if it is the second option we need to be thinking of making some changes.

Self-assessment question 20.2

Take the 16 market management matrix situations described in study sessions 3 and 4 and indicate where you would be most concerned to know how a supplier measured you and your organisation.

Feedback on page 319

20.3 Examples of supplier performance measures

This section provides examples of measures used in supplier performance measurement for both goods and services.

Learning activity 20.3

You are a small distributor of spare parts without your own IT department. Consider how you would measure the performance of a supplier who managed your IT systems.

Feedback on page 319

What do buyers want to measure suppliers on? Considerations like on time delivery, quality or cost reduction spring to mind. Whilst remembering that what is measured and what it is measured against will vary with the requirement, the organisation, the sector and the nature of the contract, figure 20.1 provides a generic 'cat's cradle' view. In this model it is possible and relevant to measure each of the factors in the left-hand column against each of the factors in the right-hand column, depending upon the needs and objectives of the organisations at the time.

20

Figure 20.1: The cat's cradle of supplier measurement

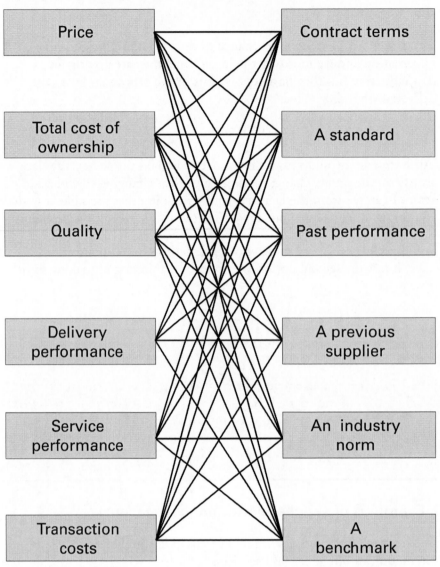

The following measures are examples of specific measures used in different industries and circumstances. They are chosen for their variety and the fact that they move away from the generic examples above.

1   Cost erosion against targets. Targets may be based upon past performance or a market need. However, electrical goods manufacturers face targets to reduce cost to enable them to compete in the worldwide market for their goods. In this industry a 7% cost reduction target was set for all suppliers in one organisation in 2002. There was little negotiation and the bonuses of everyone in the purchasing organisation did not start until more than 7% had been reduced from purchase cost.

2   Technology road maps. In high-tech industries buyers will want to see and measure the technical road map of suppliers against their own road map and market trend.

3   Compliance to environmental and CSR standards. Buyers will want to ensure that suppliers have policies, procedures and factual feedback to share in these areas.

4   Ability to integrate into supply chain. Here suppliers face demands to be able to work within the supply chain using standard systems

and protocols. This measure aims to ensure that information can be communicated accurately throughout the chain. For example, it is noted that an absolute requirement for CIPS examiners from the start of this syllabus is access to broadband or ISDN technology.

5   Customer satisfaction. Service organisations need to know how they are performing and what customers feel that they can do to improve the situation. Following a repair to a computer it is likely that you may receive a web link to complete a questionnaire on the service you have received.

In addition to the selection of robust and appropriate measures it is important that senior management support is obtained for key measures as internally and externally senior managers will meet and talk to stakeholders. If they perceive a measure as irrelevant then the stakeholders and suppliers will not work to deliver it. There can be difficulties in making measures work, particularly where a subjective element exists in the measurement process. However, repeated use of the same measure and the ability to recognise and discount personal conflicts can give useful trend information.

Self-assessment question 20.3

From figure 20.1 take delivery performance from the left-hand column and indicate how you would measure it against each of the criteria in the right-hand column.

Feedback on page 320

20.4 Examples of relationship measures

It is difficult to fully and accurately understand how the other party, a person working for a supplier, feels in a purchasing and supply relationship. If a buyer asks a seller, 'How do you see us as a customer?' sellers are tempted to give the reply that they feel the buyer wants, so they reply, 'You are a core customer to us'. This may mean that the cycle of question and answer becomes self-fulfilling and naïve buyers are told what they want to hear, whilst buyers trying to honestly understand how satisfied or dissatisfied a supplier really is can feel frustrated with the standard reply.

Learning activity 20.4

If you were to consider the issues that would make you more or less satisfied in a purchasing and supply relationship, what would they be?

Feedback on page 320

Truly attempting to assess the level of satisfaction in a relationship will be time consuming, costly and risky, for it will include an element of exposing your own feelings and logic dictates that we would therefore only invest such effort in strategic relationships. Leenders and Fearon (1997) describe a purchaser–supplier satisfaction model – refer to figure 20.2. This model

20

provides a meaningful framework for clarifying a purchasing and supply relationship. The material below, from Leenders and Fearon (1997), is reproduced with the permission of the McGraw-Hill Companies.

Assumptions

Leenders and Fearon state that the assumptions behind the model are that:

1 The two parties will have different perceptions of the same relationship.
2 The current buyer/supplier relationship can be assessed, however crudely, at least in macro terms.
3 The unsatisfied parties will attempt to move towards a more satisfied position.
4 Attempts to move may affect the stability of the relationship.
5 Attempts to move the position of the relationship can result in a move to any of the four quadrants the model contains.
6 Tools, techniques and approaches exist to assist the parties in movement within the model.

To these assumptions the author of this document adds the assumptions that both parties:

• genuinely wish the relationship to develop and
• are prepared to be honest in the information they provide.

Figure 20.2: The purchaser–supplier satisfaction model

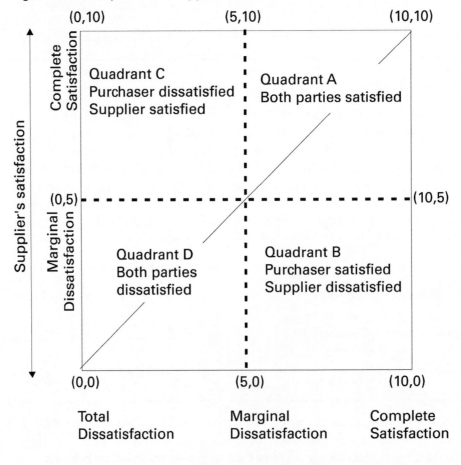

Explaining the purchaser–supplier satisfaction model

The x axis of the purchaser–supplier satisfaction model considers the buyer's satisfaction on a scale of 0 to 10 and the y axis the supplier's satisfaction, also on a scale of 0 to 10, thus arriving at four quadrants where both parties are satisfied, both parties are dissatisfied, or one party is satisfied and the other is dissatisfied. Note that the scoring methodology in the model is explained under the 'Practicalities and process' heading below.

The model could be used simply to consider the relationship as a whole. However, it is probably most beneficial if used separately across several issues within a relationship. In this way the parties would understand each other's views on a range of key issues relevant to differing aspects of their relationship. The diagonal line is seen as the fairness or stability line where both parties are considered equally well off.

The extremes of this line could relate to the market management matrix relationships:

- tactical profit to exploitable, where the score was 0 on both sides
- strategic critical to core, where the score was 10 on both sides.

Practicalities and process

The practicalities of getting an honest answer may also mean that an honest broker third party may be needed to assist the parties in determining the issues and their respective views of them separately before facilitating joint sessions helping everyone to understand where they stand at present. The timing of the analysis is also important. Within the relationship life cycle model discussed in study session 6 this analysis would ideally be undertaken within steps 20 or 22 in that model, continuous improvement or extension.

The first step in the process is to agree the key issues between the parties and the second step is to carry out the initial analysis.

The result of the initial analysis will allow everyone to understand how the other party in the relationship feels about the current situation. For example it may reveal that:

- the buyer (scoring eight) is satisfied with payment terms and the seller (scoring three) is dissatisfied
- the buyer is dissatisfied (scoring four) with typical responses to requests to schedule changes, whilst the supplier considers their responsiveness good with a score of nine
- both parties may be dissatisfied with three issues; the computer systems processing transactions between them, their current strategy plan and their ability to react to competitor pressures
- both parties may be satisfied with the joint approach to marketing over the last 12 months.

The third step is to discuss the initial analysis and *together* plan action to improve the situation. It may be that a fuller understanding of the difficulties being experienced by one party may allow the other party to

20

move on that issue, such that the scores move into quadrant A where both parties are satisfied. Equally, movement on one issue may not be possible but movement on another is. In a partnership the exercise could be repeated at two-yearly intervals.

The value of the purchaser–supplier satisfaction model

The value of the purchaser–supplier satisfaction model analysis is the:

1   information it brings out about the view of the partner or ally in a relationship
2   opportunity to be frank and open in a constructive forum
3   opportunity it affords both parties to develop further over time. Whilst it may not be possible to change immediately, this analysis will be a key input into the long-term development of the relationship
4   ability to recognise and value the amount of agreement between the parties. It may be that a given issue is considered as a score of six by buyer and seller alike, meaning that both are marginally satisfied. The opportunity therefore exists to develop a good situation into an excellent one
5   generation of trust between the people involved in the relationship
6   opportunity it brings to take the partnership concept from theory into practice.

Self-assessment question 20.4

Assume that a purchaser–supplier satisfaction model analysis has been undertaken with a key component partner using an independent third party to talk to both parties. As the buyer you are unaware of any problems in the relationship. At the initial meeting to review the issues the supplier had reflected on the issue of the current cost reduction strategy as 'leaving my organisation considerably out of pocket' with a score of 2.5. Your score was 8.5 reflecting that the current cost reduction strategy was 'delivering major benefits'. The situation is therefore within quadrant B of the purchaser–supplier satisfaction model.

How would you react to this observation from your partner?

Feedback on page 320

Revision question

Now try the revision question for this session on page 323.

Summary

- Measurement on its own will not deliver relationship benefits, but it can lead to recognition of areas in which both parties can improve.
- Measure what is vital in a simple and robust way.
- Try to understand how suppliers measure buyers.

- Relationship measures are primarily appropriate for strategic supply situations.
- Active relationship measurement can take the concept of partnership from theory into practice.
-

Feedback on learning activities and self-assessment questions

Feedback on learning activity 20.1

Performance measures may include on time delivery, quality or cost reduction.

Feedback on self-assessment question 20.1

In a partnership measures would include innovation, cost reduction, the relationship and how it is developed, process cost reduction, competitive position against others and road map.

In an adversarial relationship measures would include price, in absolute terms and against the market, delivery and availability.

Feedback on learning activity 20.2

1 Payment on time.
2 Sticking to the contract terms and conditions.
3 The number of changes to the contract.
4 The number of queries raised on invoices.
5 The quality of communication.

Feedback on self-assessment question 20.2

You would be most concerned to know how a supplier measured you and your organisation in the following relationships:

- Criticality of the requirement drives our concern to know in these cases:
  - Strategic critical to core
  - Strategic critical to development
  - Strategic critical to nuisance
  - Strategic critical to exploitable
- Risk of non-supply is the driver in these cases:
  - Strategic security to exploitable
  - Strategic security to nuisance
  - Tactical acquisition to nuisance.

Feedback on learning activity 20.3

Measures could include:

- responsiveness to requests for help
- system up time as a percentage

20

319

- how helpful the supplier's people were
- how well the supplier's people understood your software
- time to fix problems
- advice on a development path
- cost of service.

Feedback on self-assessment question 20.3

The feedback in each case below relates to a separate situation, not the same situation.

The contract – measure against what is agreed in the contract and its schedules. If next-day delivery is agreed, does it happen?

A standard – delivery must be to the goods receiving stores. Does this happen?

Past performance – previously we have received a 15-day delivery service on these items, now we seek to move to a five-day lead time.

The previous supplier – we changed supplier because the previous supplier would not move from their 22 day lead time, the improvement will be 10 to 12 days.

The industry norm is overnight delivery, how many times do we receive this service from our supplier?

A benchmark – we understand that our competitors have moved to a shorter delivery from their supplier. Can we match this target or improve upon it?

Feedback on learning activity 20.4

You might have said trust, honesty, reliability, quality, meeting targets, cost reduction, innovation, secure terms and conditions – a whole range of issues will exist.

Feedback on self-assessment question 20.4

1 I wish you had told me earlier.
2 I didn't realise that you were suffering.
3 Can you quantify the damage?
4 What can we do together to improve the situation?

An output from this situation may be a redistribution of the benefits of the cost reduction strategy or an adjustment in other ways to reduce the imbalance which obviously exists. To ignore this situation now you are aware of it would be to advertise that you did not value your partner.

Revision questions

Revision question for study session 2

Define the term 'stakeholder'. From your own experience, identify five stakeholders in the process of purchasing and determine what each of the stakeholders you identify would seek from the process of purchasing.

Feedback on page 325

Revision question for study session 3

Describe how buyers and sellers engaged in an adversarial relationship treat each other.

Feedback on page 325

Revision question for study session 4

Compare and contrast the relationship issues in a partnership relationship with an arm's-length relationship from a buyer's point of view.

Feedback on page 325

Revision question for study session 5

Identify and briefly describe three e-purchasing tools and indicate:

(a) in which type of relationship you would use the given tool
(b) two benefits that the tool would bring to the purchasing organisation employing it.

Feedback on page 326

Revision question for study session 6

Differentiate the activities of the buyer and the seller in the initiation part of the relationship life cycle model.

Feedback on page 327

Revision question for study session 7

Define corporate social responsibility (CSR) and indicate how each of the following areas within the umbrella of CSR impacts buyers purchasing goods from a low-wage economy:

(a) environmental responsibility
(b) human rights
(c) ethics and ethical trading.

Feedback on page 328

Revision question for study session 8

Contrast and compare lean manufacturing with what is referred to as traditional manufacturing.

Feedback on page 328

Revision question for study session 9

Identify the issues to be considered by a buyer when planning a supplier appraisal process.

Feedback on page 329

Revision question for study session 10

Describe the factors that will condition a supplier's view of a supplier appraisal process.

Feedback on page 329

Revision question for study session 11

Assume that you work for a private sector organisation. Your organisation is about to purchase a computer system costing £500,000. Take five issues within the purchasing process and indicate how they would be different if your organisation was bound by the EU procurement directives.

Feedback on page 330

Revision question for study session 12

Debate the following statement: 'Reciprocal trading is normally a bad thing for purchasing organisations'.

Feedback on page 330

Revision question for study session 13

Identify four areas of risk for the purchasing organisation to consider when changing supplier. For each risk indicate:

(a) what the consequence could be if the risk materialises
(b) how you would work with the old and new suppliers to minimise the risk in each case.

Feedback on page 331

Revision question for study session 14

Define the term 'outsourcing'. Explain why organisations in many sectors choose to outsource.

Feedback on page 331

Revision question for study session 15

Describe how buyers' and sellers' objectives differ throughout the life cycle of an outsourcing relationship.

Feedback on page 332

Revision question for study session 16

Compare and contrast laid back and aggressive cultures. Outline the difficulties they will present to a new purchasing professional.

Feedback on page 333

Revision question for study session 17

Explain why maintaining purchasing and supply relationships with suppliers in different parts of the world is more difficult.

Feedback on page 333

Revision question for study session 18

Tiering is a concept used in manufacturing.

(a) Using diagrams, indicate how a manufacturer may tier their supply base.
(b) Indicate what benefits the concept of tiering brings to organisations who use it.

Feedback on page 334

Revision question for study session 19

Explain why a purchasing organisation, already satisfied with the performance of a supplier, should proactively work with a supplier on supplier development projects.

Feedback on page 335

Revision question for study session 20

Explain the objective of measuring supplier performance. Identify principles that you would use to steer your approach to measuring the performance of a supplier.

Feedback on page 335

Feedback on revision questions

Feedback on revision question for study session 2

Start with a definition of stakeholder. 'Stakeholders are people working in different functions of organisations who have an ongoing interest and influence on the process of purchasing.'

1   Engineers will require quality, dependability, something to fit their specific needs and a role in supplier selection.
2   Accountants will require low-cost, long payment terms which they will choose to vary at their whim, low inventories and demonstrable procedures.
3   External customers will require goods and services to meet their standards, delivered when they need them.
4   Quality engineers will require evidence of quality procedures and records from suppliers, the ability to sample and test goods and services and improvements in performance.
5   Sales people will require their customers' needs to be met, more benefits to sell to their customers, descending unit costs to increase margins, a clear development road map.

Feedback on revision question for study session 3

First, define an adversarial relationship. An adversarial relationship is one where both the buyer and the seller seek to maximise their position in any given supply opportunity, even to the detriment of the other party or parties.

Whilst working in this relationship, both parties will:

- supply information on a 'need to know' basis
- provide minimum warning before a competitive process starts
- only do what they 'believe' they have agreed
- limit their concern to their own needs. In an extreme situation. a buyer may not change a contract even if the supplier could go bankrupt
- exhibit inconsistent attitudes/behaviour
- treat the other with a lack of care and even outright hostility and/or aggression
- be unsure as to the extent that trust exists between them and feel the need to check upon what has been promised by the other party.

Feedback on revision question for study session 4

Define both relationships.

A partnership relationship is a commitment between a buyer and a supplier to a long-term relationship based on trust and clear mutually agreed objectives. Sharing risks and rewards is fundamental through the common goals of:

- continuous improvement
- an improved competitive position
- the elimination of waste
- acceleration of innovation
- expansion of markets
- the growth of profit.

An arm's-length relationship is one where a buyer buys infrequently from a supplier, and does not have high volumes or the need for a closer relationship. The arm's-length relationship is one where the given deal is, once again, worth more than the relationship and both parties will:

- retain information to release as needed, with minimum warning before the competitive process starts, whereas in a partnership the information flow and transactions between parties is optimised
- only go as far as the agreement they have made with the supplier, whereas in a partnership there is cost transparency, the purchasing organisation being aware of the cost structure of the supplier and the supplier being aware of the proportion of the purchasing organisation's cost which the service or goods they provide accounts for
- limit their concern to their own needs, but want to ensure that the supplier is around for them in the future, whereas in a partnership joint project teams tackle problems, technical and market opportunities and intuitive development can be seen in action
- treat the other party with respect, but recognise business may be transient, whereas in a partnership the relationship feels as if 'we' are in this for the long term! It can be 'for better or worse' to succeed together
- trust each other to keep their side of the bargain, but not expect them to go beyond it, whereas in a partnership the partners trust each other to the extent that buyers exclude other suppliers and suppliers exclude other buyers; the two parties focus on each other, rather than the supply market.

Partnership relationships are ones where the highest level of trust exists and the duration is long term. The relationship is worth vastly more than any one deal or issue between the parties.

Feedback on revision question for study session 5

The three tools selected are data warehousing, a collaborative development forum and an electronic reverse auction.

1   Data warehousing. A data warehouse is a structured replica of an organisation's transaction data specifically designed to facilitate speedy and accurate enquiry and reporting. This tool could be used in a range of relationships from adversarial, where it would gather and

maintain data and give a sense of advantage over the supplier, to a partnership, where the data warehouse would hold information from both organisations. The advantage of this facility is the access to up-to-date, meaningful and relevant data which can be used to make business decisions which themselves can provide competitive advantage. A second advantage is that the data warehouse will ensure that the same information is available at different parts of the purchasing process.

2   A collaborative development forum is a secure website set up between buyers and suppliers for technical stakeholders and others to participate in the design and development of products and services between the organisations concerned, excluding other organisations and even restricting internal access to technically sensitive developments. This tool would be used within a partnership relationship and its benefits are that design cycles can be greatly reduced and new ideas generated by technical people from both organisations working together.

3   Electronic reverse auctions, in their various forms, provide an electronic environment for suppliers to bid for one item, a group of items or a whole package of goods and services. This tool would be used in a transactional or adversarial relationship situation and its benefits are lower cost and inducing competition.

Feedback on revision question for study session 6

The initiation segment recognises that in some cases this process will be a development of a previous sale, that there will be a 'fall out' as this segment progresses once:

- sellers identify the most positive prospects for them
- buyers better understand what is available in the market.

Both parties will legitimately seek to use their own process to control movement around the cycle and this may lead to conflict.

Seller's steps:

- Develop offerings which they perceive will meet the needs of the market.
- Make sure that they can be found by searching buyers, particularly via websites which may track buyer's activity within them.
- Create a need. Make buyers, particularly untrained ones, aware of situations, problems and opportunities which can be met by their services.
- Conditioning. Using conditioning techniques to help the purchasing organisation see the sellers offering as the one for them.

Buyer's steps:

- Identification of need. Understanding and examining the basic need.
- Specifying the need. Quantifying and specifying the need generically.
- Searching. The supplier selection processes used by buyers to start to identify potential suppliers.

- Conditioning. Combating sales conditioning and also conditioning sellers towards the buyer's needs.

Buyers and sellers come together when serious discussion is undertaken.

Feedback on revision question for study session 7

CSR actively manages the economic, social, environmental and human rights impact of its activities across the world, basing these on principles which reflect international values, reaping benefits both for its own operations and reputation as well as for the communities in which it operates.

When purchasing from a low-wage economy, buyers would need to consider whether:

(a) in making their purchases, suppliers were using processes which polluted the atmosphere, or whether by-products were being disposed of properly
(b) the people producing the goods had rights like freedom of association, health and safety procedures, support from trade unions and reasonable working conditions. The issue of child labour would need to be covered here too
(c) in securing the deal with the organisation concerned they were behaving ethically in giving and receiving gifts, the use of copyrighted materials of other organisations and the treatment of the workers concerned.

Feedback on revision question for study session 8

By 'traditional' manufacturing it is meant that all of the resources used to manufacture goods designed by the manufacturer for the market are optimised by focusing on the economies of scale derived from maximising the output of the physical, material and human resources available to produce at the lowest cost of sale possible. The characteristics of traditional manufacturing are:

- finished goods produced to forecasts with options minimised but still available
- machines and facilities run to economically produce batch quantities in long production runs
- stock is seen as an essential part of the production process
- stock held just in case it is needed
- production processes planned and run by production teams, other processes seen as supporting processes
- business processes focused on doing everything possible to reduce production process cost.

By 'lean' manufacturing it is meant that goods are produced firstly only when a customer needs them and secondly to a standard where the value perceived by the customer governs quality in terms of goods and process.

Processes and parts of the product that do not add what is perceived as value are considered waste and eliminated. Lean manufacturing can be contrasted with the above approach by the following features:

- the elimination of waste, the eight wastes, including stock
- producing only when customers order goods
- a focus on customer value
- removing layers within organisations
- continuous improvements
- batch quantities as low as one
- quality and right first time approaches.

Feedback on revision question for study session 9

It is vital to plan any important process and supplier appraisal is no exception. The issues are presented below in the form of questions.

- What is the objective of the appraisal? This appraisal may differ from other appraisals.
- How many suppliers should/must we appraise? The more suppliers, the more time and cost.
- What will be the scale of the appraisals? The greater the scale, the more time and cost.
- What are our resources? Are they adequate? Do we have enough people to complete the process effectively? If not, perhaps we need to change the scale or the number of suppliers.
- Do we have senior management support? If senior management do not support us then funds and people may not be available to us and the process may fail.
- What is our experience of appraising suppliers? The less experience we have, the more carefully we need to prepare.
- What is the time required and the time available? If we do not have enough time to do the job properly, then scale it down or fight for other resources.
- What is the current status of our relationships with suppliers?
- Where are the suppliers located? This has clear cost, time and risk impacts.
- Will the benefit of the process be greater than the cost? This is a common sense check.

Feedback on revision question for study session 10

A supplier's view of a supplier appraisal process will be conditioned by:

- their interest in winning the business
- the information they are given on the whole supplier selection process
- the information they are given on supplier appraisal process
- their knowledge of the purchasing organisation and the people concerned
- their experience of previous supplier appraisals
- the time they are given to prepare for the appraisal

- the timing of the appraisal visit
- the buyer's reaction to a suggestion of an alternative time frame
- the likely cost of the exercise to the supplier
- what they feel about the likelihood of winning the business
- the extent to which they will have to share confidential information
- their view of the customer within the supplier preferencing model.

Feedback on revision question for study session 11

1   Time: Without the procedures the time taken to place a requirement with a supplier in given circumstances could be shorter.
2   Cost: Following the procedures could cost more in terms of human and systems resources than would otherwise be the case.
3   Choice and the requirement for the perception of fairness to all: The private sector could choose to develop a solution with one provider without involving any other organisation, simply because they feel that the provider is the one for them. In the public sector all organisations must be made aware and given an equal chance to bid for the work. Reference to OJEU would be appropriate.
4   Fixed duration: Private sector organisations can commence and maintain unending relationships if they believe that is appropriate. The public sector must set a time limit on each relationship.
5   Selection criteria: Private sector organisations do not have to make bidders aware of selection criteria, but public sector organisations must do so.

Feedback on revision question for study session 12

There is no right or wrong answer here, the question demands a definition, followed by an argued case for and against reciprocal trading and then a conclusion one way or the other.

Definition: 'Reciprocal trading is a business situation where two organisations both buy from and sell to each other.'

Points for include that reciprocal trading is acceptable where:

- there is no coercion
- both parties are in agreement
- there is mutual benefit
- there is transparency
- additional business can be won because of it
- it is in the greater good of the organisation.

Points against include that reciprocal trading is unacceptable where:

- one party uses coercion or manipulation
- one party is forced to use the services of the other
- there is a greater cost than benefit to the relationship
- there is no transparency

- additional business is lost because of it
- it is not in the greater good of the organisation.

Feedback on revision question for study session 13

Risks can include:

1 The core activity of the organisation being impacted by the non-delivery of components. The consequence could be that service delivery or production stops. This would be minimised by working out a cut-over plan with both old and new suppliers, temporarily increasing stocks and having samples of the new supplies before cut-over.

2 The core activity of the organisation being impacted by the poor quality of goods and services provided. The consequence could be that service delivery or production stops. This would be minimised by supplier appraisal with the new supplier, temporarily increasing stocks and receiving and using samples of the new supplies before cut-over.

3 The failure of systems to interface with each other. The consequence could be that orders are not received by the supplier, who then does not commence manufacture in time to meet the customer's needs. Here testing the systems before their live use would be appropriate.

4 The learning curve, which may mean that suppliers are not sure what they have to do or, in the case of services, not sure where they have to go. The consequence could be that service or delivery take much longer than expected, causing shortages. It may also mean that the performance of initial deliveries may take much longer than subsequently required.

Feedback on revision question for study session 14

Definition: 'Outsourcing is the retention of responsibility for the delivery of services by an organisation, but the devolution of the day-to-day performance of those services to an external organisation, under a contract with agreed standards, costs and conditions.'

1 The supplier can save us money, over and above the best we can do. Cost benefits accruing from suppliers here should include:
   (a) economies of scale from their greater purchasing power and preferred supplier arrangements in the area
   (b) more efficient and productive use of people and other resources from their greater experience and greater volume.

2 The area is not considered 'core' business. Once the non-core activities are outsourced, management time will be free to focus on core activities.

3 Improving return on net assets (RONA). RONA is a measure of how a business utilises its assets to make money by comparing sales with assets. If the assets are sold to an outsourcing supplier, the organisation:
   (a) has less assets but the same sales turnover. As a percentage the turnover will therefore be higher
   (b) has to make less provision to replace the assets through depreciation
   (c) will have a single inflow of cash.

4 The high pace of technical change may mean that the purchasing organisation will prefer to use a specialist supplier who will be able to

better develop the resources to meet the changing needs of the business and in doing so reduce the buyer's exposure.

5   We need a better service. The supplier may simply have the expertise when internally we are amateurs.

6   The supplier may be able to provide a 'one stop shop' consistently across all of the sites of the organisation.

7   It may not be possible for our organisation to obtain the skills necessary to run that area of our business effectively.

Feedback on revision question for study session 15

Five stages similar to the ones identified below should be identified and comments made about the buyers' and sellers' objectives in each of the stages.

1   Bidding and negotiation, through to reaching an agreement: Buyers' objectives include the minimisation of risk through a secure contract, meeting the business needs as expressed in the specification and obtaining service and value for money.
Sellers' objectives include reaching an agreement, minimising risk and obtaining an appropriate margin.

2   Transition and initial service performance: For the buyer, early delivery of benefits from outsourcing will be a key objective here; as well as time in both the sense of urgency and achieving the agreed plan, uninterrupted supply of service and people issues will be the focus.
For the seller, implementing the transition on time will be an objective; to some extent the supplier may 'throw money' at issues to meet the schedule and not start off by being late. Sellers will share the need for early success to prove their worth to the organisation and to do this they may select 'low hanging fruit' as a clear demonstration of their value. Factors like maximising economies of scale as soon as possible will also be clear objectives. Identifying future economies of scale is also a key driver at this stage for suppliers.

3   Ongoing performance: For the buyer, maximising the promised benefits in line with the stated objectives, delivered as hard and soft savings and/or improvements to services, will be key here. Continuous improvement and benefits flowing from further improvements will also be an objective for the buyer.
For the seller, making and increasing target margin whilst keeping the internal customer stakeholders happy are key combined objectives for the supplier throughout this stage of the contract.

4   Approaching renewal: The buyer's objective here is to learn from the experience of the previous selection and the experience of working with the supplier throughout the years of the agreement to improve the benefits accruing to them.
The supplier's objectives will (presumably) be to secure a continuation of business. Keen suppliers will point to future trends and improvements that their expertise will allow them to make, working with the buyer. Renewal for suppliers may also include recovering costs that they have not been able to recover previously.

5   Termination and handover: Once contractual issues are resolved with one or both suppliers, the buyer's objectives here return to those of the

transition and initial performance phases, where uninterrupted supply, time and people issues are again important for the buyer.

Once termination is formally confirmed, the seller's objective will be to exit professionally, at minimum cost and with minimum bad feelings or bad publicity.

Feedback on revision question for study session 16

A laid back culture is one where there is tolerance of individualism and an apparent lack of drive; however, appearances can be deceiving. It may include:

- technical experts who are absolutely assured of their eminence in their profession may give the impression that they are unconcerned about commercial and relationship aspects
- a small family firm, secure in its position in a local community may also not see the need to extract the last penny out of a deal with a supplier
- use of contacts and the old boy network to source customers and suppliers.

An aggressive organisation is one marked by its readiness to challenge or fight, which may be a characteristic of the market in which it exists. Typically the organisation will find it difficult to trust employees and suppliers, relationships will be towards the adversarial end of the relationship spectrum. The organisation will always seek more for less.

Within the laid back culture the organisation will find what may be considered as typical purchasing and negotiation strategies as inappropriate, for the culture will fear they will upset suppliers and internal customers.

Within the aggressive culture the purchasing person attempting to implement partnership and alliances will have a difficult time as others may feel that they cannot trust suppliers. The person proposing practical action like sharing information and sharing costs and benefits may themselves be considered untrustworthy or unsound by colleagues in this environment.

Feedback on revision question for study session 17

- Communication: There are different time zones.
- Language: Not everyone speaks the same language.
- Geographical distances: This impacts four factors:
    - Transport costs can be significantly more when obtaining delivery from another continent.
    - Delivery time can be significantly more when obtaining delivery from another continent.
    - Packaging requirements may need to be more robust to take account of the type of journey.
    - Length of time that communication takes to reach the other person. Today this consideration has almost been eliminated when organisations have access to high-speed internet connections.
- The political and economic stability of the nations and organisations which may form our sources of supply.

- The differing legal systems the nations have evolved and which law will be the one under which the contract will operate.
- Organising payment when one party does not want to release the goods until they get paid and the other party does not want to pay until they receive and examine the goods.
- Differing cultures and ethical standards.
- Duties and taxes may be imposed and need to be accounted for by someone.
- The issue of using different currencies, which may fluctuate.
- Inflation rates may need to be factored into the cost model.
- Holidays: Different countries have public holidays at different times and this will impact communication and delivery.
- Supplier management costs: The cost of a visit to a supplier on another continent will be much greater than a journey 50 miles down the road.

Feedback on revision question for study session 18

(a)   A supply base before tiering may look like this:

Figure 21.1

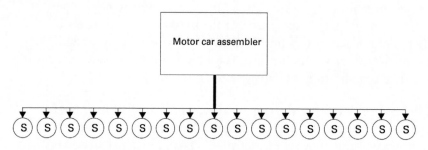

A supply base after tiering may look like this:

Figure 21.2

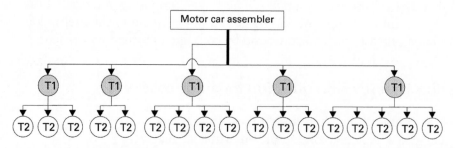

(b)   To the purchasing organisation the advantages of tiering a supplier base are:
    (i)   There is less administration. At the mundane level of space required to store records of suppliers, less records will be required.
    (ii)   There will be fewer transactions with the purchasing organisation.
    (iii)   Coordination is easier. Imagine the additional coordination required to get individual parts from several suppliers to the main subcontractor.
    (iv)   Suppliers have their own trusted specialist subcontractors. T1 suppliers may have a close relationship with several key suppliers to them. In asking the T1 supplier to organise the delivery and even

the design of components, the purchasing organisation is able to harness this expertise.

(v) Closer, better relationships with fewer key suppliers.

(vi) The closeness and duration of the relationship makes the investment in technology to design, produce and transact the relationship worthwhile.

(vii) With effective supplier tiering less stock will be required within the supply chain.

Feedback on revision question for study session 19

Buyers should undertake supplier development to improve the current position to meet their business objectives. Specific reasons include:

- The recognition that goods and services are a greater proportion of total business cost now that outsourcing is common.
- The need to develop our supply base to deliver better in terms of goods and services or in terms of the way suppliers interface with us.
- The fact that technology has increased and become more specialised; we can't, shouldn't, won't make everything. We should encourage our suppliers to be specialists.
- The fact that we don't have a monopoly of ideas and cannot 'know it all'.

Feedback on revision question for study session 20

The objective of supplier performance measurement is: 'to obtain and distribute relevant and timely data on the performance of both suppliers and buyers, using the minimum resources'.

The principles that follow are vital considerations before specific measures are determined.

- Measure what is vital, concentrate on strategic goods and services.
- Use measures that are relevant to the needs of our stakeholders and our business.
- 'KISS' – meaning 'keep it simple stupid'. Simple measures tend to work and absorb fewer resources.
- Measures must be robust. They must work again and again.
- Effective measures are 'owned' by suppliers' key people.
- Listen to suppliers' ideas. It is probable that the supplier will have their own ideas and know measures that will work successfully.

References and bibliography

This section contains a complete A-Z listing of all publications, materials or websites referred to in this course book. Books, articles and research are listed under the first author's (or in some cases the editor's) surname. Where no author name has been given, the publication is listed under the name of the organisation that published it. Websites are listed under the name of the organisation providing the website.

Barrat, C, and M Whitehead (2004) *Buying for Business*. Chichester: Wiley.

Cadbury, A (1992) *Report of the Committee on the Financial Aspects of Corporate Governance*. London: Gee.

CIPS (2004) *The Ethical Decision: an executive guide to CSR for purchasing directors*. London: CIPS

Compton, HK, and DA Jessop (2001) *The Official Dictionary of Purchasing and Supply Terminology for Buyers and Suppliers*. Cambridge: Liverpool Business Publishing.

Crocker, B, and S Emmett (2006) *Relationship Driven Supply Chain: Creating a Culture of Collaboration throughout the Chain*. Aldershot: Ashgate Publishing.

Davis, T, and R Pharro (2003) *The Relationship Manager: the next generation of project management*. Aldershot: Gower Publishing Company.

DTI (2004) *Draft Regulations on the Operating and Financial Review*. London: DTI.

Drucker, PF (1982) *The Changing World of the Executive*. London: Heinemann.

Eastern Shires Purchasing Organisation: http://www.espo.org

Gilmour, I, and I Bilson (2004) *Profit Growth and Risk*. London: Spiropress.

Google: http://www.google.com

Leenders, MR, and HE Fearon (1997) *Purchasing and Supply Management*. Chicago: Irwin.

Lysons, K, and M Gillingham (1996) *Purchasing and Supply Management* 6th edition. Harlow: FT Prentice Hall.

The Merriam-Webster Online Dictionary: http://www.merriam-webster.com

Moore, M (1988) *Commercial Relationships*. Liverpool AP.

Monckza, RM, R Trent and R Handfield (1998) *Purchasing and Supply Chain Management*. Cincinnatti, Ohio: International Thompson Publishing.

Moran, K (1997) *Investment Appraisal for Non-Financial Managers*. London: Pitman.

The Office of Government Commerce: http://www.ogc.gov.uk

Purchasing magazine

Purchasing and Supply Management magazine (published by CIPS, the forerunner of *Supply Management*)

Russil, R (1997) *Purchasing Power*. Harlow: Pearson.

Steele, P, and B Court (1996) *Profitable Purchasing Strategies*. London: McGraw Hill.

Womack, M, and D Jones (1996) *Lean Thinking: Banish Waste and Create Wealth in Your Corporation*. New York: Simon and Schuster.

Yahoo!: http://www.yahoo.com

Index